INDIANS PLAYING INDIAN

INDIANS PLAYING INDIAN

Multiculturalism and Contemporary Indigenous Art in North America

Monika Siebert

THE UNIVERSITY OF ALABAMA PRESS

Tuscaloosa

The University of Alabama Press
Tuscaloosa, Alabama 35487-0380
uapress.ua.edu

Hardcover edition published 2015.
Paperback edition published 2022.
eBook edition published 2015.

Typeface: Caslon

Cover design: David Nees

Paperback ISBN: 978-0-8173-6067-2

A previous edition of this book has been cataloged by the Library of Congress.
ISBN: 978-0-8173-1855-0 (cloth)
E-ISBN: 978-0-8173-8798-3

To my parents,
Janina and Henryk Siebert
and
Barbara and Harald Paumgarten

Contents

Figures

Acknowledgments

It is an honor and pleasure to thank here the many people and institutions that offered support as I researched and wrote this book.

For professional mentorship, for sharing research and ideas, for inspiring conversations, and for invaluable commentary on drafts, I thank Paul Achter, Bert Ashe, Crystal Bartolovitch, Sacvan Bercovitch, Tim Barnard, Alan Braddock, Laura Browder, Abigail Cheever, Steve Cohan, Philip Deloria, Susan Edmunds, Danuta Fjellestad, Winny Fluck, Brigitte Fluck, Jan French, Robert Gates, Terryl Givens, Michael Goode, Libby Gruner, Roger Hallas, Brian Henry, Ray Hilliard, Shari Huhndorf, Suzanne Jones, Monika Kallan, Arnold Krupat, Amy Lang, Anne Lounsbery, Peter Lurie, Joyce McAllister, Rob Nelson, Marwood Larson-Harris, Scott Lyons, Keren Omry, Jolene Parker, Malea Powell, Anthony Russell, Nicole Sackley, Louis Schwartz, Siobhan Senier, Julietta Singh, Kathleen Skerrett, Nathan Snaza, Werner Sollors, David Stevens, Christian Thorne, Lynn Weiss, Karenne Wood, Eric Yellin, and Doug Winiarski.

To Amy Howard, Elizabeth Outka, and Kevin Pelletier I'm indebted in ways that my words here can hardly approximate. Brutally honest members of a work-in-progress group, they have been my dream team for more than five years now. They read the manuscript cover to cover and over many hours of conversations transformed my thinking and writing, all along extending unreserved support and enduring friendship.

I'm grateful to the University of Richmond for a series of summer research fellowships and a sabbatical support grant at a crucial moment of manuscript completion and to the Virginia Foundation for the Humanities for the spring 2013 residential fellowship, which allowed me to revise the manuscript and prepare the book for production. I thank the English Department at the University of Richmond for providing an academic home like no other and for funding travel to present work at a variety of conferences. And I thank Emily Tarchokov for cheerful administrative support in things large and small.

For the invitations to share my work in public fora, I thank Katy Hoke of the University of Richmond's School of Arts and Sciences; Danuta Fjellestad and Erick Assard of Uppsala University's Swedish Institute for North American Studies; Ivonne Fuentes Wallace and Whitney Leeson of Roanoke College's International Critical Study Group; Anne Spencer and Karenne Wood at the Virginia Foundation for the Humanities; and Eric Anderson and Annette Trefzer at the Society for the Study of Southern Literature.

I'm grateful to Ashleigh Greene Wade for invaluable research assistance. Jessica Swope and Laura Holliday, incomparable editors both, wrestled with my prose without complaint and with impressive results. I thank them both for taking the manuscript on and making it much better. I'm indebted to Betty Tobias and Marcia Whitehead at the Boatwright Memorial Library at the University of Richmond for finding and making available rare texts and resources. I thank Melissa Foster and her team at the University of Richmond's Technology Learning Center for assistance with preparing illustrations for the book. A special thank you to Francisco Cuevos, who spent long hours at the computer and printer one afternoon, and to Umur Solarcan, Julian Libihoul la Fontaine, and Sam Abrahams, who helpfully assisted.

Very special thanks go to Dan Waterman, my editor at the University of Alabama Press, for seeing the promise in a budding project and for stalwart support through the years of getting that first idea into a full-fledged book. To the press's two anonymous readers, I'm indebted for invaluable commentary, which inspired a fundamental revision of the manuscript's first draft. The editorial team at the University of Alabama Press, especially Penelope Cray, Carol Connell, and Joanna Jacobs, patiently shepherded the manuscript into a meticulously edited and beautifully designed book. I first encountered Teri Greeves's art at an inaugural exhibition at the National Museum of the American Indian in Washington, DC, soon after the museum's opening in 2004. As I marveled at *Kiowa Ah-Day*, a spectacularly beaded pair of Converse sneakers in the "Our Lives" exhibit, little did I imagine that one of her stunning and moving pieces would one day grace the cover of my book. I thank Terri, for kindly allowing me to use her "We Gave Two Horses for Our Son" as my first invitation to the readers to consider the aesthetic and intellectual complexity of contemporary indigenous art.

Earlier versions of chapter 2 and chapter 5 appeared as "Zacharias Kunuk's *Atanarjuat* and the Ideological Work of Indigenous Filmmaking" in *Public Culture* 18.3 (Fall 2006) and "Repugnant Aboriginality: LeAnne

Howe's *Shell Shaker* and the Predicament of Indigenous Self-representation in the Age of Multiculturalism" in *American Literature* 83.1 (March 2011), respectively. I thank Duke University Press for permission to include these materials here.

I'm blessed with many loving families; although scattered across the globe, they sustain me in all of my endeavors. I thank my parents, Janina and Henryk Siebert, for their unconditional love and support, for their patient indulgence of my dreams and passions, and for the invaluable countless hours of childcare when I was first honing my research and writing skills. Everyday I'm inspired by, and I aspire to, the standard of caring and liberating parenting that they have modeled. My brother, Piotr Siebert, has been an incomparable companion and indispensable support at many junctions in my life; our heated debates about history keep my argumentative spirit alive. His family, including Agnieszka Pawlonka and Janek Siebert, has been a new and much appreciated source of joy. Katarzyna Ziółkowska is a lifelong friend and a constant vivid presence, despite the distance. Aleksandra Ziółkowska grants me the pleasures of watching a second daughter grow into a beautiful and talented young woman. I will always be grateful to my aunt and uncle (and "second parents"), Barbara and Harald Paumgarten, for making my American education possible and for providing, together with their daughters, Maja Paumgarten and Christina Paumgarten and their families, John, John Jr., Harald, and Sophie Parker and Christopher, Alexander, and India Campbell, a caring and supportive home on the other side of the Atlantic. My Richmond family—Elizabeth Outka and Trip, Tom, and Kate Pollard; Elizabeth, Mark, Mariah, and Nick Gruner; Kendra Vendetti and Kevin, Emerson, and Lisette Pelletier; Nathan Snaza and Julietta and Isadora Singh; and Amy Howard and Robert and Meseret Nelson—has been an infinite source of support, friendship, love, and joy.

This book is dedicated to my parents, but it is a gift from my daughter, Maria, whose intelligence, kindness, and grace inspire me every single day.

INDIANS
PLAYING
INDIAN

Introduction

Indigeneity and Multicultural Misrecognition

On November 2, 2012, No Doubt, a popular contemporary band fronted by Gwen Stefani, released a new music video to its fans on Facebook. Directed by Melina Matsoukas, a Grammy-winning music and commercial video director, "Looking Hot" offered a cowboys-and-Indians-themed narrative to accompany the recent release of their single by the same title. Featuring Stefani in the lead role as an Indian woman, the video rehearsed the classic depiction of American Indians that has been solidified in settler popular culture over the past couple of centuries: Plains warriors astride horses on the background of western prairies, a beautiful captive woman pandering to the cowboy's, and the spectator's, gaze, and the assembly of props complete with feather headdresses, ceremonial staffs, tipis, arrows, wolves, smoke signals, and an array of Indian-chic clothing, all relegating the continent's indigenous peoples to a mythologized American past. The video met with immediate condemnation by scores of commentators, indigenous and non-native alike, as an inexcusable example of cultural misappropriation and a disappointing rehash of the most hackneyed Indian representational stereotypes.[1] And even though it was defended by some of No Doubt and Stefani's most loyal fans as a harmless bit of aesthetically dazzling creative play or a deliberately ironic performance poking fun at Indian stereotypes rather than perpetuating them, just a day after the video's release, the band issued a public apology and removed it from its official website; within days, "Looking Hot" disappeared from the internet altogether.

One more example in a long history of cultural appropriation of indigenous images, "Looking Hot" was not particularly remarkable in itself. Its obvious fascination with Indian nobility, mysticism, and aesthetic and erotic appeal reflected the twisted emotional economy of settler *playing Indian*, with its simultaneous admiration for the glorious Indian past and willful disregard for contemporary indigenous realities.[2] What is remarkable about the entire incident is how quickly No Doubt issued an apology for "Looking Hot" and removed it from circulation—and how effectively their swift response put an end to the brewing controversy while, ironically, earning the band points for cultural sensitivity. One of the effects of the multiculturalist reformation that occurred in North America in the late twentieth century is that instances of cultural misappropriation and playing Indian of the kind evidenced in No Doubt's video are now readily recognized and condemned, most spectators having been successfully educated into respect for cultural diversity as the very glue that binds North American democracies. And even though such condemnations are routinely met with accusations of political correctness by those contemporary Americans who did not pay sufficient attention in their general education classes, apologies for inappropriate trespasses on others' cultural turf have become the publicly sanctioned norm and are deployed with reliable frequency.

No Doubt's apology is typical of this newly emerged genre, and it supplies clear testimony to how the multiculturalist politics of recognition has helped remake the vocabulary we use when speaking about indigeneity in North America. That it has been shaped by the rhetoric of cultural difference as a social good is evident in the apology statement's emphasis on the band's commitment to "diversity and consideration for other cultures" as well as "respect, unity and inclusiveness"; in its references to "Native American people, their culture and history" and "the Native American community"; and in its presumption that the primary harm experienced by indigenous people today amounts to a sense of insult caused by disrespect for their cultures and can thus be remedied by a respectful recognition of their cultural distinctiveness.[3] Yet, far from undoing the offenses of cultural misappropriation, such apologies bring harm of their own by further solidifying this pernicious approach to understanding indigeneity. Their reliance on the conception of indigeneity as culture obscures the unique political and legal contexts that shaped indigenous historical and contemporary realities; they imply that indigenous peoples are cultural minorities rather than sovereign nations with long political histories. Such apologies exemplify a new but already widespread phenomenon I call multicultural misrecognition, one related to but in crucial ways distinct from cultural misappropriation.

In *Indians Playing Indian: Multiculturalism and Contemporary Indigenous Art in North America*, I explore both the predicament that multicultural misrecognition poses for indigenous nations and people and the innovative ways in which indigenous artists in a range of media have responded to this predicament. As I define it, multicultural misrecognition consists in the substitution of cultural meanings for political meanings of indigeneity—that is, in the replacement of the concept of *indigenous nations* with that of *indigenous cultures* in contemporary popular, and often also scholarly, discourse. By transforming indigenous peoples into Native Americans, multicultural misrecognition equates them with other ethnic minorities to sustain the myth of America as a refuge to the world's emigrants. It enfolds the many distinct colonized nations into the American polities—Canadian and US—as one more homogenized population group accorded cultural citizenship, that is, the right to national belonging irrespective of their cultural difference rather than as a reward for cultural assimilation.[4] Multicultural misrecognition erases the multidimensional political history of indigeneity in favor of an essentialized cultural difference at a moment when, after decades of activism, indigenous peoples have successfully reinserted the concepts of sovereignty, of nations-within-a-nation, and of government-to-government relations into political and legal discourse in North America, though in different ways in the United States and in Canada. These concepts, however, remain unknown to the broader public, which—schooled on multicultural curricula—admires Native American culture and misunderstands, or altogether ignores, unique indigenous political realities, past and present.

This misunderstanding has far-reaching consequences. It renders contemporary indigenous activism on behalf of political, legal, and economic self-determination incomprehensible to much of the settler public, which often dismisses such efforts with suggestions that *Indians should just get over it already*. It determines how indigenous cultural production signifies in the public arena. If the logic of multiculturalism prohibits settler Americans from playing Indian, as the "Looking Hot" incident clearly shows, it now requires that indigenous peoples themselves play Indian to help legitimate the multicultural democracies they cannot help but inhabit. The current flowering of indigenous literature, cinema, and visual arts is typically taken as evidence that Canada and the United States have successfully broken with their colonial pasts, characterized by the expropriation and displacement of indigenous peoples, to become thriving nations of many cultures, where Native Americans enjoy full freedom to represent their cultural difference. Widely available Native American art, authenticated and protected by identity licensing laws,[5] bears witness to this representational freedom and the multicultural credentials such freedom implies.

Although certainly a welcome respite from the long history of assimilatory pressures on American minorities, multiculturalism turned out to be to a large extent a false promise to indigenous peoples. While it reinforces a long tradition of Indian representation in the national cultural imagination, now with added perspectives of Native American artists themselves, it perpetuates those cultural scripts of Indianness that thwart indigenous nations' aspirations to attain a degree of political and economic independence beyond control over cultural representation. Ironically, it becomes the task of those working in the realm of cultural production, the same realm that routinely perpetuates Indian stereotypes, to confront multicultural misrecognition and to rearticulate the political meanings of indigenous history and experience. Herein, then, lies the urgency of the central question addressed in *Indians Playing Indian*: by what means do contemporary indigenous artists capitalize on the possibilities for the creative expression of indigenous specificity offered by multiculturalism while resisting national incorporation via multicultural misrecognition?

I coined the phrase "multicultural misrecognition" to emphasize that the phenomenon it describes grows out of the ideological imperatives of multiculturalism—and the culturalization of social identities in particular—and that such a reduction to culture constitutes a fundamental misunderstanding of historical and contemporary indigeneity. The currently available concept of cultural misappropriation, useful as it is in many important ways, fails to flag the common misunderstanding of indigeneity as cultural identity; on the contrary, in its reference to cultural property rights, it solidifies the perception of indigenous peoples as Native Americans rounding out the American ethnoracial pentagon.[6] As the "Looking Hot" video incident demonstrates, redemptive attention to cultural misappropriation does not identify, let alone correct, this fundamental misperception. Indigenous peoples in North America are routinely mistaken for cultural minorities, even in the absence of inappropriate use of their images or objects of their material culture. Condemnations of cultural misappropriation may result in the removal of offensive materials and practices, but they do not change how the public thinks about indigenous peoples and their historically developed relationships to North American nation-states. By contrast, multicultural misrecognition as an analytical lens allows us to refocus the discussion of contemporary indigenous representation away from condemnations of settler playing Indian and toward the broader and more salient issues of recognition, both cultural and political.

Thus the main insight of *Indians Playing Indian* comes in two parts. While this book offers in the introduction a diagnosis of the contemporary moment and the conditions of representation with which multicultural misrecognition confronts indigenous artists, the weightier point I want to make about the ideological functions of contemporary indigenous art accrues by examples. In the book's five chapters, I explore a wide range of artistic responses to the predicament of multicultural misrecognition by focusing on sites and texts that explicitly address the dangers of multiculturalist cooptation of indigenous cultural difference on behalf of nation-building in the United States and Canada. Each chapter showcases a different medium—museum exhibition, cinema, digital fine art, sculpture and multimedia installation, and fiction—and explores a specific rhetorical strategy deployed to jam the interpretive mechanisms of multicultural misrecognition and to recover political meanings of indigeneity. While these strategies are distinct in the ways I explore below, they share a common pattern and a common aim: they evoke and engage the stereotypes solidified in settler Indian representation in a rhetorical performance we could call Indians playing Indian. They do so to expose the limitations of the culturalist conceptions of indigeneity and to clear space for the much-needed public recognition of the political historical and contemporary realities of indigenous lives.

Since the political meanings of indigeneity have been so successfully obscured by the pervasive operations of multicultural misrecognition, I turn below to a brief account of the history of recognition of indigenous peoples in North America, an account that highlights the gradual but deliberate shift from political recognition in the early colonial period to cultural recognition in the present. I begin with the contemporary moment and the ideological functions of indigenous misrecognition in the context of multiculturalism. To provide a genealogy of the present moment, I then backtrack to the early colonial period to recover the precedent of indigenous sovereignty in the diplomatic practice of the time and to the early republican period to trace the first attempts at circumscribing this sovereignty in the process of national consolidation during the nineteenth and early twentieth centuries. I describe the emergence of modern ethnology and culturalist conceptions of indigeneity and how the popular visual media, from early painting to photography and film, helped first inspire and later disseminate these conceptions. My primary focus in the narrative of these shifts in recognition is on the United States, but I note where Canadian practice diverges in significant ways.[7] I conclude this section by describing some of the many instances and forms of political and legal resistance to the erasure of indigenous nations by American Indian leaders and intellectuals from the early nineteenth century to the present. A thorough understanding of the rhetorical strategies explored in *Indians Playing Indian* depends on a good grasp of the basic facts of indigenous political history in North America. This history serves as a foundation for this art's insistent appeal for the recognition of indigeneity as a unique political phenomenon rather than as merely one more cultural identity among many others.

Recognizing Indians: From Politics to Culture

Multicultural misrecognition as a coinage derives from the concept of the politics of recognition, the ideological and ethical heart of North American multiculturalism. The politics of recognition—that is, recognition of diverse cultural identities in the context of constitutional democracies via the concept of cultural citizenship, a group-based right—is a contemporary phenomenon. It was institutionalized in the 1982 Canadian Constitution, in a clause defining Canada as a nation of multicultural heritage. In 1992, the Canadian philosopher Charles Taylor theorized it as an ethical obligation and a human right in a seminal essay, which gave the concept of "The Politics of Recognition" its name.[8] Although absent from US foundational legal documents, which famously enshrined the concept of individual rights, in practice it currently pervades public discourse on social relations in the United States as well. A fighting creed during the so-called culture wars in the 1980s, by the 1990s, the politics of recognition had been appropriated by the American democratic states as a tool of nation-building, multiculturalism having replaced the earlier melting-pot ideology. By 1997 the preeminent American sociologist of race and ethnicity, Nathan Glazer, would famously, though reluctantly, claim that *We Are All Multiculturalists Now*.[9]

Contemporary American multiculturalism emerged in the late twentieth century in the wake of the new social movements advocating on behalf of equal political and cultural rights for a variety of minority groups. It promised representational liberation to all of America's historical and contemporary others and depended on a far-ranging appreciation of cultural distinctiveness, rather than cultural assimilation, as a crucial constitutive of the American past and present. Multiculturalism put a premium on difference as a resource that promised to expedite national integration, and it admitted previously marginalized groups to the national imaginaries. Thus it quickly became the dominant model for social relations in North American states that were fashioning themselves as nations of immigrants nurturing their diverse cultures while pledging allegiance to a specific political ideal of representative democracy. Suspended immediately after 9/11 in favor of mobilizing pronouncements recalling the early twentieth-century cry "Americans All!" deployed in the context of the increased immigration of people seen as racially other, multiculturalism was quickly redeployed in public discourse as a way to distinguish North American democracies, and the United States in particular, from fundamentalist Islamic states (Yúdice 340).

In the twenty-first century, multiculturalism operates in changed conditions, characterized by the war on terrorism, an increased concern with national security and the policing of borders, heated debates over immigration reform, and renewed attention to class difference and the redistribution of resources brought on by a series of severe economic downturns. Yet through all of these adjustments to changing geopolitical, economic, and social conditions, and despite the fact that it is frequently criticized for its pernicious ability to deflect questions of socioeconomic inequality (for example, by Žižek, San Juan, Fraser, and Benhabib) and political representation (for example, by Povinelli and Yúdice) in favor of the celebration of cultural difference, multiculturalism remains crucial to the self-representation of Canada and the United States as fully credentialed contemporary democracies. However, because of its dependence on culture as the main conceptual reference point, multiculturalism presents a unique set of problems for indigenous peoples, who have experienced a history of colonization rather than one of immigration. While the multiculturalist politics of recognition has offered a way to break with the more shameful aspects of the colonial past in the United States and Canada and granted previously marginalized groups access to the settler national imaginaries, it has led to a fundamental misperception of indigenous peoples and their relationship to the American nation-states and other American population groups. And while this misperception bolsters the settler states' projects of national consolidation, ironically, it undermines the explicit imperative of the politics of recognition as formulated by Taylor: the ethical obligation to properly recognize all population groups for who they are. Devoid of the acknowledgment of the unique political distinctiveness of indigenous nations, the multicultural mandate of inclusiveness continues, rather than puts an end to, colonial coercion.

Diplomacy, Treaties, and the Political Conception of Indigeneity

Apologies for cultural misappropriation, such as that of No Doubt following the release of the "Looking Hot" video, are informed by a contemporary understanding of recognition as tied to cultural citizenship. And yet, while explicitly linked to multiculturalism's conceptual presumption about the primacy of culture to the formation of the modern self and social identities, multicultural misrecognition of indigenous peoples as Native Americans has a historical genealogy. It stems from two contradictory yet related developments: the long history of European and American depictions of the continent's indigenous peoples, which has resulted in the hypervisibility of Indians in the settler national imaginaries; and more than two centuries of federal policies that have made contemporary indigenous nations invisible and their political history on the continent unknown to the general public. However, uniquely in North America, formal recognition of indigenous political separateness, or sovereignty, reaches back to the first decades of European arrival on the continent. It furnishes an extended precedent for the international diplomatic exchanges of recognition, one that the North American multicultural democracies prefer to leave in the past and that indigenous nations insist on resurrecting, commemorating, and acting upon. Its formal expression is a record of several hundred treaties concluded between European, and later American, governments and indigenous nations. Today, these historic treaties are often considered in contradictory terms; they are evoked to assert the recognition of indigenous sovereignty in international law, on the one hand, and pointed to as evidence of a deliberate limitation of this sovereignty in US and Canadian legal and administrative practice, on the other.

This contradictory perception begins to make sense if we keep in mind the distinction between the treaties concluded in the early colonial period—that is, prior to 1776—between indigenous nations and European states, and those negotiated with the US federal government through 1871, when the US Congress unilaterally put an end to treaty-making. In the context of international law and diplomatic practice at the time, colonial-era treaty-making between indigenous nations and European governments testified to the commonly accepted understanding that the former were politically separate entities exercising self-government and control over their territories. Early treaties regulated trade, political alliances, and land cessions; as such they functioned to recognize the prior rights of indigenous nations, even if the actual agreements involved relinquishing some of those rights. The pervasiveness of treaty-making practice, manifested in the large number of treaties, "gives clear evidence," argues historian Howard Berman, "of broad European recognition of the international personality of the indigenous peoples of that time and place" (131).[10] Importantly, Berman points out, these treaties did not constitute political recognition for North American indigenous nations, because "as political communities created by the original inhabitants, Indian societies possessed inherent, preexisting sovereign rights and conducted political relations in their own interests on the international plane" (131). By contrast, the very same treaties were the source of European rights on the continent, for they served as the formal recognition of spheres of influence in America by legitimating territorial and trade claims of European states against each other while also specifying their economic and political relationships to the indigenous nations.

This understanding of early treaty-making has persisted among North

American indigenous nations and is embodied in the Guswenta, or the Two Row Wampum Belt. The Guswenta is a record of a treaty negotiated between the Haudenosaunee, known to the Europeans as the Iroquois Confederacy, and Dutch settlers in the Hudson Valley in the early 1600s. Represented by a wampum belt featuring two purple beaded stripes, one depicting the Haudenosaunee and the other the Europeans, running parallel to each other on a white background, the Guswenta is glossed by Haudenosaunee elders as a record of an agreement to coexistence guaranteed by the mutual policy of noninterference. To this day, the Guswenta and the principles it represents are upheld by the indigenous nations of the American Northeast as the originary formulation of settler-indigenous relations on the continent. A fixture of political memory and of present practice among the Haudenosaunee, the Guswenta has been recently memorialized at the National Museum of the American Indian in Washington, DC, in a bronze sculpture titled *Allies in War, Partners in Peace* and donated to the museum by the Oneida Nation of New York. Tellingly, the sculptor placed the Guswenta in George Washington's right hand.[11]

When the United States emerged as a political entity in 1776, it inherited the practice of treaty-making from the British Crown. Treaties served several important purposes for the newly proclaimed republic. They helped the recently constituted government to establish and assert its political legitimacy with regard to England, France, Spain, and other governments competing for influence in America. As Frederick Hoxie observes, "ironically, Indian treaties were originally a badge of sovereignty for the national government" (90). Successful treaties allowed the federal government to avoid costly wars on its frontiers and assert its authority over that of the individual states. Treaty negotiations offered opportunities for the new nation to demonstrate in practice its political philosophy via the concepts of the contract as a model for social relations and of free consent to enter such contracts regarding political associations (Konkle 3). While the United States was solidifying its existence as a political entity and staking claims to territorial sovereignty in North America, many of the indigenous nations continued to carry on diplomatic relations with European courts and governments through the end of the Napoleonic era (Berman 187).

However, even while engaging in treaty negotiations in order to consolidate its political existence, from its beginnings the United States deliberately limited indigenous sovereignty in order to exert sole control over land and natural resources. The process of such limitation begins in 1783 with the Treaty of Paris, when representatives of the United States managed to exclude indigenous nations from peace negotiations following the Revolutionary War, both as participants and as potential claimants to American territories.[12] It continued with the US Constitution, which in the Commerce Clause differentiated Indian tribes from both the states and the foreign nations, thus circumscribing their status as sovereign nations upheld in treaties. This definitional limitation progressed further with the Marshall Court decisions in the 1830s, which asserted native title to the land but defined indigenous nations as "dependent domestic nations," effectively sealing the removal of indigenous nations from international diplomacy. It culminated in the abrogation of treaty-making in 1871 and concluded with the assertion of the US Congress's plenary power over Indian nations in the 1903 *Lone Wolf v. Hitchcock* decision.[13] This trajectory exemplifies a shift in US-Indian relations from recognition of both parties' political sovereignty to the subjection of indigenous nations to US colonial rule.

Treaty-making stopped in 1871, but the complex dynamic of recognition continued to structure indigenous-settler relations, though it shifted to a different plane. The abrogation of the treaty process effectively denied the indigenous nations their sovereign status, allowing for their treatment as colonized people and for consolidated efforts at integrating them into the US administrative, political, legal, social, and cultural matrix. These efforts included establishing missionary and federal agents on reservations; education in boarding schools; administrative acts such as the 1887 General Allotment Act, which aimed to put an end to collective landownership on reservations, the 1885 Major Crimes Act, which sanctioned federal incursions into tribal jurisdiction on reservations, and the 1924 Indian Citizenship Act, which, for the first and only time in US history, extended (or, as its critics would charge, imposed) US citizenship on an entire population group without their consent.[14] In a historical precedent to contemporary multiculturalism, the Indian New Deal era's official cultivation of Indian cultural difference coupled with the passage of the Indian Reorganization Act was part and parcel of the federal project to integrate Indian peoples into the administrative and economic fabric of the United States (Pfister). This process of administrative integration continued via the federal termination and relocation policies of the post–World War II years, which in a reversal of the Indian New Deal aimed to end tribalism by reorganizing terminated tribes as corporations and by encouraging the migration of individual Indians to American cities. During this extended period, from 1871 through the 1950s, indigenous peoples ceased to be viewed as citizens of independent nations and became members of minority groups to be assimilated into American society as individual bearers of rights and obligations (political citizenship), and eventually, by the second half of the twentieth century, as members of yet another ethnic group comprising the multicultural nation (cultural citizenship).

Art, Anthropology, and Cultural Conceptions of Indigeneity

As the idea of the Indian nation and the indigenous nations themselves were being politically and literally undermined, settler artists began to create images of Indians that cast them in an elegiac mode, nostalgically commemorating a civilization lost to the inevitable historical progress manifest in the proper settlement of the continent and the eventual emergence of modern democracies. Partners in diplomacy from the seventeenth through the mid-nineteenth centuries, indigenous peoples increasingly became subjects of a representational resurrection that cast them as emblems of a noble but vanishing race, as ethnological case studies—at first in civilizational development and later in cultural difference—or they were reinvented as First Americans.

The conceit of resurrection through the artist's imaginative abilities originated in the early nineteenth century with George Catlin, the painter of numerous portraits known as the Indian Gallery and the multivolume *Letters and Notes on the Manners, Customs, and Conditions of the North American Indians* (1841), who routinely fashioned himself as an Indian redeemer while taking rhetorical pleasure in descriptions of Indian death.[15] Catlin's amateurish representational rescue efforts found their scientific counterpart in 1879 with the establishment of the American Bureau of Ethnology, a federally funded institution charged with the mandate of salvage ethnography.[16] With the government's funding, ethnographers fanned across the American West in an effort to describe, transcribe, translate, and record the presumably last and fast-fading remnants of authentic Indianness. Collectors followed, the most notorious and rapacious among them being Gustav Heye, the Indian enthusiast whose enormous collection eventually joined the Smithsonian Institution as the National Museum of the American Indian. In the process, the politics of indigenous recognition ceased to be strictly political and moved from the diplomatic stage to a variety of cultural stages—the World's Fairs, the private collections of curiosities, the museum, the gallery, the national statuary, and the silver screen—where the exhibits of indigenous material culture testified to the civilizational progress of so-called Man.

The mandates of salvage ethnography continued to animate the work of later artists. For example, the American photographer Edward Curtis authored numerous portraits of noble but presumably vanishing Indians in the early twentieth century; today ubiquitous in coffee-table books, in calendars, on wall posters, and on T-shirts, they remain the most widely circulated images of American Indians in the world.[17] Filmmakers Robert Flaherty and H. P. Carver directed, respectively, *Nanook of the North* (1922) and *Silent Enemy* (1934), pseudo-ethnographic films that readily translated the settler society's powers of destruction into those of artistic resurrection by recreating on celluloid the vanished authentic Indian worlds.[18] In popular entertainment, the *Wild West* shows staged by Buffalo Bill Cody from 1883 until the development of cinema helped disseminate the idea of the Indian as an emblem of ancient nobility throughout North America and Europe. Theatrical re-creations of the recently fought battles of the Indian wars, often featuring actual participants—most famously Sitting Bull—reenacting their days of military glory, these shows encouraged in the general public a perception of Indians as historical anachronisms obsessively taking pride in their past and stubbornly refusing to adapt to modernity (Deloria, *Indians in Unexpected Places*, 66). However, in an ironic foreshadowing of the imperatives of multicultural misrecognition, participation in these shows likely taught indigenous actors that playing Indian in ways that were recognizable to the settler publics might be the best preparation for American modernity.[19] Further, a range of what we would today call "media initiatives," under the auspices of John and Rodman Wanamaker, a father and son from a family of financiers and owners of department stores in Philadelphia and New York, melded the ideological imperatives of the Catlin-Curtis and Cody projects with an important new twist. While staging the departure of the Indian from the American political scene and preserving the images of his noble race, the Wanamakers, through the efforts of their "agent for culture and education" Joseph Kossuth Dixon, birthed the transformation of the vanishing Indians into the First Americans.[20] Dixon pressed the agenda of Americanizing the immigrants arriving in large numbers in the early twentieth century, through the displayed examples of the Indian. Additionally, the idea of First Americans served to extend the United States' historical genealogy into antiquity—combining the best of the Indian noble race and the best of Western modernity—and helped rewrite the colonial conquest into the nationalist narrative of progressive historical evolution and a political future as a universal democracy.

These representations of the Indian in popular visual media in the late nineteenth and early twentieth centuries emerged during an era of profound epistemological reshuffling, especially with regard to dominant conceptions of human difference. Major political, economic, and social changes around the turn of the century—such as an end to slavery and the Indian wars, Reconstruction, increased immigration from new regions of Europe, urbanization, and the development of mass popular culture—effectively undermined the dominant concepts and hierarchies, such as slave/master and savage/civilized, that had previously organized knowledge and social reality (Evans 4). As race was increasingly circumscribed to skin color, the anthropological concept of culture gained currency in specialist as well as popular discourses (5). Scholars usually credit Franz Boas with bringing about this shift from race to culture and from evolutionary diachronic models of civilization, which aimed to account for change, to contextual synchronic models of cultures, which offered static representations of diverse ways of life and modes of thinking (Elliott xxv). Inspired by Boas's culture concept, ethnographic conventions in genres raging from scholarly writing to amateur visual representation left no room for depictions of indigenous political agency, whether historical or contemporary. Instead, this new ethnographic approach transformed living historical peoples into objects for scientific study and aesthetic contemplation, objects that served as emblems of the modern American civilization's past.

This particular mode of Indian representation, one obscuring the political history of indigenous nations in favor of the conceptions of the vanishing noble race or of Indians as First Americans, has proven enduring; it has morphed into the full-fledged multicultural misrecognition of the present moment. The goal of the meticulous representational resurrection of indigenous worlds as yet unchanged by European colonialism or encountering that change still from the position of their own epistemological strength survives in contemporary examples such as Kevin Costner's 1990 *Dances with Wolves*, Bruce Beresford's 1992 *Black Robe*, or Terrence Malick's 2007 *The New World*, to offer just a few better-known cinematic instances. As with their precursors, these films nostalgically re-create precontact indigenous societies only to ultimately depict their destruction. The inevitability of that destruction, now blamed regretfully on European colonialism rather than on the necessity of civilizational progress, and the belief in the redeeming potential of the settler representational media remain virtually the same. As with their predecessors, these films refuse to represent any connection between historic indigenous peoples and their contemporary descendants. By the early twentieth century, Boas's anthropology had freed indigenous peoples from the earlier evolutionary narratives only to trap them in the static representations of their presumably authentic but now vanished cultures. The mainstreaming of multiculturalism and its politics of recognition in the late twentieth century solidified the hegemony of the Boasian culturalist understanding of group-based human difference. The films mentioned above and my opening example of No Doubt's apology for their "Looking

Hot" video are just some of the many available examples of the hold this culturalist conception of indigeneity has on the contemporary settler public.

By contrast, contemporary feature films by indigenous filmmakers often insist on just such a connection and continuity between indigenous pasts and presents, as in an example I discuss in chapter 2, the Inuit Isuma Productions' 2001 feature *Atanarjuat (The Fast Runner)*, which frames the story of a precontact Inuit band with outtakes depicting Inuit filmmakers, producers, and actors engaged in the performance of their usable past. No more mere objects of settler redemptive efforts, the Inuit appropriate the settler representational medium and conventions to confront multicultural misrecognition with aesthetically savvy interventions. The appeal of indigenous peoples as First Americans survives in many of the contemporary Canadian and US public narratives of multicultural democratic consolidation, such as, for example, the National Museum of the American Indian, which opened in 2004 on the National Mall in Washington, DC. However, as I discuss in chapter 1, it has to compete there with the political conceptions of indigeneity asserted in the tribal galleries curated by members of contemporary indigenous nations.

Indigenous Political Resistance

Indigenous nations and people have always resisted this incorporation by political erasure and cultural resurrection, and they typically have done so by evoking the historic treaties, and the political sovereignty they presumed, as an emblem of their status on the continent. While the general settler discourse on Indians shifted from politics to culture, many indigenous nations have never stopped acting and speaking as independent nations. The early chapter of indigenous resistance to US federal efforts to limit indigenous sovereignty unfolded in the courts, the press, and the public lecture circuit in the early nineteenth century as the Cherokee Nation, along with the Seminole, Creek, Choctaw, and Chickasaw Nations, resisted attempts to remove them to Indian Territory. In the context of arguments about the inherent racial difference and inferiority of American Indians current at the time, indigenous intellectuals, such as William Apess and George Copway, understood that any articulation of indigenous difference functioned ultimately to justify political disenfranchisment of indigenous nations. Instead, they used the evidence of the treaties concluded with the US government to argue for their prior recognition as political sovereigns. But the histories of indigenous nations they penned included accounts of the successful appropriation of European and American institutions, such as representative government, press, and plantation slavery, as a way to show these nations' ongoing fitness for nationhood and thus to write them into the political future on the continent (Konkle 6). Before the era of cultural difference as a social good, indigenous intellectuals used evidence of acculturation as an argument for preserving indigenous political sovereignty as recognized in the treaties.

Following the 1871 halt to treaty-making, the 1903 assumption of plenary power by the US Congress, the pacification and confinement to the reservations of Plains nations, the allotment of tribal lands, and the resulting demographic crisis in Indian Country, American Indian intellectuals at the turn of the twentieth century could hardly hope to successfully argue for indigenous political independence. Nevertheless, against the then-dominant vanishing-race discourse, they insisted on inserting indigenous people into settler modernity. American Indian ethnographers, anthropologists, folklorists, and writers such as Ella Deloria, Archie Phinney, Zitkala-Sa, Arthur S. Parker, Charles Eastman, and Francis La Flesche politically supported the Americanization of Indians through educational and economic assimilation via boarding schools, allotment of tribal land, and US citizenship. In the written accounts of tribal societies, they deployed the culturalist model, thereby contributing, however unintentionally, to the settler public belief in the moribund nature of indigenous traditionalism. However, while operating firmly within the Boasian model, far from dutifully recording Indians' vanished pasts for future generations' study and nostalgic admiration, these writers questioned the model's usefulness for articulating indigenous modernity, on which they unequivocally insisted (Elliott 127). Caught between the earlier social Darwinism and the Boasian culture concept, in order to account for historical and cultural change—that is, for indigenous entry into settler modernity—these writers often had to rely on the earlier civilizational progress narrative (147). Their choice between history and culture, in other words, was political, a gambit calculated to resist the vanishing facilitated by the conceptual models of modern ethnology. While, in the spirit of the period, they took up the project of accounting for indigenous difference in terms of culture rather than unique political status, as writers and activists, they argued for the continued presence of indigenous peoples as equal citizens in a modernizing United States.[21]

Indigenous sovereignty reemerged during the 1960s and 1970s in the political rhetoric of pan-Indian organizations, such as the National Congress of American Indians (NCAI), the National Indian Youth Council (NIYC), and the broader American Indian Movement (AIM). In response to the success of the federal termination policies,[22] NIYC and NCAI defined sovereignty and tribalism in their political platforms as foundational concepts for indigenous activism in the twentieth century.[23] In a series of widely publicized actions, such as fish-ins, road blockades, and occupations of federal property and lost historic indigenous lands, AIM activists invoked the authority of the treaties to remind the federal governments and the general public about the inherent sovereignty of indigenous nations and the historic recognition of that sovereignty in North America.[24] In the context of the United States' repeated attempts to discount these treaties as anachronisms, AIM political activism attempted "to re-establish treaty documents as powerful and authoritative and as binding on the contemporary settler nation" because it saw them as legal precedents for the reassertion of indigenous rights to land and other resources (Allen, *Blood Narrative*, 19–21). This strategy paid off: insistence on the recognition of the enduring legality of the treaties bore fruit in American national politics when, in 1970, President Nixon officially ended the termination policy. It continues to pay off as every US government from the Clinton administration to the current Obama administration customarily reiterates its commitment to tribal sovereignty and to the government-to-government relationship with indigenous nations, even though they rarely act on it.[25] In the 1970s and 1980s, treaty-based activism in US legal courts resulted in the upholding of the provisions of several historic treaties,[26] the important effect of these court battles being the repeated reassertion of tribal sovereignty and treaty rights, and their solidified legal precedent.[27]

This particular history of indigenous recognition, with its twinned efforts at political erasure (and indigenous resistance to that erasure) and cultural resurrection, has led to disparate conceptions of indigeneity in the spheres of legal and diplomatic practice, which take the political nature of historical and contemporary indigeneity as a given, and in the sphere of popular culture, which remains wedded to the understanding of indigeneity as culture or ethnicity. It explains why settler entertainers issue earnest apologies for the offenses of cultural misappropriation to "the Native American community" at the same time as presidential candidates reaffirm government-to-government relations between the US federal government and indigenous tribal governments as a routine gesture in their political campaigns. More importantly, however, this history offers an archive of historical facts that are encoded in a variety of ways in contemporary indigenous art. Reading contemporary fiction by indigenous writers or appreciating contemporary indigenous visual art, whether in the museum, gallery, or movie theater, with this history in mind allows for an interpretive insight that breaks with the vastly limited understanding—misunderstanding, really—encouraged by multicultural misrecognition.

Because the multiculturalist politics of recognition encourages the exploration and celebration of cultural differences as a form of patriotic citizenship, cultural production in all of its varied forms provides a vast interface for exchanges of recognition between settler and indigenous participants, enabling interventions to be made on a much larger scale than in other realms of social engagement. Contemporary settler publics flock to museums, art galleries, and cinemas in far larger numbers than they do to Supreme Court hearings or meetings of political caucuses involving indigenous political and legal issues. Broad engagement with cultural production allows for intervention right where multicultural misrecognition takes place, at the source of the predicament, so to speak. Contemporary indigenous artists have capitalized on the current interest in their work to confront multicultural misrecognition. They do so by orchestrating fruitful interpretive impasses that play with cultural stereotypes of Indianness, and thus exploit the disjunction between culturalist and political understandings of indigeneity—and their coexistence and dissonance in contemporary public discourses. These conceptual impasses disrupt the interpretive mechanisms of multicultural misrecognition by making such misrecognition explicit and by shining light on its ideological ramifications. Because cultural production is the sphere where the culturalist conceptions of indigeneity are most commonly and forcefully perpetuated, it is here where they can be most effectively confronted. As spectators and readers, we can appreciate these confrontations—provided we are able to pry ourselves away from the interpretive mandates of multicultural misrecognition and instead consider indigenous cultural production in its proper political context. The varied forms of art explored in my book teach us how to do just that.

To demonstrate how the disjunction between the culturalist conception of indigeneity and the political conception of indigeneity operates in public forums, I turn first to the most visible recent engagement with the question of contemporary indigenous representation: the National Museum of the American Indian (NMAI) in Washington, DC. Chapter 1 focuses on what I call the dialectic of recognition—that is, the tension on display at the museum between the recognition of indigenous peoples as sovereign nations and their recognition as First Americans. First written into law in 1989, the NMAI was conceptualized in the 1990s in wide-ranging collaboration with indigenous communities across the Americas. Since its opening in 2004 it has been at the center of ongoing debates over the forms of contemporary indigeneity and its recognition by the state and federal governments and by the general public. The NMAI straddles the period of the emergence of multiculturalism, its mainstreaming in the late twentieth century, and its reassertion in the early twenty-first, functioning as a kind of barometer of contemporary indigenous representation. I propose that this tension between culturalist and political conceptions of indigeneity constitutes the NMAI's most valuable and enduring contribution to contemporary debates over indigenous recognition, because it both maps in detail the workings of multicultural misrecognition as a rhetorical predicament faced by contemporary indigenous artists and highlights some of the strategies these artists and curators have developed to confront this predicament.

In chapter 2, "*Atanarjuat* and the Ideological Work of Indigenous Filmmaking," I move from the public space of the museum, constructed via multiple curatorial agencies and responding to the mandates of both settler and indigenous constituencies, to a different kind of collective effort at indigenous recognition. I turn to *Atanarjuat (The Fast Runner)*, the Igloolik Isuma Productions' debut feature, because it is the first film written, directed, acted, and produced locally by indigenous filmmakers to gain international recognition and accrue a complicated reception history as simultaneously a quintessential Inuit and Canadian film. Thus it offers an opportunity to explore indigenous negotiation of multicultural misrecognition in the context of full indigenous creative and administrative control in Canada, a country that, unlike the United States, wrote multiculturalism into its constitution but, like its neighbor to the South, displays marked reluctance to acknowledge the political ambitions of indigenous nations beyond the scope of the Canadian federation. I suggest that in *Atanarjuat*, Isuma's filmmakers deploy their own brand of the dialectic of recognition by elaborating a concept of contemporary indigenous authenticity as a deliberate performance that facilitates a variety of political projects for multiple constituencies, speaking simultaneously to the specificity and universality of Inuit history and the present.

Historically, settler Indian representation has been carried on particularly prolifically in the visual arts, from early American painting and photography to the first moving pictures and beyond, resulting in a vast encyclopedia of images and visual representational modes that helped develop the discourse of the vanishing Indian and that continue to subtend interpretive mandates of multicultural misrecognition. The examples of the NMAI and *Atanarjuat* reveal that the creative appropriation of these images of Indian past constitutes an effective strategy for disrupting multicultural misrecognition. Digital fine art is a genre that engages with the settler visual, and in particular the photographic, archive more extensively than other forms of contemporary cultural production and thus allows for a comprehensive investigation of the rhetorical uses of this archive in the context of the multiculturalist appetite for visual displays of indigenous cultural difference. Thus, in chapter 3, "Palimpsestic Images: Contemporary American Indian Digital Fine Art and the Ethnographic Photo Archive," I explore the work of Dugan Aguilar, Hulleah Tsinhnahjinnie, and Pamela Shields, three contemporary digital artists/photographers who deploy a similar strategy of multifaceted layering of settler archival images and photographic conventions, an approach I call palimpsestic representation. I argue that palimpsestic representation allows today's indigenous artists to capitalize on this ideologically weighty visual inheritance to evoke the truth of indigenous historical experience obscured in settler photography precisely by incorporating fragments of the settler visual archive into their works to reveal contemporary indigenous realities as saturated with officially suppressed political histories.

Even as it capitalizes on the subversive potential of the settler photographic archive, palimpsestic representation remains wedded to a settler representational system. So in chapter 4, "Of Turtles, Snakes, Bones, and Precious Stones: Jimmie Durham's Indices of Indigeneity," I turn to an artist and a body of work that explore the utopian possibilities of what I call insubordinate indigenous art—that is, art that signifies outside of settler technologies of meaning, even as it is aimed against them. Durham's is a playful yet serious utopianism that never loses sight of its vision even as it pays careful attention to the rhetorical complexities of contemporary exchanges of recognition. One of the earliest indigenous critics of multiculturalism, Durham remains largely unknown to the American public and is very rarely a subject of scholarly analysis. It is a pity, not only because of the acutely insightful commentary he has offered on the impact of multiculturalism in the art world but also because his sculptures and multimedia installations deploy a rhetorical strategy—indexical representation—that is particularly effective in exposing and subverting multicultural misrecognition. By using found objects such as animal bones, turtle shells, and precious stones as indexical rather than symbolic or iconic signs, Durham dips into a different kind of archive available for indigenous self-representation. This archive of what I call indices of indigeneity allows the artist to bypass, to some extent, the settler signifying systems and to experiment with a utopian possibility of unfettered indigenous self-representation, even as his astute critique of the American rhetorical ground defined by multicultural misrecognition undermines such utopian potential of indigenous art.

The last of the case studies turns to the genre typically seen, along with the museum, as paradigmatic of European modernity: the novel. Unlike

Durham's turtle shells and coyote skulls, which help stage strategic escapes from settler interpretive frameworks, the novel embeds indigenous writers in the representational medium perhaps most inhospitable to traditional tribal forms of creative expression, which are rooted in orality, performance, and a far more complex conception of chronology than the one that underwrites standard Western narrative fiction. In chapter 5, I examine the deployment of what I call the gruesome authentic in LeAnne Howe's 2001 novel *Shell Shaker* as a strategy of forestalling multicultural misrecognition and as part of a larger narrative experiment to enact indigenous cosmology via the western medium of literary fiction. American Indian literature has been at the foreground of what critics have described as the American Indian Renaissance, which dates back to the early 1970s and is very much in evidence today. While many contemporary American Indian writers have met with critical success and wide readership, Howe's work is known only to a few specialists in the field of American Indian literature. Part of this neglect has to do, in my view, with the radically experimental nature of her narratives and with her unwavering allegiance to the political conception of indigeneity. For the very same reason, I believe it is critical to introduce Howe to the larger scholarly and general publics.

While I elucidate the consequences of multicultural misrecognition for indigenous artistic expression, ultimately my aim is to identify and describe medium-specific formal strategies that American Indian artists have developed to remind American settler publics about their peoples' long histories on the continent and their ongoing status as sovereign nations rather than as ethnic minority groups clamoring for inclusion in American nation-states. I also seek to model a critical approach that acknowledges the opportunities multiculturalism presents as well as the dilemmas it poses for contemporary indigenous artists. While I begin my discussion with the National Museum of the American Indian and Isuma's debut feature, *Atanarjuat (The Fast Runner)*, textual sites that have achieved global circulation, I also introduce a wide range of artistic media and some lesser-known figures in hopes that other scholars will expand their teaching repertoires to include these or similar voices. Settler representation of North America's indigenous peoples has historically unfolded in a variety of media, and so have contemporary indigenous responses; we should pay attention to as many of them as we can. And as we do so, we should strive to retrain our interpretive acumen away from the pervasive imperatives of multicultural misrecognition and toward the complex and innovative ways in which contemporary indigenous art makes available the rich political histories and complex contemporary realities of indigenous experience in North America. When we refuse to pay attention to the political, we are risking misapprehension of the complicated pasts and the potential futures of both indigenous and settler nations in North America, along with the fundamental conditions and possibilities of their inextricable relations. My book is an attempt to listen to the political in contemporary indigenous art in an interpretive mode that itself resists multicultural misrecognition.

I

Indigeneity and the Dialectic of Recognition at the National Museum of the American Indian

> There is established, within the Smithsonian Institution, a living memorial to Native Americans and their traditions, which shall be known as the "National Museum of the American Indian."
>
> Public Law 101–185, 101st US Congress, 1989

> We are thus a new kid on the block—the 18th of the Smithsonian Institution's world-renowned museums. . . . We define a moment of reconciliation and recognition in American history, a time for Indian people to assume, finally, a prominent place of honor on the nation's front lawn. It is our most fervent hope that we will be the instrument of enlightenment, helping our visitors learn more about the extraordinary achievements of the indigenous people of the Western hemisphere. We also hope that Native people will look upon the museum as a truly Native place, where they are welcome and honored guests.
>
> W. Richard West Jr. (Southern Cheyenne and member of the Cheyenne and Arapaho Tribes of Oklahoma); Founding Director, NMAI, *The NMAI Guide*, 2004

On September 21, 2004, in the largest gathering of indigenous peoples in Washington, DC, ever, more than twenty-five thousand people from more than five hundred nations and communities throughout the Americas converged on the National Mall to celebrate the opening of the National Museum of the American Indian (NMAI). Forming a grand procession, the participants marched by the Museum of Natural History to the NMAI's brand-new building—a symbolic, and ironic, graduation from one interpretive framework to another—to hear the NMAI's founding director Richard West welcome all indigenous peoples home and all others to a "Native Place." Taking his cue from the 1879 plea of Hinmatoowyalahtqit, or Chief Joseph, for "the white man to live in peace with the Indian" for they are "made by the same Great Spirit . . . they are brothers," West declared the NMAI to be "a symbol of hope, centuries in the making," a place where "at long last, the culturally different histories, cultures, and peoples of the Americas can come together in new mutual understanding and respect," prompting "the true cultural reconciliation that until now has eluded American history" (qtd. in Calloway 594). West's hyperbolic optimism, along with the contagious enthusiasm of all participants,[1] offset for a moment the obvious question hovering above the crowds gathered on the National Mall that day: Given the troubled history indigenous peoples have had with the American nation-states and with that premiere institution of Western hegemony, the museum, why had so many come to celebrate yet another opportunity for the United States to promote itself as a multicultural democracy? The colonial state, the museum, multiculturalism—numerous writers have denounced all three as inimical to the political aspirations of indigenous nations in the Americas, aspirations that these nations have been increasingly successfully bringing before international fora, such as the United Nations, in the late twentieth and early twenty-first centuries.[2]

By handing control over the exhibition of indigenous material culture and art to indigenous peoples themselves, the Smithsonian Institution publicized the creation of the NMAI as an opportunity to break with the long and shameful history of Western museological practices.[3] With its public commitment to work "in collaboration with the Native peoples of the Western Hemisphere and Hawai'i to protect and foster indigenous cultures, reaffirm traditions and beliefs, encourage contemporary artistic expression, and provide a forum for Native voices," as the NMAI website puts it, the museum officially recognized the continued indigenous presence on the continent and contracted to foster cultural expressions of such presence. Despite these declarations the number of indigenous people on the governing board of the museum and among the museum's employees did not constitute a majority,[4] so the NMAI embarked on an extensive collaboration with indigenous nations and communities across the hemisphere in order to fulfill the founding principles for the new museum. This collaboration resulted in *The Way of the People,* completed in 1993, a set of guidelines detailing the representational imperatives facing the architects charged with designing the Washington, DC, and Suitland, Maryland, sites, guidelines that would also help direct future curators of the collections. To serve as an ongoing record of the museum's legitimacy, these consultations were extensively described in the Smithsonian Institution's *Spirit of a Native Place,* a collection of essays by people involved in the creation of the museum that was published in 2004 to coincide with the opening. Across these documents and numerous printed materials available in the various branches, press releases, and on the museum website, the issue of Indian control over the collections and exhibitions has emerged as the most valuable aspect of the museum, a defining characteristic, and a kind of public relations mantra often reiterated in writing about the museum's popular and critical reception. When hailed by commentators, the NMAI has been praised foremost "as an institution that represents an important move away from the past—a museum about Indians controlled by Indians" (Alvin and Nagel 7).[5] When faulted, the museum has been criticized for its handling of specific organizational and thematic issues but usually only after an acknowledgment of its pioneering approach to curatorial control.[6] The Smithsonian Institution's officials publicized the transfer of administrative control over the former Gustav Heye collection and over future exhibitions to indigenous people not only to declare a shift in specifically museological practice but also as incontrovertible testimony to a larger achievement: the NMAI was a material expression of an unprecedented "moment of reconciliation and recognition in American history" (*The NMAI Guide* 7). The museum was thus to mark two beginnings: a new museological practice and a new period in US-Indian relations, the two linked in a causal relationship, with the former testifying to the latter.

The public response to the opening of the Washington branch of the NMAI has been varied. While many early mainstream press commentators complained about what they saw as radical departures from established conventions of museum exhibition, scholars of museum and American Indian studies responded by applauding the NMAI's policy on curatorial authority and by arguing that the museum successfully deployed an indigenous perspective, especially in the architecturally distinctive building and site.[7] Very soon, however, scholarly assessments became more critical, as many began to see the NMAI as an example of missed opportunities, a failure of will on the part of the curators. While these commentators fully accepted the NMAI's founding presumption about the ideological potential of "a museum about Indians controlled by Indians" and praised the design of the building and the grounds, they took issue with the content of the permanent exhibits. The main charge has been that the curators have failed to present an indictment of US colonialism and a comprehensive account of indigenous resistance.[8]

What this critical assessment misses, however, is an analysis of the limitations of the museum both as a genre and as an institution (despite Hilden and Huhndorf's early instructive example concerning the Heye Center in New York) and the acknowledgment of the structural constraints posed by establishment multiculturalism. The criticism of the NMAI indicts the curators' script as inadequate while omitting from the analysis the nature of the stage—that is, the rhetorical conditions of engagement already in place and the interpretive constraints of multicultural misrecognition in particular.[9] As I argue in the introduction, the United States and Canada have embraced multiculturalism because it supplies a useful tool for national integration. Deploying the politics of recognition has allowed these states to translate their colonial histories into uplifting narratives of national and ideological triumph repeated in the autoethnographic accounts of each ethnic group's overcoming of past prejudice and subordination. Minority writers and artists have readily embraced and supplied these multiculturalist narratives of representational liberation because they offered visibility in the national imagination as cocitizens rather than second-class citizens. The state-sponsored performances of cultural difference by ethnic groups have testified to the vision of North American democracies as nations of multiple cultures in an ongoing project of reformation toward an equitable future. Multicultural democracies dwell on their colonial pasts, if at all, only in order to celebrate their irrevocable passing. The ultimate proof of this passing is the ascendancy of multiculturalism as a model of cultural relations, fully evidenced in the hypervisibility of minority cultural production in the public sphere. In the case of indigenous peoples, however, engagement with the politics of recognition leads to what I have called multicultural misrecognition, that is, an interpretive framework that reduces indigeneity to culture, and as a result obscures the colonial status of indigenous nations. Because the majority of criticism leveled at the NMAI took the premises of multiculturalism for granted, ignoring multiculturalism's ideological imperatives altogether, it failed to appreciate that an engagement with the politics of recognition diverts attention from historic and ongoing colonialism. As a result, this criticism remained blind to the inventive ways in which the NMAI both invites and resists multicultural misrecognition by staging a tension between the conceptions of indigeneity as culture and as nationhood. This rhetorical move, a kind of dialectic of recognition, paradoxically opens up space for critiques of colonialism within the very framework designed to conceal it. By sustaining rather than resolving this tension, the NMAI offers an instructive example of the complexity of indigenous representation in the age of multiculturalism.

The NMAI and the Ideological Mandates of Multicultural Misrecognition

It's surprising that the critics of the NMAI overlooked the extent to which the museum accommodates multicultural misrecognition. The rhetoric accompanying the arrival of the NMAI in Washington and onto the American museological stage makes plain that the recognition taking place via the erection of a museum devoted to and controlled by American Indians on the National Mall is far more complex than a straightforward return, reclamation, and reconciliation; the irony of American Indians returning to Chesapeake Bay as "the new kid on the block" (*Guide* 7) is hard to miss. Richard West's commentary, during the opening ceremonies and in museum publications, manifests these complexities and allows us to appreciate the pressures of multicultural misrecognition at work. Paying attention to his language reveals precisely how the conception of indigeneity as culture works to bypass the history of colonialism in order to deliver a multicultural United States. For example, in *Spirit of a Native Place* West explains that the NMAI "represents the long overdue recognition of the contributions Native peoples and communities have made and continue to make to American civilization" and declares his belief that "the museum will be an invaluable resource for learning about cultures that were here at the very beginning of this country and are woven into its heritage"; that "for the first citizens of this hemisphere" it "will serve as a center of affirmation"; that "the museum will be here for a very long time"; and that while "what goes on in it will change over time, as it should, there will always be this place—this Native Place. As long as this country is here, it will be here" (65). West reiterated these sentiments during the opening ceremony speech, when he declared that American Indians "have lived in these lands and sacred places for thousands of years" and are thus "the original part of the cultural heritage of every person hearing these words today." And though he admitted that indigenous people "have felt the cruel and destructive edge of the colonialism that followed contact and lasted for hundreds of years," speaking in the first person plural, he declared: "We have survived, and from a cultural standpoint, triumphed against great odds. We are here now—40,000,000 indigenous peoples throughout the Americas and in hundreds of different cultural communities. And we will insist, as we must, that we remain a part of the cultural future of the Americas, just as we were a part of its past and fought so hard to be a part of its present" (qtd. in Calloway 594). West's rhetoric suggests that the NMAI supplies a happy ending to a long, traumatic history; the museum's opening marks a new era in exhibitionary practice and in indigenous-settler relations. On behalf of the United States, it offers a testimony to a new coming to terms with the nation's colonial history; as colonialism is banished to the past tense in West's speech, this history is safely transcended in the nation's multicultural present, manifested for all to see by the newest building on the National Mall. Like the final missing tile placed in an otherwise complete mosaic, erected on the last available piece of land on the Mall, the NMAI completes the public image of the nation by helping to transform indigenous peoples into the First Americans. As an added bonus, it extends the genealogy of North American nation-states well beyond the age of discovery, conquest, and settlement. For indigenous peoples, the NMAI provides the recognition that has supposedly eluded them for so long, and with this recognition a promise of a more equitable future.

The sticking point is the nature of this recognition—that is, the question of what exactly is being recognized. As I explore in the introduction, the kind of recognition extended to America's indigenous peoples has undergone a dramatic shift from the recognition of political sovereignty in diplomatic exchanges in the eighteenth and nineteenth centuries to the recognition of American Indian cultural difference in the twentieth century. The late twentieth century saw a consolidation of the culturalist conception of indigeneity—ironically, precisely at a time when American Indian activists succeeded in reinserting the concepts of national sovereignty and government-to-government relations into political and legal discourse and in acting with visible results in international fora such as the United Nations. Richard West's deference to culture as the defining concept for thinking about indigenous pasts and futures manifests the extent to which multicultural misrecognition structures the public exchanges of recognition between contemporary indigenous nations and the North American democracies.

The NMAI promises recognition that is cultural rather than political. The museum will foster indigenous cultures, not nations; it will reaffirm traditions and beliefs, not indigenous governance systems; it will encourage the expression of artistic, not political, aspirations. However celebratory, West's language, and the Smithsonian Institution's broader public relations discourse that this language represents, is telling in its rhetorical choices, its omissions and qualifications, and its equivocal use of terms such as *nation*, *people*, *country*, *civilization*, and *America*. West appropriates the rhetoric of the multicultural nation—*cultural* standpoint, *cultural* heritage, *cultural* communities, *cultural* future—to make claims for indigenous visibility. He deploys the language of citizenship but divorces it from indigenous nationalist aspirations. The NMAI will celebrate American Indians as "the citizens of this hemisphere" rather than as citizens of the Onondaga Nation, the Lakota Nation, or any other of the many indigenous nations of the United States or Canada, federally recognized or not, status or nonstatus. The NMAI will showcase indigenous contributions to American civilization and "this country" rather than unfold narratives of indigenous national formation.

However broadly "American civilization" might be conceived, spatially and temporally, ultimately it gets reduced to "this country," which is not America or Indian Country, but the United States, the colonial state guarantor of the recognition extended to indigenous peoples. And this particular moment—"the beginning of this country," be it 1492, 1607, or 1776—rather than centuries or millennia[10] before European colonization, remains the relevant historical marker of the hemisphere's civilization, even from West's explicitly indigenous perspective.

West's central metaphor of the NMAI as the "meeting ground on the nation's front lawn" is especially emblematic of the peculiar kind of recognition extended to indigenous people by the Smithsonian Institution and, by extension, the government that funds it. The phrase is simultaneously honorific and insulting; it promises agency only to enfold it in a larger structure of control. Historically, the term evokes early diplomatic exchanges between indigenous nations and colonial governments, such as, for example, those that took place on the front lawn of Johnson Hall in today's New York state, where the emissary of the British Crown negotiated with the Haudenosaunee in the eighteenth century. The NMAI itself is a meeting ground where indigenous people and settlers can seek reconciliation under cultural guidance from First Americans. But this meeting ground is located on the nation's front lawn, the National Mall, down the hill from the watchful perch of the Capitol. It is a Native Place—the last patch of symbolic Nativeness in a continent gone American—but one contained within national borders, those of the United States. Here, in West's words, Native people are "honored and welcome guests." The Native Place on the nation's front lawn is a home to America's indigenous peoples, but one in which they are welcome to feel like guests—and guests who are on display. Native Americans are acknowledged as partners, authorities even, engaged in cultural dialogue; they also become exhibits in the great museum of the United States as a multicultural democracy, for which the National Mall is the most visible "vitrine."[11] The recognition extended by West, speaking on behalf of the NMAI to America's indigenous peoples, is premised on the latter's reconciliation to the circumscribed nature of indigenous sovereignty within the United States or Canada—the coupling of recognition with reconciliation, one the guarantor of the other and vice versa, being the essential multiculturalist gambit.[12] The Smithsonian Institution's official rhetoric surrounding the opening of the NMAI suggests that far from acknowledging that indigenous nations have longstanding separate political identities, the museum provides a way of integrating indigenous peoples into the body politic of the nation as separate cultures rather than as nations within it, an exemplary instance of multicultural misrecognition.

The Legacy of the Museum as an Institution

The predicament posed by multicultural misrecognition exerting its pressure on the NMAI is further compounded by the historical legacy of the museum as an institution and its representation of the world's indigenous peoples. Much of the scholarly work in museum studies in the last two decades shares a consensus on the ideological role of the museum. Although at present ubiquitous throughout the world—from the cosmopolitan metropolis to the small town, from the state capital to the reservation cultural center—the museum is considered one of the primary founding institutions of European modernity. Having originated in cabinets of curiosities and princely collections at European aristocratic courts, the museum proliferated during the eighteenth century and emerged as a public institution in the early nineteenth. Over the next century and a half it was instrumental in the formation of the modern nation-state and the consolidation of European empires at the expense of indigenous populations across the globe.[13] Visual culture's equivalent of the novel, which in Benedict Anderson's famous formulation helped usher in imagined communities—modern nations—in place of societies structured by kinship or feudal obligations, the public museum served to transform these communities into national, and eventually imperial, audiences; it educated—or, if you prefer, disciplined—them into specific conceptions of the state, nation, empire, and the modern order of things (Preziosi 519). While making the public visible through its rituals of participation and civic engagement, the museum served a fundamentally conservative role by encouraging political passivity among its visitors (Duncan 283).

The museum's defining modes of procedure—acquisition, ordering, and exhibition of art and material culture—have reflected and reinforced the centrality of the system of objects and the culture of spectacle characteristic of the modern capitalist West.[14] Because it operates primarily by substituting the reality of the exhibited collections for that of lived social relations, the museum as a genre has tended to reify historical processes into representable essences and totalizing narratives. This process of abstraction from historical specifics operates in art museums, where aesthetic appreciation is premised on lack of familiarity with the social context, as well as in ethnographic ones, which in an effort to depict authentic cultures to metropolitan publics end up suppressing the complex lived experiences of tribal peoples, along with their ever-changing art (Clifford, "Histories of the Tribal and the Modern," 643). As they construct the special nature of European modernity in sharpest relief, ethnographic museums present cultural differences produced or reproduced through curating as preexisting, inherent cultural diversity (Prakash 209). In the process, they obscure the historically unequal relations of power that enabled the traffic of bodies and things for exhibition from the colonial periphery to the imperial center in the first place. Indigenous peoples typically serve in these representations as adjuncts to narratives of civilizational development, of which the focus and the final point is the West.

This generic and institutional propensity of the museum to obfuscate global historical processes, along with the material and power inequities resulting from them, and to reinforce the centrality of the West to its representational practices has turned out to be its sturdiest characteristic, surviving even the series of reforms in exhibitionary practice undertaken in the second half of the twentieth century under the auspices of multiculturalism and its promise of equal representation. Many critics have insisted that far from transforming the museum, its late twentieth-century reinvention offered only superficial reformation, and that it ultimately, and ironically, entrenched existing perspectives and practices. For example, in his well-known critique of the 1992 National Gallery exhibit "Circa 1492: Art in the Age of Exploration," Homi Bhabha argues that despite new exhibition techniques stressing the coevality of represented cultures and the historicity of the indigenous, "the angle of visibility" in the museum has not changed. He points out that "what was once exotic or archaic, tribal or folkloristic, inspired by strange gods, is now given a secular national present, and an international future," and he charges that "sites of cultural difference too easily become the part of the post-Modern West's thirst for its own ethnicity" (240). Furthermore, as Ania Coombes has suggested, "it is precisely under the banner of a form of multiculturalism that those exhibitions, uncritically celebrating cultural 'diversity' through the primary strategy of displaying culturally hybrid objects from once colonized nations, can claim immunity from addressing the specificity of this experience" (490) and, I would add, from addressing their own implication in the global processes of subjugation. Contemporary multiculturalist "curatorial projects end up supporting the centrality of the Western museum" (Bhabha 240). Equally importantly, I would suggest, such projects promote the magnanimity of contemporary multicultural democracies that have broken with their shameful colonial pasts, have ceded the cultural, but not the political, stage to the once oppressed, and are now, as is demonstrated in these exhibits, equal partners in the global democratic project. The multiculturalist panacea of equal representation ends up evoking, in the service of the Western museum and the nation-states it articulates, a "misleading rhetoric of equality" (Coombes 490), which implies equivalence of difference, sliding once again into segregationist essentialism (Bhabha 240). Despite a more thorough and historicized incorporation of the ethnographic other in contemporary museological exhibitions, the West remains the center and the reference point structuring the representation of the rest of the world.

Although broadly denounced as the most successful imperialist tool, the museum has not only persisted through the late twentieth century and into the twenty-first but also flourished, its contemporary ubiquity across the world the incontrovertible testimony to its staying power. Three-quarters of the currently operating museums have been founded since World War II (Hudson 86), the majority of them in decolonized nations in Asia and Africa, on indigenous reserves and reservations in North America, and in aboriginal communities in Australia and New Zealand. Given its long legacy of exploitation in acquisition and misrepresentation in exhibitionary practice, the museum would appear too compromised as a genre and an institution to inspire such widespread interest among the world's indigenous populations. And yet, the museum is a site of potential for indigenous peoples for the same reason it has been criticized in recent museum studies—its role in mobilizing imagined communities of diverse kinds, in building and legitimizing political entities such as nations. Indigenous nations want museums as places where cultural heritage is preserved and made accessible for appreciation through staged visual narratives of historical development; in the case of tribal museums in particular, as narratives of perseverance or recovery, they function as "powerful identity-defining machines" (Duncan 286). As such, they become indispensable to indigenous nations struggling to overcome the demographic, economic, and social impact of genocide and the continuing effects of colonialism while asserting their historical status as sovereign political entities. Museums can recover and articulate suppressed national histories and legacies. They offer an arena where embattled indigenous nations can exercise control over their very constitution and definition. They make communities visible as nations to themselves and to other national and international publics. The number of newly opened tribal museums in North America readily testifies to the indigenous nations' willingness to appropriate the museum in their nation-building projects. In a refusal of standard museological practice in the West, these institutions are often renamed cultural or heritage centers, but they are intended to function as museums, albeit reformed ones, particularly in their potential for national self-definition. The example of the Mashantucket Pequot Museum and Research Center is perhaps the best, and definitely the most visible, recent example of the constructive potential the museum offers to contemporary indigenous nations.[15]

As mainstream critics condemn museums for their participation in nationalist and imperial projects and their collaborative operation in globalized capital markets,[16] and as many indigenous critics condemn historical and contemporary museums and art galleries for misrepresentation, indigenous nations continue to create tribal museums in efforts to consolidate their communities and assert their national and political separateness. But they have also invested financially and intellectually in the National Museum of the American Indian at the Smithsonian Institution, despite its federal oversight. If the rapid development of tribal museums is motivated by a desire to have full—administrative and curatorial—control over indigenous national representation, the investment in the NMAI would appear to make little sense, given that despite its public rhetoric, the museum is a federally funded institution negotiating mutually exclusive demands for indigenous recognition. This investment does become more intelligible once we consider the colonial state's national museum as a space of negotiation where indigenous nations can seek recognition of their presence and sovereignty by the colonial state—Richard West's "meeting ground" in that historically specific sense. Located on the National Mall, in the US national capital, the NMAI certainly offers the highest visibility quotient. The museum's commitment to hemispheric and pan-Indian representation, along with its inadvertent participation in the American politics of recognition, however, makes it a particularly difficult stage for staking claims to indigenous sovereignty. The museum's very name captures the rhetorical dilemma perfectly, with "National" implying, ambiguously, a variety of references, from the colonial nation-state to the numerous indigenous nations seeking their re-recognition as such. The museum becomes a meeting ground where the primary exchange of recognition is thoroughly contradictory: as the community and the NMAI curators seek to reassert indigenous sovereignty, the museum's existence within the particular geography of the National Mall cannot help but corroborate the vision of the United States as a multicultural nation and its specific understanding of the settler-indigenous relationship, which folds American Indians into the polity as yet another ethnic group.

The NMAI's curators have not been oblivious to this dilemma. For example, Jolene Rickard, a Tuscarora artist and art historian who curated several of the opening exhibits, has long recognized that a museum functions primarily in the service of the colonial state and that inclusion of indigenous art in national museums is "simultaneously a colonizing act and a decolonizing act" (115). Given this fundamental structural predicament, she has asked: "How can we insert different worldviews or philosophical positions into a museum space? How do the interconnected artistic and political needs of First Nations function in any national museum?" (115). As long as indigenous nations continue to experience political, economic, and cultural subordination to the colonial states, she points out, inclusion of their work in these states' cultural institutions will continue to pose special difficulties (116). How can a concept of an indigenous nation be articulated on the representational stage of the colonial state? What thematic and formal choices would such articulation assume? Is a viable assertion of indigenous national sovereignty possible within the framework of multiculturalism? How can the political meanings of indigeneity be asserted in the climate of a desire for its cultural meanings? Rickard's answer to these questions is to focus relentlessly on the concept of indigenous sovereignty. She argues that "an understanding of the term 'self-determination' as 'sovereignty' is as critical a framing for Indigenous artists and art as the 'gaze' is to the gendered discourse. The fundamental issue is the exposure of an inequitable power relationship. By making sovereignty part of a national and international dialogue, museums shift the boundaries of control for the maker, the Native Nation, the gallery, and society" (118). Such exposure necessarily has to take place on the nation-state's museological stage, where it will achieve greatest visibility. It has to take place in the national rather than the tribal museums, because indigenous nations hardly need to be convinced about their sovereign political status. It is the mainstream public that must be invited to consider these questions, especially as it engages in the rituals of good citizenship made possible by the Smithsonian Institution just down the hill from the US Capitol. Museums remain of interest to American Indian nations because they facilitate the reinvention and assertion of American Indian tribes as contemporary nations. The National Museum of the American Indian, in particular, provides a highly visible national and international forum to press this agenda in the colonial state's capital. As Karen Coody Cooper put it, "the ironic symbolism [of the museum's location] is not missed. American Indians want to be visible to the nation's lawmakers, never to be forgotten again, and [they] also want to keep an eye on the US government" (166). The NMAI relies on the museum as the nation-building institution in order to interrupt the celebration of one nation with a reminder of the existence of others in its midst.

In the remainder of this chapter, I investigate how the NMAI takes up the genre of the museum and reforms it to make it more suitable for articulating a range of issues of interest to indigenous peoples. Viewed through the lens of multicultural misrecognition, the NMAI emerges as engaged in a complicated nexus of strategies designed to make visible and to subvert the erasures demanded by multiculturalism. While the museum's public relations materials and opening ceremonies, as I described above, invite multicultural misrecognition as the primary interpretive framework, many of its individual exhibitions undertake a critique of US imperialism, expose the continued colonial nature of US-Indian relations, assert indigenous political separateness, and attempt to reeducate a public raised on stereotypes of Indianness perpetuated in popular culture. Furthermore, the NMAI engages in tribal nation-building by showcasing the work undertaken in tribal museums, reforms museological practices of representing indigeneity, and tackles the contradiction of representing the museum venture as a collaboration with the United States while chronicling the history of conflicts between indigenous nations and American federal governments. Most importantly, the NMAI allows contemporary indigenous nations to participate in the current politics of recognition by adjusting the terms of such participation away from the interpretive effects of multicultural misrecognition. It does so primarily, as I argue below, by harking back to the historical precedent of the early treaty-making period. The discourse of indigenous nationalism and of historic treaties in the museum offers an antidote to the notion of cultural rather than political citizenship asserted so emphatically in the museum's public relations materials and in the concepts of the Native Place and First Americans in particular.

Historic Treaties and the Political Conception of Indigeneity

Upheld as testimonies to European recognition of the prior inherent political autonomy of North America's indigenous nations and decried as a colonial tool of dispossession, treaties remain complicated but apt symbols of indigenous sovereignty as circumscribed by North American democracies. Within the existing colonial framework, they furnish the only politically viable tool for asserting indigenous sovereignty, for holding on to the land base and other material resources, for demanding the return of lands lost, and for claiming gaming rights as an engine of economic development on reservations. Vine Deloria Jr.'s take on the subject is emblematic of this predicament: repeatedly in his writing, Deloria exposed treaties and government-to-government conceptions of indigenous-settler relations as a political expedient for the colonial state, and yet he also supported evocation of historic treaties as useful to indigenous nations in securing access to resources and to some forms of self-determination.[17] Any deployment of historic treaties on behalf of indigenous sovereignty at the turn of the twenty-first century has to contend with this complicated historical context. As the understanding of indigeneity has shifted from political to cultural representation throughout the twentieth century, most dramatically in the late twentieth century with the rise of multiculturalism and the idea of *cultural citizenship*, the concept of *indigenous nations* has grown ever more obscure to a mainstream American public enamored of *Native culture*, despite occasional court rulings honoring the historic treaties and the presumption of indigenous political autonomy they embody. In a political and cultural climate in which recognition has come to mean acknowledgment and respect for cultural identity, treaties hark back to the pre-1871 period in which recognition unfolded on the diplomatic stage. Contemporary insistence on historic treaties aims to wrench indigeneity away from culture and return it to politics, to extricate the Indians from the museum and other cultural stages and to return them to the diplomatic meeting ground, so to speak.

To attempt such a shift from cultural to political recognition in a national museum of a colonial state is an enterprise wrought with paradoxes, given the museum's historical predispositions to cultural essentialism and colonial incorporation. As indigenous art and history are appropriated by the multiculturalist democracies of North America, and as Indians become celebrated as "First Americans," the NMAI functions primarily as a testimony to the state's recognition of indigenous cultural difference and therefore of indigenous peoples' cultural citizenship within the contemporary (colonial) states. And yet, the NMAI's very location on the National Mall and directly across from the Capitol opens up the possibility, however symbolic, for the recognition of the presence of indigenous nations as political actors who are once again negotiating in the colonial state's capital. By evoking the admittedly contradictory iconography of this particular location, the context of historic treaty negotiations allows us to see the NMAI as more than a venue for assertions of Western incorporative universalism. Potentially, it can function as a meeting ground where the political autonomy of indigenous nations could be asserted once again. The NMAI thus itself functions as a contemporary instance of historic treaty-making, one in which different mechanisms of recognition work simultaneously in complementary and contradictory ways. Paying attention to how historic treaties are used at the NMAI allows us to specify the complex ways in which indigenous sovereignty—that is, the political idea of the Onondaga, or Cherokee, or Lakota Nations—is obscured in contemporary North American multicultural democracies and how it can be evoked and asserted.

How this complex dialectic of recognition, or the specific ways in which political and cultural conceptions of indigeneity contend with each other, plays out at the NMAI has much to do with the museum's location, its architectural design, and its multiple curatorial agency. I've described above the symbolic valences of the museum's placement on the National Mall in Washington, DC, and its potential for asserting both the diplomatic relationship between two political entities and the circumscription of indigenous sovereignty within the colonial state via the concept of cultural citizenship. This dynamic of simultaneously asserting and obscuring the political dimensions of indigeneity operates as well within the building itself. The museum's distinct common and exhibition spaces reflect the mandate to represent all indigenous peoples across the hemisphere as a demographic sharing common historical experiences and contemporary realities. At the same time, they also aim to represent the many indigenous nations as distinct from each other and as engaging in a variety of political relationships with the colonial states they inhabit.

The museum tackled this complicated mandate via a unique layout design for its exhibition spaces and an original approach to curatorial agency. The museum spaces unfold in a concentric pattern. Three large exhibition areas designed according to the same spatial principle constitute the building's core. The "Our Lives" exhibit treats contemporary indigenous issues; "Our Peoples" tackles the past; "Our Universes" presents cosmologies. Each main area is divided into two separate sections: a central cluster of displays highlighting pan-Indian issues, referred to as permanent exhibits and curated by the NMAI curators, and a surrounding area, a perimeter of sorts, divided into eight distinct spaces, referred to as community galleries, each devoted to a specific nation or tribal community and curated by a committee of the tribal members working in cooperation with the NMAI curators. These main areas are supplemented by "Windows on Exhibitions," small galleries curated by the NMAI team and dispersed throughout the building's several floors; these exhibitions highlight different kinds of objects in the museum's collections. The museum also offers space for changing exhibitions curated by invited curators. The main common gathering spaces, including the Potomac Rotunda at the museum's entry, two separate theaters, Mitsitam Café, and the museum store all continue the overall aesthetic design of the museum. Thus, curatorial agency in the museum is dispersed between museum professionals and nonprofessionals, and between architectural and curatorial teams, on the one hand, and individual curators, on the other. In the discussion that follows, I specify the curatorial agency at work in each exhibition or display I analyze by referring to community galleries' tribal designations and by naming individual curators, or curator teams, whenever possible.[18] My point, however, is not to attach either the cultural or the political conceptions of indigeneity to particular individuals or teams responsible for the design of the museum and its exhibits, but rather to elucidate the complex ways in which these two divergent forms of indigenous recognition contend with each other throughout the museum, regardless of the political and theoretical stances of the various curators.

To press the political conception of indigeneity, the NMAI deploys the discourse of the historic treaties in a variety of ways, from permanent and community exhibitions on specific treaties and their ramifications for past and contemporary indigenous realities to the general iconography evoking the concept itself that recurs throughout the common spaces of the building and in the museum's promotional materials. Some of the above strategies successfully deliver a political understanding of indigeneity; others end up subsumed by the idea of indigeneity as culture. For example, the guide to the museum, available to all entering visitors free of charge, reproduces Public Law 101–185, an act of Congress that established the NMAI as part of the Smithsonian Institution in 1989, along with several maps of the Chesapeake Bay and Potomac River region, the capital, and the National Mall. Part of what the guide calls "the reclamation of a Native Place," Public Law 101–185 is formatted to mimic a founding legal document, its design following the same aesthetic conventions as the historic treaties displayed in the museum exhibits. However, in keeping with the rhetoric of the opening day speeches from Smithsonian Institution and NMAI officials, the description of Public Law 101–185 emphasizes the cultural citizenship of indigenous peoples and eschews any mention of their political status, testifying to the fact that merely invoking the treaty iconography does not necessarily subtend a political conception of indigeneity. The *Spirit of a Native Place* collection describes Public Law 101–185 as launching a museum where "Native People [can] celebrate and share their achievements and aspirations as Americans and citizens of the world" (183)—not as citizens of their nations. The language of Public Law 101–185 itself also carefully avoids the subject of indigenous nationhood. Instead it describes "cultures indigenous to the Americas," "Native American history and art," "Native American peoples," "the cultural legacy, historic grandeur, and contemporary culture of Native Americans," "Indian tribes," and "Native communities" (Public Law). When it is used, the word "nation" refers to the United States only; it never designates American Indian peoples. Rather than evoking indigenous nationalism, the iconography of the treaty appears in the guide only to point toward the idea of Native American cultural citizenship, in ways similar to Richard West's opening ceremony address.

The museum's permanent exhibitions, however, use the treaties to highlight a political conception of indigenous nations. For example, "Our Peoples" features an extended exhibit on historic treaties titled "Stated Intentions: Treaties as Instruments of Dispossession and Survival." The exhibit notes that the indigenous nations were negotiating treaties with European governments since contact, but it focuses on treaties signed with the US federal government since 1776 in order to offer an account of this government's subversion of the earlier tradition of treaty-making. The exhibit's narrative argues that treaties were expedient diplomatic tools aimed initially at forging alliances with indigenous nations to protect the fledgling US government from frontier wars and territorial challenges from other European contenders on the continent; later, with the military dominance of indigenous nations waning, they were used to extract territorial cessions. The exhibit further notes that though treaty-making was abrogated by the US Congress in 1871, the treaties constitute a historical testimony to indigenous sovereignty: "treaties are living documents that support our sovereign people and our survival," asserts Leslie Wheelock, one of the exhibit's curators.

If the central exhibit of "Our Peoples" emphasizes both the treaties' role in the federal government's dispossession of indigenous nations and their potential to support these nations' contemporary claims to resources and rights, its community galleries present the treaties as legal documents that established the historic and continuing political relationship between indigenous nations and the federal government. For example, the Yakama Nation exhibit foregrounds the 1855 treaty, which brought fourteen separate bands together and "retained 1.2 million acres of homeland." The exhibit describes how the annual celebration of "Yakama Nation Treaty Days" honors the treaty as a foundational event in Yakama national history; the Yakama see their "treaty as an empowering document" that "recognized and reaffirmed [their] rights and sovereignty." The exhibit's narrative affirms the Yakama's prior inherent sovereignty—"we were here since time immemorial . . . long before the signing of the treaty"—and insists on a specific understanding of the treaty not as a source of that sovereignty but rather as a tool to support the tribal government's decision on behalf of the nation. The accompanying account of the "closed area," a sacred place reserved for Yakama ceremonies and inaccessible to outsiders, in this context, provides a model for territorial sovereignty guaranteed by government-to-government agreements. A framed newspaper article about the creation of the closed area—"Indians Get Mt. Adams"—supplies a useful contrast between public perceptions of tribal rights and the curators' stress on Yakama nationhood.

In a similar focus on sovereignty and its deliberate limitation, the Kiowa exhibit juxtaposes the 1867 Medicine Lodge Treaty with the 1903 Supreme Court decision *Lone Wolf v. Hitchcock*, which declared that the US Congress had complete constitutional authority over Indian affairs and that it could abrogate treaties negotiated with indigenous nations. The exhibit's intent is to uphold the treaty as a primary legal document recognizing the Kiowas' sovereignty and right to self-determination, including control over their territory, and to denounce the Supreme Court decision as a breach of an established, and still binding, political and legal order. The treaties stake claims to modern political relations with the United States and show that such relations have plenty of historical precedent. Pressing the related point about the prior and inherent nature of indigenous sovereignty, the chronologies of some of the community galleries in "Our Peoples"—for example the Tohono O'odham's "Long ago through 1900s"—make a point of situating indigenous nations within a continental time not bound by the Western calendar, emphasizing their prior occupancy of the land and their long political existence independent of the current colonial state. Furthermore, the Kiowa community gallery, along with those of the Tohono O'odham and Cherokee Nations (including the Eastern Band, which remained in Georgia after the removals) and the Seminole Tribe of Florida, stands in contrast to the community galleries of the Tapirape in Brazil and the Nahua and Wixarika in Mexico. The latter, having never signed treaties with the Portuguese or Spanish colonial governments, cannot resort to the language of nationhood and sovereignty and must turn instead to the discourse of cultural continuance and ancestral genealogies to describe their contemporary experience. The presence of treaty documents in the North American community galleries, especially in light of their absence from those of indigenous communities in South America, underlines the unique political and legal status of indigenous nations in the United States and Canada and the historic practice of recognizing their nationhood.

But it is the "Our Lives" exhibition that most insistently emphasizes the links between the historic treaties and contemporary indigenous nationalism. This exhibit reaches for early treaties, such as those negotiated in the early seventeenth century between the Pamunkey and the English in Virginia, or between the Haudenosaunee and the Dutch in the Hudson Valley, to offer a historical genealogy for contemporary objects such as the Haudenosaunee passport displayed in the Kahnawake Mohawk community gallery and the Certificate of Degree of Indian Blood (CDIB) card and Fritz Scholder's *The American Indian* painting included in the permanent exhibit. National sovereignty, for which the Haudenosaunee passport serves as a material emblem, is the focal point of the Kahnawake gallery. "When something happens, we react in a way that asserts our self-determination as a people and our sovereignty as a nation," declare the Kahnawake community curators. In this context, the well-known account of Mohawk high-rise ironworkers in New York and other American cities becomes an opportunity to assert the Mohawks' treaty-guaranteed right to unrestricted movement across the US-Canadian border rather than their adaptability to modern American industry.[19] Mohawks' labor migrations, their jaywalking across the border, function as an exercise of Mohawk sovereignty. Mohawk assertions of nationalism stand in contrast to the neighboring account of the emergence of Nunavut in the Canadian Arctic, the first Canadian province with an indigenous (Inuit) governing majority. This account makes clear the new territory's administrative subjection to the Canadian Constitution and the Canadian Charter of Rights and Freedom. The Inuit country, in other words, represents the integration of the Inuit into the Canadian federation rather than their national emancipation.[20] It offers an example of administrative incorporation on par with the economic integration of the Seminoles through the federally developed tourism and cattle industries depicted in the "Our Peoples" exhibition.

Curated by Jolene Rickard, the central exhibit of "Our Lives" accounts for such disparities by focusing on the issue of continued negotiations between indigenous nations and European nation-states in North America and by stressing the political nature of contestations over rights and resources. For example, the section on 1960s activism highlights a shift in Indian self-perception from tribalism to nationhood and chronicles the reemergence of specific national identities such as Diné, Ho-chunk, Skarure, Piscataway, Muscogee, and Unangan. Other sections treat CDIB cards, blood quantum, negotiations over Indian identity politics, gaming, control over natural resources including hunting and fishing rights, language preservation, and other cultural revitalization initiatives—all as examples of treaty-guaranteed exercises in self-determination. A side note by the curator explains the dual citizenship of American Indians, as members of both settler nations and indigenous nations, and advocates for the right to self-government for all indigenous peoples across the world. It also stresses the need for an international political forum, such as the United Nations, to serve as a stage for redressing indigenous nations' grievances against colonial states. Rickard thus harkens to the early treaty period, when Indian affairs unfolded on the international diplomatic stage rather than as part of domestic policy in the United States and Canada.

This emphasis on the long history of diplomatic relations between indigenous and European, and later American, nations recurs in different locations in the museum beyond the "Our Lives" and "Our Peoples" exhibitions. For example, an exhibit on tomahawks, pipes, and peace medals, one of many under the heading "Windows on Exhibitions," glosses those objects as emblems of mutual recognition among political sovereigns from Europe and North America. Because they were exchanged as gifts on the occasion of diplomatic engagements, the large number of peace pipes and tomahawks—which, the accompanying narrative points out, were manufactured in England—attests to the pervasiveness of political relations between indigenous nations and European courts and governments. Presidential medals gifted to leaders of indigenous nations by the US government offer a visual chronicle of the transformation such relations underwent after 1776. Initially a testimony to the mutual recognition of "Indian nations and the US government as equal powers," the medals bear engravings of the heads of American presidents and symbols of friendship and cooperation. These gradually give way to visual assertions of the inherent value of the American way of life, such as apotheoses of agricultural labor. Ultimately, the medals decline in importance in the late nineteenth and early twentieth centuries as the military and political balance in North America shifts and the United States claims complete territorial control over the mainland. Once again, the goal of the exhibit is to use the material evidence at the museum's disposal to remind visitors about the unique political status of the indigenous nations in North America and to imply that a return to the early model of political relations in North America is the only internationally legal way to resolve America's "Indian Problem."

This implication is forcefully manifested in what is effectively a presidential medal in reverse, the contemporary bronze statue titled *Allies in War, Partners in Peace* gifted to the NMAI by the Oneida Nation of New York and displayed on the museum's ground floor. The life-size statue features a group of historical figures: Polly Cooper, an Oneida woman who, the accompanying narrative informs the visitors, saved American revolutionaries from starvation by teaching them how to cook corn; her contemporary, Oskanondonha, an Oneida wampum keeper; and General George Washington. The statue commemorates a specific historic event: the Oneidas' four-hundred-mile march from Oneida Territory to Valley Forge, Pennsylvania, to deliver food to starving American soldiers during the Revolutionary War. Rhetorically, it asserts Oneida national sovereignty. The artist has placed in General

Washington's right hand the Guswenta, which for Oneida and other nations of the Haudenosaunee Confederacy is a record of a treaty of mutual noninterference concluded by them with Europeans during the early colonial period. The statue implies that the Guswenta continues to define and govern relations between the contemporary Oneida Nation and the United States, or at least that it should do so. The description accompanying the sculpture further explains that the statue "honors the bonds of friendship that were forged between the Oneida Nation and the fledgling US during the Revolutionary War." A performative speech act of a kind, *Allies in War, Partners in Peace* is a gift, which gifts a particular treaty and the historical memory of diplomacy it embodies back to the United States. Extended in a highly visible national space such as the NMAI, it asserts a friendly relationship between two discrete and equal partners; moreover, it highlights the obligation of the United States to continue the friendship, especially in view of the Oneidas' siding with the Americans during the war for independence at the risk of breaking the Haudenosaunee Confederacy. The statue is a reminder of the political relationship between the US government and the Haudenosaunee, of the obligations of a contracted agreement, and ultimately and most importantly, of the Haudenosaunee Confederacy's prior political independence and its recognition by the European courts and early American governments.

Ideological Functions of Museum Objects

The political, rather than cultural, understanding of indigeneity evoked by the deployment of historic treaties is reinforced by some of the NMAI's exhibition strategies, particularly in two of the three permanent exhibitions: "Our Lives," the account of contemporary indigenous experience in the Americas; and "Our Peoples," its historical equivalent. These strategies include a refusal of traditional ethnographic displays of material culture and an insistence on metacritical reflection on exhibitionary practice, an insistence that transforms the NMAI into a museum about the conjunction of museology and indigeneity. By the late twentieth century, traditional ethnography in museums had come to refer to display practices first developed and instituted by Franz Boas as a preferable alternative to the evolutionary approach of earlier periods. In an effort to move away from the hierarchical tenor of exhibitions narrating civilizational progress from primitive societies to the modern West and to consider particular cultures in their proper environmental contexts, the Boasian synchronic approach produced indigenous people as essences frozen in tradition and apparently impervious to change, except as a result of adulteration by necessarily foreign modernity; thus Boas ironically contributed to the perception of American Indians as vanishing anachronisms. The NMAI's community-curated galleries, charged as they were with presenting a comprehensive but limited snippet of their contemporary nations, needed to consider the conventions of museological display that they inherited and the conflict between evolutionary models that narrate change and culturalist models that emphasize wholeness and authenticity at the expense of transformation. Their challenge was to represent historical change without reverting to the pre-Boasian evolutionary model of civilizational progress and without celebrating this change as a process of assimilation but instead to account for it in the context of colonialism and indigenous resistance. Accordingly, these exhibits often represent progress—in its Western understanding as industrial development, for example—as a bane to indigenous modes of life, however changed they have become during the centuries of colonialism. The exhibits are poor in objects and rich in text and visual materials such as photographs, reproductions of legal documents shaping the life of each nation, and press coverage on critical contemporary issues. When objects are displayed, particularly in the "Our Lives" exhibition, they are rarely actual historical artifacts; instead, they are reproductions of historical objects by contemporary artists or contemporary objects, such as beaded basketball sneakers, Métis Nation coffee mugs, or Indian Miss Chicago beaded headdresses, fully testifying to the culturally hybrid nature of contemporary indigenous everyday life. However, rather than representing a capitulation to Western epistemological frameworks, this stress on modernity is combined with an emphatically indigenous point of view. The community galleries insist that the indigenous present is always a negotiation between appropriating modernity and preserving traditionalism, or a conscious practice of translating traditionalism into its viable contemporary forms in a kind of "changing same," a concept first evoked by Paul Gilroy with reference to the evolving social and cultural forms of African identity in the Black Atlantic.

The attempt to move away from the generic West-centric focus of the museum while showcasing indigenous modernity as continuity is firmly at the center of Jolene Rickard's work as a curator. Rickard has been particularly concerned with the fact that the North American national museums typically represent Canadian and US American history as "the significant measurement—the bookends" of indigenous experience, thus making it impossible for the viewing public to see indigenous experience as "proceeding and ongoing." She has been interested in the possibilities of "inverting the colonial framing of Aboriginal history within a contact-narrative timeline" and in situating "American and Canadian history, or even modern world history . . . within an Aboriginal timeline" (117). These concerns of inclusion, sovereignty, and competing but overlapping histories determine her curating decisions in the "Our Lives" exhibit. The entry to this exhibit showcases rhetorical strategies she employs to respond to this challenge. The entry is framed on both sides by a video installation featuring images of contemporary American Indians walking by, as if in a street crowd from which all non-Indians have been digitally removed, behind a slightly reflective surface. Entering the exhibition, the visitors become part of the installation, walking side by side with indigenous people, seeing themselves reflected among the projected images. The interactive aspect of the installation is hardly innovative in contemporary museums, where the visitor's active participation is the norm. What's new and radical in Rickard's conception is the specifically self-reflexive impact of the installation on the museum visitors. The exhibit turns such visitors, who usually are merely observers, even if of the participant kind, into the objects of exhibition by forcing them to contemplate their images as superimposed on those of the Indians passing by. Museum visitors join a procession that is already taking place; they arrive at, happen upon, life and history in progress rather than posturing as its originators. In Rickard's words, then, they are inserted in the ongoing indigenous historical framework. The exhibit marks the visitors', and the Europeans', late arrival on the American stage, be it museological or continental. An entry into the exhibition—in itself a civic duty in the context of the Smithsonian Institution's mission—is framed as an act of joining in or as an intrusion into an already peopled world. For what now seems merely an imaginative moment of wishful thinking, but what historically constituted a reality for much of the colonial period, the newcomers become a minority in a society constituted by others. In a telling departure from the social dynamics of contemporary multicultural societies, where the people descended from European settlers are Americans and everybody else provides ethnic color, at the entry to "Our Lives" indigenous peoples are the norm and visitors are supplementary.

The refusal of traditional ethnographic display conventions has led the NMAI curators away from the usual treatment of objects in museological practice. For example, unlike its counterpart in New York City, the Gustav Heye Center at the Custom House, the Washington NMAI has dispensed with the staple of ethnographic exhibits developed to feature objects of material culture in their environmental contexts: the diorama.[21] As I describe above, the NMAI's permanent exhibitions include relatively few objects and rely instead on textual and visual materials. If objects are exhibited, they tend to be contemporary and to deploy hybrid aesthetics. Instead of "authentic" objects—that is, ones uncontaminated by settler materials, techniques, or ideas[22]—amassed in the museum's archives, visitors are asked to contemplate displays of a bombardier used by the Métis for ice-fishing, a Haudenosaunee passport, administrative forms for work release due to indigenous religious holidays, and so on—all documenting changes in indigenous material practices in response to American colonialism. When historical objects from the Heye collection are exhibited—as they are in the "Windows on Collections" exhibits, the central exhibit of "Our Peoples," and occasionally individually throughout the museum—their display departs significantly from traditional museum practices.

Such departures from the existing conventions of museological display have been resentfully noted by museum reviewers, who have complained that "nowhere at the NMAI" are visitors "asked to pause to consider an object, to study it, to admire it, ask questions of it," that "the curators . . . have little faith in the power of objects to convey meaning," and that "the Heye Collection isn't really here at the NMAI" (Conn 70–71). Such assessments are patently inaccurate: there are plenty of objects to contemplate at the NMAI. More importantly, however, these critics misunderstand the basic function of these innovative exhibits: that is, their critique of the usual exhibitionary practice, with its metonymic logic, its holy grail of adequate representation, and its commitment to the ethnographic imperative of producing knowledge about authentic cultures rather than about historical changes affecting all social worlds. At the center of the very idea of the museum, metonymic logic presumes that an object, or often an arbitrary collection of objects, extracted from its specific environment and arranged in a display case, can stand in for the culture within which it originally functioned.[23] It is in the process of such exhibition, and not before, that these objects—the Plains headdress, the Eastern seaboard wampum, the Northwest Coast totem pole—gain iconic status, becoming authoritative tokens fully and evidently imbued with cultural essences in order to serve as conduits for the settler understanding of the indigenous; they become culture, quite literally, reified under the museum glass. As such they are crucial to creating an illusion of the adequate representation of a particular cultural formation, which is the main prerogative, mandate, and constant worry of ethnographic museums.

The object exhibits at the NMAI deliberately teeter between the ethnographic and the aesthetic; they are presented as evidence of an indigenous presence that is not made immediately intelligible but requires further work to be meaningful, that demands reflection on interpretative strategies that would make such meaning available in the first place. Object displays at the NMAI aim to be ideological rather than merely informative: they testify to indigenous presence on the American continent along with the inherent difficulty of the museological interpretation of this presence. For example, the "Windows on Collections" exhibits—featuring beadwork, pottery, dolls, arrow points, peace medals, and tomahawks, all grouped by type of object rather than historical or geographical provenience—function, most obviously, as introductions, sample glimpses into the much vaster collections stored in the NMAI's research center. But their mode of display communicates a subtler message as well. The glass cases in these exhibits are crammed with objects . . . and nothing else. There are no labels offering descriptions, nothing to distract the visitors from contemplating them primarily in their abundance and their aesthetic dimension—in other words, as material evidence of indigenous presence and as art rather than as material culture. Detailed ethnographic information on the objects displayed is available, but not at hand; it has to be retrieved through the interactive digital technology at several computer stands adjacent to the exhibit. The display, thus, is designed to postpone visitors' reliance on ethnographic gloss to understand what they are seeing. The general, brief narrative texts accompanying these exhibits also encourage such aesthetically oriented contemplation (the exhibit on tomahawks and peace medals described above is a notable exception). An introduction to the exhibit on beadwork is a good example of this strategy: it describes the beadwork as a "unique American creation" that continues "to delight us," a result of contact and trade, of mixing indigenous technique with European materials (the exhibit emphasizes objects dating from 1492). There is no attempt to explain the political contexts of the transatlantic trade or its impact on indigenous economies—no mention of indigenous art production for the tourist market, for example, or of the nationalist context of the contemporary beaded art. To further encourage a primarily aesthetic interpretive mode, the curators have arranged these objects into larger patterns, combining individual pieces into collage-like compositions: displays of arrow points arranged into large undulating waves or of South American gold pieces patterned into a gigantic sun are good examples of this approach, which draws attention to the curators' imaginative talents, to their work as artists rather than ethnographers.

As a result, these exhibits of archival collections project an interpretatively fruitful paradox with regard to exhibiting indigenous materials. Their refusal of traditional ethnography pitches the exhibits into the art museum's propensity to decontextualize the objects in an effort to bring out their aesthetic dimensions, a move particularly troubling in the case of indigenous artifacts. As Shari Huhndorf and Patricia Hilden point out in their critique of the Gustav Heye Center in New York City, undue attention to the aesthetic dimension of indigenous material culture turns the museum into a "boutique of valuable Indian artifacts" (169) displayed in the fashion of a high-art gallery, one designed to preempt historical reflection and, as a result, obfuscating the history of the American colonial project on the continent; a display of the Ghost Dance Shirt without any mention of the Wounded Knee Massacre is indeed an example of pernicious historical revisionism.[24] By contrast, Rickard's display design, which exhibits objects in great numbers but without the usual ethnographic gloss, brings the ethnographic and the art museum tradition into a productive conflict, prompting reflection on the desirability of existing modes of exhibition of indigenous objects in museum and art gallery contexts. Rickard's objects are not extracted from their proper ethnographic context simply to highlight their aesthetic qualities. Presented en masse, in the abundance of their historical cognates rather than as individual pieces (of art), they call forth a theoretical and methodological reflection. A different kind of commodification takes place: an arrow point no longer serves, or no longer only serves, as a singular emblem for scientific decoding; rather, it becomes a piece of a larger picture that speaks to utilitarian, historical, and aesthetic dimensions, but above all to its own ideological expediency.

This strategy prevails even in the few displays of individual historic pieces scattered in the museum hallways, such as the large-scale pottery or Plains buffalo-skin parfleche. These are placed in the more traditional museum display cases and appear singled out for their aesthetic appeal. However, as visitors contemplate these objects' beauty they also notice that the display case is a replica of a travois or a drag, a kind of sled pulled by horses to move possessions from place to place. Yes, the exhibited object is immobilized under the museum glass, but in a case that is a symbol of both mobility (transport) and indigeneity (before the European wheel technology). The pottery and the parfleche are framed—or captured, or revealed—as both portable cultural inheritance and commodified heritage that can be showcased in a museum. The display design activates all of these understandings and manages to be self-reflexive in the way it glosses the contentious debate over American Indian art and material culture and the exhibitionary order. Rickard's display strategies showcase the indigenous museum objects as cultural capital and suggest how they can be used to mobilize different understandings of indigenous experience and history; in other words, they emphasize the objects' political potential. Indigenous material culture has long been used to subtend ideological narratives: of civilizational progress, of vanishing races, of savage nobility, of radical otherness, of multicultural reformation, of indigenous nationalism. Jolene Rickard's curating aims to bring forth forcefully the sovereignist understanding of indigeneity, but it also intentionally facilitates reflection on the politics of indigenous representation and self-representation.

One such understanding emphasizes the vitality and complexity of the indigenous world, on the one hand, and the massive scale of its disruption following the arrival of the Europeans, on the other, by using the museum collections to emphasize both the abundance of the material archive and its fragmentary nature. The exhibits such as "Windows on Collections" and "Our Peoples" amass large numbers of artifacts to harness their potential as "object-lessons of documentary import" (Preziosi 518). These objects serve as evidence of numerous societies thriving before the arrival of the conquistadors, traders, missionaries, and settlers (signaled in pre-Columbian stone and gold sculpture, shell wampum, pottery); of extensive traffic in natural resources, manufactured objects, technologies, ideas, and habits between the Europeans and the indigenous nations (seen in swords, money, gold, glass beadwork, pottery); and of the persistence of indigenous peoples despite their programmatic displacement and dispossession (evidenced in treaties and bibles with beaded covers that are translated into indigenous languages). The exhibits eschew representation of ethnographically captured cultures in order to narrate the extent and effects of political and economic interests as they played out in the Americas between the indigenous and European peoples and governments. The very abundance of objects such as early stone and gold sculpture, arrow points, pottery, and shell beadwork points to the demographic history of the continent, thereby directly undermining the myths of the virgin land and new world, however residual they might have become by now, and supporting the recent adjustments upward of the continental population before 1492.

As they testify to the vitality and complexity of the indigenous world pre- and post-contact, the great numbers of archival objects exhibited serve also, perhaps unintentionally, as evidence of the massive extent of Gustav Heye's collecting project, or, as some commentators would have it, as an indictment of his grand thievery.[25] In view of several popular and scholarly accounts of Heye's rapacious expeditions to acquire collections from impoverished communities, including an episode of grave-robbing, of his unethical dealings with indigenous leaders who pleaded for the return of sacred objects in his possession, and of the collection's gradual dissipation at the hands of unscrupulous curators, Heye's collection, the very raison d'être of the NMAI, is a tricky subject for the museum's public relations department. *The Museum Guide* and *Spirit of a Native Place* strain to represent Heye as a committed collector rather than a thief; they offer a very generous account, skimming over or dismissing as apocryphal most of the accusations of unethical collecting leveled against Heye. The resulting account is utterly, and perhaps shamelessly, redemptive: Heye is praised for his "prodigious accomplishment" and "his single minded devotion," which preserved "objects that have provided inspiration and cultural renewal for Native people from communities throughout the hemisphere" (115). When Heye's "even then buccaneer ruthlessness" is mentioned, it refers to instances when he was stealing from other collectors rather than indigenous communities. Heye's redemption is, of course, part of a larger attempt to justify the continued existence of the collection, even in its new version as the NMAI, especially in view of persistent calls for the return of all museum-held objects to their original communities. NMAI officials openly acknowledge that the matter is difficult: "The relationship between museums and Native people has always been a two-edged sword, fraught with the ambiguities of collecting, preserving and displaying," declare the authors of *Spirit of a Native Place* as they register and record "the sorrow for the loss to communities that collecting represents" (127). Yet very quickly—perhaps too quickly—the replacement of that sorrow by gratitude is offered as the proper reaction to the abundance of the collection. *Spirit of a Native Place* offers a model of such emotional adjustment in the words of Susan Billie, a Pomo artist from California who visited the research branch to select objects for the Gustav Heye Center's inaugural display in 1995: "The first day I was here I felt angry that there are so many Pomo baskets so far away from home. But by the last day I began to feel grateful that there were so many Pomo baskets here, because they were preserved and now I can see them" (115). The work of making museum collecting a legitimate project requires a quick translation from "stolen" to "preserved," one that many commentators on the Heye collection are not willing to make.[26] It requires discouraging any reflection on the connection between destroyed communities and preserved objects, and it obscures the obvious realization that if it were not for the destructive effects of American colonialism on the continent, the issue of preservation would not be of much import, as the objects would remain in their original environments among thriving indigenous communities.

As is the case with the treatment of the historic treaties, visitors have to leave behind the museum's public relations discourse and enter the collections themselves for a more acute and historically accurate assessment of the relationship between indigenous material culture and the museum. There, in the "Our Peoples" central exhibit on gold, swords, and money, they will chance upon Paul Chaat Smith's account of how America's wealth established Spain as a superpower and transformed global economies, an account that concludes pointedly with a claim that nearly all of the original gold made by indigenous peoples before contact is now in the possession of museums and private collectors. The abundance of material-culture artifacts in the museum evidences the massive transfer of wealth from indigenous nations to European colonies and later to American colonial states.

And yet, importantly, the abundance of material culture displayed in these exhibits does not add up to a comprehensive archeological and ethnographic record of indigenous societies and economies. The display design that arranges these objects into patterns of waves, sun, and landscape ironically highlights the fragmentary nature of these object-lessons by insisting that only aesthetic rather than historical sense can be made from these shards of larger social orders. Too much has been lost to reconstruct the indigenous habitus in a comprehensive way. This fragmentation of the remaining material record and the outright absence of material evidence of many indigenous societies is an important point of the "Our Peoples" exhibition. While "We Are the Evidence," an installation framing the entry to "Our Peoples," lists hundreds of indigenous languages once spoken on the American continents, its accompanying text, in a now-recognizable dialectic of abundance and scarcity or wholeness and fragmentation, insists on the list's incompleteness. It reminds the visitors of the demographics of the colonial conquest—nine out of ten indigenous inhabitants of the Americas perished—and calls upon them to bear responsibility "for remembering everything, especially the things we never knew." In doing so, the installation foregrounds the difficulty of reconstructing indigenous history in the context of both massive historical disruption and a fragmented material record.

This problem of testifying simultaneously to preconquest vitality and colonial destruction, to abundance and to massive loss, structures the exhibits of the central area of "Our Peoples" called "The Storm: Guns, Bibles, and Governments" and beginning with Edward Poitras's "The Eye of the Storm" installation. Like many of the exhibits in "Our Lives" a floor below, "The Eye of the Storm" is scarce in objects: a circular glass display case at the center contains a beaded replica of a feathered wing; several stones with inscriptions or wrapped in pages from the Book of Revelation; a military staff and a hat purportedly resembling that worn by Wovoka, the Paiute prophet of the Ghost Dance; four direction markers; and a small bible. A large glassed exhibit placed on its outer perimeter, filled with small video screens running a series of images ranging from footage of natural disasters to archival photographs of American Indians, completes the work. The impression is of scarcity and stillness. The installation is framed by a text that represents the conquest as a natural event—it speaks rather vaguely of "foreign intrusions" and of "being caught in the storm of bibles, guns and government," of "storms coming and going" while life continues—and by doing so obscures the specific historic agency of European and American colonial states and their deliberately genocidal policies toward indigenous nations. Here, then, is an example of what the museum's critics meant when they faulted the curators for missing opportunities to offer a sharper critique of European colonialism in the Americas. And yet, the installation works in conjunction with the larger argument about the scarcity and fragmentation of the indigenous material archive; after the storm, the field is swept nearly clean—emptiness invokes devastation. What's left is quickly gathered into a display case, with a handful of objects arranged to metonymically stand in for the presumed-to-be-vanished indigenous world. In Poitras's hands the museum case itself becomes in turn an object-lesson in the massive extent of colonial destruction, on the one hand, and in the museum's collecting and exhibiting project's complicity in redemptive representational resurrection, not much different from those of Catlin and Curtis, on the other.[27]

If "The Eye of the Storm" obscures the historical specificity of the colonial projects of European governments in order to facilitate a reflection on the Western museum exhibition of American indigeneity, then the adjacent exhibit on gold and swords and on money and treaties returns some of that specificity, focusing on the impact of the Spanish Crown and British and US governments on indigenous nations in South and North America. NMAI's insistence on inserting the West into the museum's representation of the indigenous world is a significant departure from the traditional practice of ethnographic museums, which, as Gayan Prakash has explained, "have categorized, classified, and exhibited objects from nonwestern cultures according to universalist aesthetics and history, but nowhere in this display is the West itself exhibited. . . . the West cannot be described or captured as a set of beliefs: it shows up in offering an understanding of otherness, in giving it coherence and meaning" (210). In the "Our Peoples" exhibit, the West is eminently present as a powerfully destructive historical agent, a force thoroughly shattering these worlds to produce the fragmentary remnants showcased in the exhibition. The very fragmentation of the archival record implied throughout the collection is an indictment of Europe's presence in the Americas.

Rickard's and Paul Chaat Smith's curating produces both a reconstruction of indigenous experience in the indigenous timeline from an indigenous perspective and an indictment of the West as destructively present within that framework. The scarcity/abundance dialectic is crucial to the exhibit's ideological import: the discourse of fragmentation is necessary to indict Europe's colonial project in the Americas, but the assertions of sovereignty on behalf of the indigenous nations require narratives of political, social, and cultural coherence and continuity to warrant recognition. The demand for such manifested historical and cultural continuity is often at the center of battles over recognition, and as Elizabeth Povinelli points out, it is an impossible demand given the extent of the disruption of indigenous societies through policies of extermination, displacement, forceful assimilation, and the essentialist conception of authenticity informing the recognition process.[28] And this is precisely why the treaties—as historical documents, as American Indian nationalist discourse, and as iconographic reminders—are placed throughout the museum. The treaties come to the rescue in battles for recognition by substituting historic documents laying out mutual political obligations for the relentless demand for culturally authentic indigeneity.

In addition to showcasing the vitality of the precontact indigenous world, exposing the extent of historical disruption brought on by European colonialism in the Americas, and provoking reflection on the ideological ramifications of traditional exhibitionary practices, "Our Peoples" sets out to comment on the politics of documenting and exhibiting history. The introduction to "The Americas," a display of pre-1492 stone sculpture, makes clear that the exhibit is as much about rethinking the way history is understood and inherited as it is about recovering historical details about the pre- and post-contact periods. Paul Chaat Smith's text on "Making History"—an installation that also includes an account of the spread of smallpox and other epidemics in the Americas, Theodor de Bry's engravings recording the early period of colonization, and a collection of George Catlin's American Indian portraits—draws attention to the ideological functions of historical narratives and argues that history-making was a weapon of conquest that intentionally misrepresented or altogether ignored the continent's indigenous inhabitants. Because our understanding of history is shaped more by "who is telling the stories and who the story-teller is speaking to" than by actual events, the authorship of historical accounts—or, we could say, the ownership of history—is of great consequence. If Catlin's painting and Heye's collecting are examples of Indian history-making that manifest passion for Indian culture premised on Indian disappearance, the NMAI as "the museum about Indians controlled by Indians" where indigenous peoples can tell "their own stories in their own way and voice" offers a necessary alternative. It allows the curators to appropriate the existing European historical record—in the form of paintings, engravings, and museum collections—to offer Indian versions of Indian histories, the exhibit itself being a preeminent example of such an effort. Paul Chaat Smith's account cues visitors to the political expediency of settler representations of indigeneity, deployed at the NMAI toward different ideological ends.

Cultural Politics of the First Americans at a Native Place

The emphasis on the politics of exhibiting indigeneity and on the museum objects as ideologically expedient cultural capital works in tandem with the NMAI's use of historic treaties by shifting the issue of indigeneity from the ground of cultural authenticity to that of politically defined nationhood. However, the museum's other discursive practices obscure anew this political conception of indigeneity showcased in permanent and community exhibitions. First deployed during the opening ceremonies, the rhetoric of indigenous people as First Americans and of the NMAI as a Native Place informs much of the museum's cultural programming as well as the very design of the building and surrounding grounds, effectively enfolding the political conception of indigeneity within a broad culturalist framework.

The concept of indigenous people as First Americans accomplishes two claims at once. First, it translates indigeneity, or rootedness in place, a definitional characteristic American Indians insist upon to distinguish themselves from settler Americans, into *firstness*, a mere sequence of arrival on the continent; it takes difference of kind and turns it into difference of degree. Second, it amplifies the similarity implied in the first rhetorical move by retroactively turning "them" into "us"—that is, Indians into Americans. Historically, these claims to prior existence and to inherent Americanness emerge as responses to the pervasive myths of America as the virgin land and of indigenous peoples' radical—racial or cultural—otherness, myths that have been deployed at different historical junctions since 1492.[29] The public relations materials and press coverage of the NMAI's development, from the legal efforts to pass Public Law 101–185 to fundraising, construction, and the inaugural ceremonies in 2004, all represent the museum's placement on the National Mall as both a long-overdue indigenous return to and reclamation of a Native Place and a final, and equally long-overdue, recognition on the part of the contemporary United States, and by implication other American nation-states, of these states' fully American heritage. The museum thus renders the proper recognition of their priority to indigenous peoples and extends the historical and cultural genealogy of America beyond 1492. Richard West's double welcome—"Welcome Home" addressed to American Indians and "Welcome to Native America" to those Americans who are not indigenous—during the museum's opening celebrations is emblematic of this complicated claim of American belonging for indigenous people and Native belonging for settler Americans.

Lest it create anxiety in Americans whose ancestors settled in indigenous territories (many land claims continue to await resolution in US courts), the language of Native reclamation is mediated through the discourse of shared Americanness deployed throughout the museum, from the framing of specific exhibits to the museum's film and performance offerings. For example, the "Our Lives" exhibit is dedicated, as visitors are informed in the text displayed at the entry, "to everybody who [has] experienced discrimination." This effort to represent indigenous experience as portable from one minority group to another dispels potential worries about radical and oppositional otherness; it does so, however, by obscuring indigeneity's historical specificity, a point otherwise emphasized strenuously throughout many of the "Our Lives" displays. Here the curators depend on the museum-going tradition as a ritual that works to minimize the disjunctions or antagonisms among distinct social groups, and the differences among their individual members, in order to emphasize instead a shared, universal humanity, the Family-of-Man version of history (Preziosi 514). In a similar effort, Chris Eyre's *A Thousand Roads*, the NMAI's signature film intended as an introduction not so much to the museum collections as to its mandate to showcase the contemporary indigenous experience, features separate vignettes representing indigenous protagonists dealing with issues easily recognizable to other contemporary Americans: a successful stockbroker on Wall Street encounters a homeless fellow Mohawk on her way to work; an Aleut teenager returns to an Alaskan village as her US marine mother is deployed overseas; a Navajo gangster cleans up by learning traditional sheep herding under the tutelage of a Raven; and an Aymara healer fails to heal a dying boy in a Peruvian mountain village. All stories are structured in the same way, by casting indigenous specificity in the larger context of similarity: the Aleut girl's return to a traditional village, which to her is as foreign as it is to many viewers, is precipitated by her mother's deployment to the Middle East, an experience of dramatically increased currency in the United States of the 2000s. The Navajo Raven comes to the rescue of a teenager, who, like the captives of contemporary urban ghettos, too, is mired in gang activity but out in the Southwestern desert. The opening section on the stockbroker reduces her Mohawk identity to language and ornamental tokens of a different epistemology: after she addresses the street flute player in Mohawk, she returns to her desk and fingers a few stones she placed there, ultimately arranging them in a circle before returning to selling and buying bonds. The point of this segment is that the residual indigeneity she held onto helps her function within contemporary capitalism; her office bears all the marks of a successful career. The only moment of irony arises when we realize that her office is located in one of New York's skyscrapers, very likely erected by Mohawk ironworkers. *A Thousand Roads* depicts indigeneity as a fully private, personal reservoir of resources that enables the protagonists to function successfully in contemporary America. The exception is the Aymara healer, of course, who experiences a crisis of belief as his patient dies. In this case, the film most radically departs from offering a culturally reliable picture of indigenous practices; its representation of the boy's death and the healer's response to it obscures the traditional understanding of the healer's role as a helper in a person's passage over or back to health; in that context a death is not necessarily evidence of the holy man's failure.[30]

This message of fundamental Indian normativity, as opposed to inassimilable otherness, is further reinforced in many of the performances by contemporary American Indian artists invited regularly to the museum. A good example is a Washington, DC–based women's trio, Aki, whose concerts are pervaded by the "we are just like you, except that we're Indian" rhetoric. Accompanied by strumming guitars and African and Native American drums, Aki offers a repertoire ranging from Bob Dylan songs with "Native" chants inserted as a refrain to ballads about Internet dating. The lyrics of their signature song, "Make Us One," fully render the performance's multiculturalist tenor of humanity shared across cultural differences: "Are we so different?/ I do not think so./ You can feel the way I feel./ You can hurt the way I hurt./ It makes us one./ Many different cultures, all the same inside./ We are one world, one family." The logic expressed in the phrase "many different cultures, all the same inside" shifts the burden of signifying difference from content to form, from historically specific experiences of the various indigenous nations on the continent to the abstracted aesthetic dimensions of indigeneity as manifested in art, architecture, and material culture.

At the NMAI in Washington, DC, it is the museum grounds and building in their formulations as a Native Place that have become emblematic of this kind of indigeneity, particularly in contrast to the site of the George Gustav Heye Center in Manhattan. The historic 1907 Alexander Hamilton Custom House at Bowling Green, which houses the New York branch of the NMAI, has been criticized as a particularly poor choice for the exhibition of American Indian collections.[31] The Custom House is as unequivocal and celebratory an expression of American imperialism as it gets. An example of lavish Beaux Arts architecture, it features Daniel Chester French's ethnocentric limestone sculptures depicting the continents, which flank the building's main entrance, and generic Indian heads adorning both of the side entrances. Its massive central rotunda is decorated by Reginald Marsh's frescos celebrating the discovery and conquest of the Americas in images of transatlantic trade and portraits of Columbus, Vespucci, Hudson, Cabot, and Verrazano. Historically, it served as a location where import duties were levied. And while the resulting irony may in the end be productive, if also lost on some visitors[32]—the disjunction between the building and the exhibitions inside forcing the visitors to consider indigenous material culture in the context of European colonialism rather than as merely a collection of beautiful objects for aesthetic contemplation—this architectural mishap put considerable pressure on the architects of the building destined for the National Mall. In Washington, the architecture is meant to work differently: not to evoke contradiction, however unintentionally, but to express Nativeness, through the emphasis on form as a matter of cultural distinctiveness.

As a museum whose building itself embodies cultural specificity, the NMAI in Washington, DC, is not unique. With the rapid growth of tribal museums and research or cultural centers in the late twentieth century in North America, the idea of the museum as an opportunity to reconsolidate tribal knowledge gained wide currency as architects devised new but historically grounded architectural models to project specific tribal identities. Examples ranging from Sequoyah Birthplace Museum in Vonore, Tennessee; Camp Verde Visitor Center in Camp Verde, Arizona; Makah Cultural and Research Center in Neah Bay, Washington; Yakama Nation Cultural Heritage Center in Toppenish, Washington; to Mashantucket Pequot Museum and Research Center in Ledyard, Connecticut, and the planned Omaha Interpretive Center[33] all unfold a repertoire of specific, tribally distinguishable aesthetic markers, historical and symbolic, along with the concept of architectural integration into the natural environment. These efforts testify to the usefulness of architecture itself as an embodiment of indigenous national specificities.

However, conceived as a pan-Indian hemispheric museum, the NMAI had to respond to the mandate of representing a variety of indigenous nations and communities on the continent while also articulating the predicament of indigeneity in the Americas in general. Across the permanent exhibitions in the museum, this challenge is addressed through a specific design concept, as I described above. "Our Lives," "Our Peoples," and "Our Universes" share the same organization of space: a cluster of installations centered in the exhibition space and showcasing pan-Indian issues are surrounded by eight community galleries devoted to specific nations and communities. The community galleries are organized as separate spaces, divided by walls but arranged side by side and open to the exhibits at the center. The effect is that of a larger space—a common set of historical experiences and contemporary predicaments—shared by smaller discrete tribal universes. The exhibits strike a balance between giving their due to pan-Indian issues while insisting on the specific political identities of particular nations or the distinctiveness of hybrid American Indian communities that are not recognized as separate political entities, such as "The Indians of Chicago" or the Métis exhibitions in "Our Lives." But this kind of split attention to pan-Indian and tribally specific representation was not possible at the level of the museum's architectural design. If the national museums constructed across Indian Country could deploy architecture to evoke tribally specific aesthetics, the NMAI took the road of universalized Nativeness arrived at by the process of abstraction and homogeneization of tribally specific concepts.[34] The NMAI's Washington building does not employ any specific architectural traditions, nor does it replicate actual historical indigenous building practices. Rather, it devises its own and deploys them to convey a generalized indigenous cosmology.

In a chapter entitled "Building a Native Place," *The Museum Guide* explains the connection between the building and its surroundings: "Native people believe that the earth remembers the experiences of past generations. The National Museum of the American Indian recognizes the importance of indigenous peoples' connection to land; the grounds surrounding the building are considered as an extension of the building and a vital part of the museum as a whole. By recalling the natural environment that existed prior to European contact, the museum's landscape design embodies a theme that runs central to NMAI—that of returning to a Native place" (22). This narrative outlining the distinctive Nativeness of the museum site continues by singling out the forest, wetlands, meadow, and traditional crop areas along with the Grandfather Rocks, forty boulders that "welcome visitors to the museum grounds and serve as reminders of the longevity of the Native peoples' relationship to the environment" (23) and the Cardinal Direction Markers, four stones placed along the north-south and east-west axes and serving "as metaphors for the indigenous peoples of the Americas" (23). The building itself, according to the 1996 NMAI document, "must have a language of its own, a language that speaks for the aboriginal peoples of the Americas, a language that wraps the visitor in a different paradigm of perception" (*Guide* 24). Inspired by "the stone and masonry work of Chaco Canyon, Machu Picchu, and other Native sites" and "shaped by the wind and water," the building figures as "a distinctly Native place, one that reflects and honors the organic and emphasizes that people are part of a larger natural world" (24). It is "aligned perfectly to the cardinal directions and the center point of the Capitol dome, and filled with details, colors and textures that reflect the Native universe. A palette of colors, materials, symbols, and forms" created by the design team "imbues the building with a Native sensibility" (27). These materials, symbols, and forms are abstracted from the museum's collections and range from the sun symbols and copper wire weaving motifs in the rotunda to moon sconces in the Main Theater, shell inlays and adze-shaped wood in the museum store, and bird motifs representing the cardinal directions on the elevators. Potomac, the museum's rotunda and central gathering space, in particular, is packed with references to indigenous cosmology and material culture: sun symbols etched on the entry doors, an oculus extending to the sky, glass prisms on the south wall, axes of solstices and equinoxes mapped on the floor, copper weave installation evoking the traditions of basketry and textiles, and at the museum's opening, an exhibition on canoe- and boat-making.[35] "Filled with visual metaphors that ground the building in the Native world" (38), the NMAI becomes an embodiment of a particular fantasy: a patch of distinct Nativeness returned to the national heart of the United States, firmly and safely a part of the country's redemptive nationalist multicultural discourse.

And yet, this specifically indigenous distinctiveness of the NMAI's building emerges in a dialectic relationship to its simultaneous references to Western architecture. For example, the museum's rotunda, the Potomac, effortlessly evokes classical European architecture, from Rome's Pantheon and Romanesque churches to American classical revival and Lincoln's Memorial. The stripped-down, modernist aesthetic of the hallway galleries surrounding the Potomac recalls Frank Lloyd Wright's Guggenheim. Even in its most distinctive Native abstractness the NMAI's architectural design relies on European and settler American models. Or, at least, visitors cannot help but recognize these architectural conventions as familiar even if they were not intended as such. This referencing of recognizable Western architecture along with an articulation of specifically indigenous formal signifiers constitutes the museum's appeal: visitors get a dose of difference but are also reassured by formal architectural continuities that allow them to read the space of the museum properly as temple or national sanctum and to make the comparative leaps necessary to participate in the museum's civic ritual. This aesthetic crossover is the building's brilliant rhetorical gesture: it offers interpretive signposts to visitors and prompts them to recognize an aesthetic affinity in a kind of difference that is about similarity—the NMAI is like the Pantheon, Sistine Chapel, or Guggenheim, but Indian!

But because such referencing risks being misread as colonial mimicry, it requires a written Native gloss on the museum's website, in *The Museum Guide*, and many other printed materials. All of these glosses control for the meaning implied in architecture by unfolding a narrative of the museum's design and construction that focuses on the building as an embodiment of indigenous cosmologies and eschews any mention of its affinity with Western architectural traditions. As indigenous difference is embodied in formal aesthetic solutions, the results are vulnerable to interpretive appropriation by visitors and have to be rearticulated by curators and architects. Unless carefully and repeatedly glossed, the form cannot be trusted to provide a consistent and reliable conduit for indigenous specificity, at least not in its abstracted and homogenized version at the NMAI. The very need for the controlling gloss implies that the architecture's Nativeness is not manifestly evident beyond the most obvious references to the Southwest; it has to be interpretively constructed. The form, too, is a matter of interpretation and of politics.

The consequence of this abstraction of indigeneity to formal aesthetic markers is the sacrifice of the political discourse of national sovereignty. An abstract so-called Native Place imbued with a generalized so-called Native sensibility does not evoke the concept of contemporary indigenous nations. What it encourages instead is a general notion of Indian cultural difference rather than indigenous historical specificity in all of its differing versions across the continent. It implies cultural citizenship and invites an understanding of American Indians as a large, amalgamated ethnic group, one more to complete the image of the multicultural democracy that is the United States or Canada; in other words, it corroborates the conceptual assumptions of multicultural misrecognition. The ultimate irony in the critical reception of the museum is that the very critics who condemned the curators of the NMAI's permanent exhibitions for missing an opportunity to offer a trenchant critique of US colonialism, past and ongoing, unanimously praised the museum's architectural design—the very design, which in helping locate "Nativeness" within the larger imagined community of the nation, so effectively corroborates the vision of North American states as reformed multicultural democracies that have successfully broken with their colonial pasts.

Pushing against the critical consensus on the NMAI that elevates the grounds and building over the exhibitions, I argue that the permanent exhibitions are more successful at inserting indigenous nationalist discourse into the Western museum narrative—the stated objective of Jolene Rickard's curating efforts—and at articulating a critique of the European colonial projects and their effects in the Americas, the disappointed mandate of the museum critics. Those aspects of the museum that contribute to elaborating the central idea of a Native Place—the grounds and building, the Potomac, the Mitsitam Café, the museum stores, and the other common spaces inside—readily meet the demands of North American multiculturalism for performances of depoliticized difference; they invite multicultural misrecognition, or recognition of abstracted Native American cultural distinctiveness and not of the political separateness and historically specific practices of individual indigenous nations. In its effort to showcase the latter, the NMAI reforms some of the exhibitionary practices traditionally used to frame collections of indigenous material culture: Rickard's walk with the Indians entry to "Our Lives" and the exhibition's insistent emphasis on the contemporary, hybrid, political, and tribally specific aspects of indigenous experience; "Windows on Collections" and individual hallway exhibits that blur distinctions between ethnographic and art gallery treatment of objects; and the insistence throughout on the exhibition objects as politically expedient cultural capital. In addition, the NMAI employs traditional museological practices and concepts, such as the function of the museum as a socializing ritual, the Western concept of nation, and the measured reliance on representational adequacy, to deploy the political discourse of indigenous nations. Thus the NMAI emerges as a meeting place where the discourses of indigenous sovereignty and of the pan-Indian Native Place exist side by side.

The irresolvable tension between the culturalist concept of the Native Place and the political concept of indigenous nations may well be the most enduring and valuable legacy of the NMAI's museological experiment. As George Yúdice explains, in contemporary multicultural states, democracy is taken to mean proper recognition of the diverse cultures of the population groups comprising the nation, recognition accomplished through state sponsorship of their expression in the arts (48–49) rather than as equal access to the political meeting ground. The curators' emphasis on indigenous nations as political units rather than as cultural entities is an effort to refuse the reducing of social identities to culture, a process encouraged by multicultural misrecognition. The sovereignist argument for respect and resources does not arise from the conception of cultural citizenship but from the legal precedent of the historic treaties laying out rights and obligations on both sides of the diplomatic divide. But as the NMAI permanent exhibitions showcase the tribally specific histories, expose European and American colonialism, and deploy historic treaties to foreground the political understanding of contemporary indigeneity, the larger context of the museum—including its location on the National Mall in the United States' capital and its generic status as the premiere institution of the modern nation-state—

obscures these efforts again, folding tribal specificity into North American multiculturalism and its particular politics of recognition. The NMAI contains the more radical revisionist or outright separatist tribal narratives of community galleries and permanent exhibitions within the larger abstract and innocuous Native Place. This very enfolding of the sovereignist messages of some of the exhibitions within the abstracted Native Place of the museum and its grounds best exemplifies the possibilities and limits of indigenous self-representation under multiculturalism. What routinely gets recognized at the NMAI, despite its curators' efforts, is not the continued colonial relationship between the North American federal governments and the indigenous nations within their borders but the fantasy of an end to such a relationship, a fantasy substantiated by the very existence of the NMAI as a Native Place, even if the museum's dutiful alignment with the dome of the Capitol cannot help but hint at the rhetorical coercion underpinning this fantasy.

2

Atanarjuat and the Ideological Work of Indigenous Filmmaking

> I always say: that's the most Indian movie ever made. It's much more Indian than *Smoke Signals*. *Smoke Signals* was made for Indian people, but certainly for the other culture [as well]. When you get a movie like *The Fast Runner*, you are watching this movie and saying to yourself, this is an inside job.
>
> Chris Eyre (Cheyenne/Arapaho), in *Reel Injun*

> If the purpose of the national cinema is to represent the culture of the peoples it belongs to, then *Atanarjuat: The Fast Runner* achieves this triumphantly, both the content of the film and the manner of its telling being wholly specific to Canada, yet in the process achieving universal appeal.
>
> Edward Buscombe, *Cinema Today*

Chris Eyre's lavish praise for *Atanarjuat (The Fast Runner)* comes with the weight of considerable authority. Since the release of his *Smoke Signals* in 1998, Eyre has been credited with inaugurating a new period in the long and tangled history of Indians and cinema, a period in which American Indians write, act in, and produce their own feature films, offering much-needed alternatives to the hackneyed mainstream representations.[1] *Reel Injun*, a 2009 documentary subtitled *On the Trail of the Hollywood Indian* and directed by Neil Diamond (Cree), offers an account of the Indian's trajectory through the medium, from the perspective of indigenous actors, filmmakers, and critics. Diamond's film surveys depictions of American Indians from the silent-film era, through a variety of Indian stereotypes nurtured by Hollywood, all the way to contemporary indigenous cinema. In this trajectory, *Atanarjuat* occupies the apex as the "inside job" of an authentic indigenous film, asserted as such, in the film's concluding sequences, through a series of comments made by Eyre and others discussing the film. These assertions presume several different conceptions of authenticity. For example, the Mohawk recording artist Robbie Robertson relies on an apparently self-evident notion of purity when he declares: "Wow! I have never seen anything like that before. This is so pure in its soul."[2] For Jesse Wente, an Ojibwe film critic, authenticity means the absence of stereotypes and the presence of full indigenous authorial control. He explains: "*Atanarjuat* to me was that point when cinema was being altered to tell our stories in our way. And gone were the stereotypes of the past. Really in that one movie there's none of that nonsense. It's a gloriously sexy film set in the Arctic. . . . Finally an aboriginal cinema that isn't someone else's; the gaze is ours." Eyre, too, admires the film's ability to appear so resolutely unconcerned with that settler audience, which his own film still could not help but address. Taken together, these readings suggest that *Atanarjuat* is the best example yet of authentic indigenous cinema because it is free of settler influence: with no settler stereotypes, no settler directors, no settler actors in redface, it offers a precontact tale with no mention of the colonization to come, and thus manifests its freedom to tell Inuit stories in the Inuit way with Inuit goals and mandates in mind. When Neil Diamond sums up the film's significance by suggesting that *Atanarjuat* "captures one of the Inuits' most cherished legends and brings it to the world" and that by doing so it "has revolutionized Native cinema *and* . . . gone on to win at the Cannes Film Festival," he solidifies the view that the film's greatest achievement is its self-generated authenticity, one that depends on radical separateness from the American colonial states, even as it gets recognized and acclaimed by them and the rest of the world. In this view, the power of the film stems from its ability to enact, for the first time in the history of cinema, complete indigenous artistic autonomy.

This reception of *Atanarjuat* as wholly authentic due to its sustained focus on all things Inuit does not surprise, given the film's subject matter, aesthetic conventions, and production and distribution history. The film is a creation of Isuma Productions Inc., the first independent Inuit production company, incorporated in 1990 and based in Igloolik, a community of twelve hundred people on a small island in the north Baffin region of the Canadian Arctic. It has been marketed as the first feature film written, directed, acted, and produced by the Inuit. A cinematographic reprise of a traditional Inuit morality tale passed down orally through many generations, the film has been billed on Isuma's website and in other promotional materials as a "part of this continuous stream of oral history carried forward into the new millennium through a marriage of Inuit storytelling skills and new technology." "An exciting action-thriller set in ancient Igloolik," it promises, the filmmakers assure, "international audiences a more authentic view of Inuit culture and oral tradition than ever before, from the inside and through Inuit eyes."[3] Even as it subsequently courted international audiences in its promotional materials, *Atanarjuat* was first screened for the residents of Igloolik and follows on the heels of over ten years of Isuma's local community-oriented television productions.[4]

And, indeed, *Atanarjuat* fascinates with its successful attempt to sustain an illusion of a precontact world in what is today Canada's Eastern Arctic for its entire two hours and forty-one minutes. It unfolds as a story about an interfamily feud precipitated by an evil curse and a dispute over a woman among a small band of nomadic Inuit. But above all, the film works as a representation of the ancient Inuit material world, re-created with meticulous attention to the accuracy effect of ethnographic detail by contemporary Igloolik's craftsmen, and celebrated by the camera's loving lingering over everyday objects. Reconstructions of traditional seal- and polar-bear-skin clothing adorned by intricate embroidery; caribou bone, skin, and ligament sleds and kayaks; and snow-block igloos built in the traditional manner; as well as attention to details large and small, from the landscapes of women's tattooed faces to the physiognomy of the Eastern Arctic, uninterrupted by any signs of alternate economies—these all build the film's credibility as a re-creation of a specific economic, social, and cultural past. Here Inuit authenticity appears entirely unmarred by settler society's historically developed and politically motivated misrepresentations.

Inuit and Inuktitut-speaking[5] contemporary viewers recognize *Atanarjuat* as a retelling of an ancient lesson in ethics; the film allows them to see, rather than just imagine, the world intimated in traditional storytelling. It brings to cinematic life, in the words of the film's director, Zacharias Kunuk, "the stories we used to hear when we were children, what do we believe, and why we are here" (*Reel Injun*). The film's explanatory power alone testifies to its authenticity. But non-Inuit and non-Inuktitut-speaking viewers of *Atanarjuat* find themselves thrown into a world that does not offer them recognizable parameters of orientation: no familiar language, history, or tradition, and no native informant either. The promise of understanding held out by the English subtitles shatters with the first translated message: a declaration by an elder storyteller that she can tell this story only to those who already understand it, but to no others. The disjointed editing of the opening sections further augments the impression of being at a loss in an incomprehensible world, as the settler or Southern viewer struggles to reconstruct the plots from the offered fragments.[6] To viewers unfamiliar with the ancient tale of Atanarjuat, the storyline itself is comprehensible to the extent that it evokes the generic conventions of classical epics and their preoccupation with governable communities, which has allowed reviewers to juxtapose claims of exotic authenticity with assurances about the universal qualities and appeal of the tale, the way Edward Buscombe, a prolific scholar of world cinema, does in the second epigraph to this chapter. Ironically, the less the settler viewers understand of the film, the more likely they are to perceive it as authentic and then quickly to reappropriate it as a masterpiece of universal preoccupations and dimensions.

This attempt to cast *Atanarjuat* in universalist terms has precipitated a vigorous response from indigenous commentators who insist on the Inuit specificity of Isuma's first feature as its most vital, pertinent, and revolutionary characteristic. Thus *Atanarjuat* has been discussed as an example of Inuit "visual sovereignty" (Raheja), as an allegory of colonialism showcasing the pernicious effects of abandoning traditionalism (Huhndorf, "Atanarjuat"), as a reconstitution of Inuit traditional generational relationships and allegiances (Hearne "Telling"), and as an expression and an engine of Inuit nationalism, one whose local meanings and effects become dangerously obscured as it circulates globally (Huhndorf, *Mapping the Americas*). Much of the critical debate over the film concerns the film's relationship to the national (both Inuit and Canadian) and global contexts out of which it emerges. And the consensus arising out of this debate suggests that *Atanarjuat*'s authenticity depends on its sustained commitment to Inuit meanings and contexts and its indifference to the colonial, political, economic, and cultural environment of its production, thus echoing the comments expressed by indigenous filmmakers and critics in *Reel Injun*.[7]

And yet, as I argue in this chapter, *Atanarjuat* offers perhaps the most sophisticated conception of contemporary indigenous authenticity currently available precisely because of the way in which it anticipates, fulfills, and foils expectations of the settler public while never compromising its primary orientation to the Inuit audience. To put it another way, the film succeeds in offering a viable version of contemporary indigeneity because in its most fundamental rhetorical gestures it engages, rather than avoids, the complicated cultural field of its production and reception, a field shaped by multicultural misrecognition. To appreciate fully the ideological work of Isuma's feature debut, we must supplement its interpretation as an example of indigenous cultural autonomy with an exploration of its deliberate entanglement in the Canadian politics of recognition. Unique in the context of contemporary North American indigenous cinema, both in terms of its subject matter and its formal solutions, *Atanarjuat* raises urgent questions about the possibilities and limits of indigenous self-representation in contemporary multicultural democracies. And it does so without offering quick or easy answers; rather, it invites viewers to consider a particular kind of representational and interpretive impasse. At first the ideological valence of the film appears contradictory. This contradiction is embodied most vividly in the juxtaposition of *Atanarjuat*'s main narrative, depicting a precontact nomadic band of Inuit, and the film's outtakes chronicling the making of the feature itself. *Atanarjuat (The Fast Runner)*, as the title already hints, participates in two separate traditions of representing indigenous people. It runs from modernity into a mythic indigenous past and then veers toward contemporary Canada as it unabashedly claims the specifically Inuit present moment in the outtakes concluding the film.[8] Through this rhetorical device, which suspends viewers between different temporal realms and different ways of depicting indigenous peoples, the film highlights the issue of contemporary forms of indigenous authenticity and their representation under the conditions of multicultural misrecognition in North American democracies; as I argue in detail in the introduction, these conditions enlist recognition on behalf of national cohesion of the settler states rather than on behalf of the political autonomy of indigenous nations. In its sophisticated resistance to (and exposure of) multicultural misrecognition, the film posits contemporary indigeneity as an orchestrated performance in the name of specific political and cultural projects, which in turn serve diverse ideological functions for multiple constituencies, be they indigenous or settler. The brilliance of the film resides in its shrewd formal logic, which offers *Atanarjuat* as the Inuit inside job to one viewer and as the specifically Canadian tale of universal appeal to another.

The Formal Puzzle of Atanarjuat

With its plot unfolding in the premodern past, *Atanarjuat* differs markedly from contemporary indigenous films in North America. Other works directed by indigenous filmmakers or based on texts by American Indian writers situate their plots in the contemporary United States or Canada and depict indigenous individuals and communities negotiating material and cultural legacies of American imperialism.[9] These films' ideological work is plain to see. On the heels of a long history of settler representations of indigenous peoples as vanishing emblems of a premodern past (think of such historical dramas as *Dances with Wolves* [1990], *Black Robe* [1991], or *The New World* [2005]; the entire US western genre; or early ethnographic film), contemporary indigenous films represent American Indians in the context of the American present. In their uncompromising portrayals of current reservation or urban realities, of communities and individuals suffering from unemployment, poverty, alcoholism, and alienation, alongside stories of material survival and cultural resistance and revival, contemporary American Indian films have aimed to reinsert indigenous people into the historical time and material realities of present-day North America. And yet, because of the unvarnished treatment of these subjects, such novels and films often meet with sharp critique by indigenous intellectuals for serving up negative stereotypes of American Indians to settler audiences or for their inability to narrate the indigenous present from an uncompromisingly indigenous point of view.[10]

In this context, Isuma's choice in *Atanarjuat* to shed the trappings of modernity, with its necessary settler presence, and to invoke instead an Inuit world that is inspiring in its completeness can be read as an effort to articulate a categorically indigenist point of view, one that explores the advantages of speaking from a time and place when Europeans weren't even a rumor yet. Locating the narrative far enough in the past to bracket completely the settler presence and its impact, *Atanarjuat* refuses to narrate the obliteration of the traditional way of life.[11] Instead, it indulges in a fantasy of a world as-yet-not destroyed by the soon-to-encroach colonizing power, a kind of reality no longer possible in the current moment. Yet for that reason, one wonders about the contemporary uses of such representations. However attractive such a vision might be, considering the long tradition of an allochronic representation of indigenous peoples in Western visual media, most flagrantly and famously evidenced in photographs by Edward S. Curtis,[12] an insistence on the mythic indigenous past could appear as a troubling choice. In Curtis's photographs and his 1914 film about the Northwest's Kwakwaka'wakw, *In the Land of the Head Hunters*, as in a host of other ethnographies of the early twentieth century, indigenous authenticity is associated with the period before the arrival of the colonizing armies and settler communities, as if the very fact of conquest annulled any possibility of continuous authentic indigeneity. For this reason, American Indian commentators have worried that an insistence on narratives of the past diverts attention from the present, that it encourages an acceptance of things as they are and invites continued ignorance of the ongoing struggles of indigenous peoples to reclaim their land (Lyons, Scott R., "Rhetorical Soverignty" 461). *Atanarjuat*, then, poses a question: Why would an Inuit film company dedicated to building independent Inuit media—dedicated, more broadly, to Inuit cultural and economic empowerment—commit itself fully to a representational strategy so compromised by mainstream ethnographic and popular film and so thoroughly criticized by American Indian intellectuals clamoring for inspiring representations of contemporary indigenous life? What useful ideological work does a sustained image of an indigenous preconquest past make possible beyond the current critical truism about the need of indigenous communities to reclaim mainstream representational modes in order to record indigenous history from indigenous points of view?

The puzzle posed by *Atanarjuat* does not end with the questions above, however, because whatever useful ideological work an ancient tale told by Inuit themselves performs, the film seems to undermine that work in its final moments. *Atanarjuat* concludes with outtakes showing Inuit actors and filmmakers in contemporary garb availing themselves expertly of that most modern means of representation, the digital film camera. The effect of these several clips is to shatter whatever illusions of utopian access to the real the film's main narrative might have inspired in viewers. They do so primarily by insisting on the *re*-creation of traditional cultural practices, on the Inuit past as a carefully staged performance. They display Inuit technological expertise, which immediately showcases their thorough embeddedness in contemporary mainstream life—black leather jackets, portable CD players, digital cameras, and all. Unlike in the widely circulated images of an aboriginal man in a loincloth drinking from a Coke bottle or South American Indian men and women in traditional dress wielding cameras, there is nothing extraordinary here; at stake is the very ordinariness of the situation. The outtakes take for granted the unique cultural dexterity of the actors and filmmakers: they move in and out of Inuktitut and English, in and out of historical and contemporary clothing, in and out of representations of the contemporary and ancient Eastern Arctic. By doing so, they pose the question of where the authentic can be located: then *or* now, then *and* now, or perhaps, precisely in the negotiation of these two temporal realms.

What is unprecedented in *Atanarjuat* is the juxtaposition of these two representational strategies: the allochronic diegesis, which locates the Inuit firmly in the precontact past, and the metafictional outtakes, which insist that the Inuit are indeed coeval with contemporary settler Americans. The self-reflexive moment of showing outtakes, a gesture that firmly implicates the indigenous filmmakers within the present moment and establishes them as authors of their own representations, is fairly widespread in indigenous cinema.[13] It is often identified as a rhetorical move crucial to indigenous filmmaking, which distinguishes itself from author-oriented settler culture cinema by insisting on its community-authored nature and its function as a form of social action, what Faye Ginsburg has called "embedded aesthetics." Zacharias Kunuk's and Isuma's earlier video work has been fully invested in that aesthetic. His 1989 *Qaggiq* (*The Gathering Place*) and 1991 *Nunagpa* (*Going Inland*), both productions for the local Inuit TV channel, combine historical reconstruction narratives with representations of how settler economy and culture changed Inuit communities.[14] Isuma's later productions, including *The Journals of Knud Rasmussen* and *Before Tomorrow*—features that complete *The Fast Runner Trilogy*—and the most recent documentary, *Inuit Knowledge and Climate Change*, continue that representational tradition by exploring the effects of the intertwining of Inuit and settler societies, whether these effects are deleterious, as in the case of the disappearance of shamanism, or inspiring, as in the case of Inuit expertise on global warming. In this context, *Atanarjuat* represents a departure from Isuma's prior and subsequent cinematographic practice because it formally separates the historical reconstruction from the narrative of the Inuit present. The outtakes do interrupt the illusion of an autonomous precontact world, but their unmasking of authentic indigeneity as performance is maximally delayed; in fact, it risks being missed altogether by impatient viewers who leave the screening rooms as soon as the final credits begin to roll. This peculiar double rhetorical gesture of showcasing the painstaking reconstruction of a precolonial past characterized by Inuit economic and social self-sufficiency, only to contradict or complement it with a brief concluding narrative of the Inuit's inextricable and even joyous participation in the Canadian and global present, is without parallel in contemporary American Indian filmmaking. And yet, at first it appears to be merely a cinematic footnote rather than a defining feature of the entire undertaking. In what follows I argue that the apparent disjunction between the film's main diegesis and the outtakes is a deliberate rhetorical strategy, Isuma's own brand of a dialectic of recognition aimed at mapping the contradictions embedded in the effort to represent contemporary indigeneity in the context of pervasive multicultural misrecognition.

Rhetorical Sovereignty

One immediately available way of making sense of this apparent formal disjunction I identify in Isuma's celebrated first feature would be to suggest that *Atanarjuat* engages in a deliberate exercise of what Scott Lyons has called rhetorical sovereignty, a people's right to determine "their own communicative needs and desires, to decide for themselves the goals, modes, styles, and languages of public discourse" (462). With its insistence on Inuit-controlled production and cultural authenticity all the way down to an exclusive use of Inuktitut, *Atanarjuat* is a good example of rhetorical sovereignty, which "requires above all the presence of an Indian voice, speaking or writing in an ongoing context of colonization and setting at least some of the terms of the debate" and "ideally employ[ing] a Native language" (462). Here the outtakes function precisely as one such effort to set the terms of discourse on indigeneity: they show the Inuit representing their usable past within the context of contemporary multicultural Canada—and doing so with the financial support of its governmental institutions.[15] However, Lyons's insistence that "the pursuit of sovereignty is an attempt to revive not [an indigenous] past, but [indigenous] possibilities" (449), along with his emphatic reminder about the colonial conditions of any indigenous action in North America, puts additional pressure on the film's primary interest in reconstructing the past and representing it in a mythical, rather than historical, mode.

And yet, if we do read the outtakes as a gesture of rhetorical sovereignty, *Atanarjuat* will appear as a succession of narrative strategies, each deployed to contest dominant settler modes of representing the Inuit. The outtakes bring the body of the film into their project of autoethnography, self-consciously deployed. By asking viewers to reevaluate what they have just seen, they invite recognition of the film as something other than a quixotic pursuit of an uncontaminated Inuit past, one condemned to mimic conventional representations of the indigenous that are all too familiar from settler popular culture and early ethnography. In *Imperial Eyes,* Mary-Louise Pratt described as autoethnography texts created by subaltern peoples in response to their representations in the settler cultures. Because it partially incorporates and appropriates the colonizer's idiom, an autoethnographic text is not an authentic form of self-representation, argues Pratt; rather, it constitutes the group's point of entry into metropolitan literate (and for our purposes, cinematographic) culture. As such it presents minority artists with advantages and limitations. It offers them an opportunity to speak back to the dominant culture in an idiom that that culture already understands. At the same time, though, this strategy runs the risk of reinforcing the reigning ideology, not to mention the economic and social systems this ideology sustains, the very systems that have historically been inimical to the survival of indigenous peoples. By reiterating, and thus legitimating, those very categories of thought, this strategy makes it harder to imagine, let alone put to use, a radically different worldview as a viable alternative to the dominant social and cultural arrangements.

The debate over orality versus literacy as proper modes of indigenous expression illustrates this predicament well. In one of the earlier critiques of contemporary Native American fiction, Paula Gunn Allen charged that the very transition into English and the written text constituted a radical departure from the indigenous worldview and a capitulation to the signifying systems of the colonizer. It has been the task of the youngest generation of American Indian scholars to point out the dangers of such a categorical stance. Craig Womack, in his study *Red on Red*, for example, sees writing as complementary to the oral tradition. In his attempt to legitimate a separate Native American literary and cultural criticism, he finds it necessary to recuperate the written tradition for contemporary indigenous intellectuals. Scott Lyons, too, has argued against equating Indian authenticity with orality, a logic that implies that "a writing Indian is no Indian at all" ("Rhetorical" 495). For Lyons, arguments that juxtapose orality and literacy erase contemporary Indians as Indians just as effectively as mainstream attempts at their assimilation. Thus modern and contemporary indigenous writers and artists have confronted a particularly vicious trap that is a defining dilemma of all autoethnographic texts. Their assertions of traditionally indigenous forms of expression, such as orality, as defining Indian authenticity effectively cast literate Indians as cultural half-breeds. And yet a turn to majoritarian conventions of expression seems inevitable because claims to political and cultural sovereignty have to be addressed to the colonizer and in their very formulation depend on the colonizer's political discourse.

Atanarjuat develops innovative strategies to steer through these dilemmas. Its autoethnographic investment is evident, and it begins with the simultaneous employment of Inuktitut and digital video technology. While Inuktitut privileges the putatively subaltern subject by shifting the discourse onto indigenous linguistic terrain and positions non-Inuktitut-speaking viewers as outsiders without easy entry into the film's fictional world, in Kunuk's own estimation, the digital camera technology resolves the contradiction between orality and literacy. It allows for the untarnished entry of traditional Inuit storytelling into contemporary media, bypassing altogether the question of textuality as a supposed marker of civilization.[16] Digital video makes it possible to render traditional storytelling not through a written text, with all the concessions such translation would require, but through a visual and auditory representation of traditional storytelling. Isuma's filmmakers speak to metropolitan subjects but get to define the mode of this dialogue; in an openly metafictional gesture, the concluding outtakes break away from the historical narrative to represent its very production. These concluding shots of actors and filmmakers at work force us to reenvision the entire film as a project in representing not only an authentic indigenous past but also, and more importantly, contemporary indigenous people making collective decisions about what counts as their usable past and exercising their agency in depicting it in their way. The film's promotional materials make clear that the process itself involved a conscious give-and-take between what the filmmakers perceived as divergent, though not irreconcilable, cultural conventions. While the authors declare that their intention "was not to impose Southern film-making conventions on their unique story, but to let the story shape the filmmaking process in an Inuit way," they also insist that they "wrote the script by a unique process of cultural authenticity that was bi-lingual and bicultural through most of the stages of the production." Eight versions of the Atanarjuat's legend told by Inuit elders were combined into one narrative recorded both in Inuktitut and English and then edited by a Toronto-based story consultant. By a similar process of Inuit and settler collaboration, "all costumes, props, and sets for *Atanarjuat* were handmade by local artists and elders based on meticulously researched traditional knowledge, drawing both on Inuit oral history and the journals of Captain William Edward Parry, leader of the British expedition to Igloolik in 1822." Thus, the producers explain: "The artistic research and production for the film was a reappropriation of ancient knowledges from Southern museums and books." The autoethnographic strategy became here "a means of bringing traditional skills and technologies back to the Inuit of Igloolik" (Isuma website).

The filmmakers' use of the Parry expedition journals and other such settler materials raises a thorny issue of authenticity but may have surprising ideological benefits. Allison Griffiths has pointed out that while the appropriation of the settler culture's ethnographic archive by contemporary indigenous peoples is wrought with paradoxes, it often has fulfilled significant political functions. She explains that even though "stereotypes [pervading these archives] depend on mythical construction of cultural difference for meaning, they have nevertheless provided peoples with a model of self-representation which they can exploit for their own political ends" (322). One well-known example of this kind of appropriation of settler ethnographic material is Maine's M'kmaqs cultural survival films, which function as "a form of native rights advocacy, documenting traditional arts and crafts, strengthening cultural identity and informing the public of their existence and ongoing struggles" (322). In a similar intertwining of cultural and political representations, the production of *Atanarjuat* in the late 1990s overlapped with a ten-year-long legal process leading to the creation of Nunavut Territory in 1999, the first Canadian territory governed de facto by an indigenous majority. Isuma's film was scheduled to premiere at the official celebrations of the Nunavut's constitution, but its release was postponed due to delays in funding. In this political context, the producers of *Atanarjuat* turn to settler knowledge, preservation, and representation, such as Parry's journals and Canadian ethnographic museums, to re-create the precontact social and economic life around Igloolik in the Eastern Arctic in order to assert a distinct culture in contemporary Canada at the moment when Nunavut, with its 80 percent Inuit population, emerges as a self-governing political entity.[17]

The re-created tale of Atanarjuat itself testifies to a conscious autoethnographic strategy as well. The film deploys this strategy in at least two critical ways: it attempts both to tell a universal tale recognizable to the world beyond the Eastern Arctic and to represent properly the nomadic Inuit in a way that pushes back against settler ethnographic conventions, most famously on display in Robert Flaherty's 1922 film, *Nanook of the North*. The fact that the majority of mainstream press reviews have consistently described *Atanarjuat* both as an Inuit *Iliad* or drama of Shakespearean proportions and as a consciously scripted alternative to *Nanook* testifies to the success of this tactic. And a deliberate tactic it is, if we are persuaded by Malea Powell's argument in "Rhetorics of Survivance: How American Indians Use Writing." Powell suggests that American Indian intellectuals such as Sarah Winnemucca Hopkins and Charles Eastman used mainstream discourses of Indian identity and deftly anticipated their white audiences' desires and expectations as shaped by current literary conventions in order to garner sympathy and support for concrete rhetorical, cultural, and political projects. This tactic necessarily required these intellectuals to assume a position between the specific tribal cultures and the settler American culture and to appropriate the politically ambiguous and often compromised figure of the civilized Indian. It also allowed them, however, to mark themselves as subjects within the dominant discourse rather than as being merely subject to it. For Powell, as for Womack and Lyons, autoethnographic strategy presents contemporary indigenous intellectuals with particularly useful, though rhetorically tricky, opportunities. If we bring Powell's argument to *Atanarjuat*, it is easy to see that the outtakes work to stake such an in-between positioning as well as to foreground indigenous agency and subjectivity in the present: no longer objects of a settler ethnographic discourse, the Inuit imagine their own past. From this perspective, the Atanarjuat tale works more as a shrewd deployment of recognizably settler narrative conventions, both filmic and literary, than as an effort to elide them. The South, which disappeared from the diegesis, reappears at the level of form.

The most evident among these settler conventions is the ethnographic one, dating back to well before the invention of the kinetoscope[18] and coming to some culmination in Robert Flaherty's *Nanook of the North*, the first feature-length film about the indigenous people of the American Far North. Griffiths points out how cinema "took over the project of naturalizing racial hierarchies inherited from other nineteenth-century visual technologies" (249), and Flaherty's film is certainly emblematic of that effort. Silent and in black and white, the film tells the story of a hunter, Nanook, and his family, following them through a visit to a trading post, a seal and walrus hunt, the building of an igloo, and scenes of food preparation, washing, and getting ready for sleep. The entire film is animated by the concept of the benevolent native informant and trading partner who freely and happily serves up his life for documentation. As if aiming to sadden and bemuse at the same time, *Nanook of the North* is also curiously pervaded by Charlie Chaplin's tramp aesthetic, as well as by a sense of nostalgia, "the melancholy spirit of the North" in the words of the scriptwriters. The opening title card notifies viewers that the protagonist died two years after the completion of the film, starving during an unsuccessful hunt. But the viewers do not need to be concerned, because *Nanook of the North* has toured the globe. Filmic representation stands in here for the actually existing indigenous person: as one Nanook replaces the other, the entire story becomes a story of cinematic triumph, not ethnic disaster, an exercise in salvage ethnography—that is, a concerted effort to document the everyday life of a putatively vanishing people.

Atanarjuat explicitly takes up specific narrative segments of *Nanook*. The visual allusions pile up: dogs get kicked, raw meat gets eaten, knives and sled runners get licked, igloos go up, the camera lingers over the ethnographic detail of tattooed faces and hand-crafted tools. And yet, while reproducing these documentary conventions, the film offers a subtle critique of them, by replaying some scenes with a difference and omitting others completely. For example, in the "getting ready for bed" scene in *Nanook*, the ethnographic verges on the pornographic, as early twentieth-century viewers can be both titillated by the display of a woman's bare breasts and excused for this titillation at the same time because the indigenous woman is figured as an ethnographic specimen rather than as a person. *Atanarjuat* stages an identical scene very differently by focusing on intrafamily dynamics rather than on ethnographic detail. The morning bed routine is a pretext to illustrate Atanarjuat's second wife Puja's perfidy as she attempts to seduce her husband's willing brother only to be discovered by his wife. Thus, what in *Nanook* was one more testimony to the supposedly timeless routine of a not-quite-people becomes in *Atanarjuat* an opportunity to play out a specific plot of planned revenge, and later, a pretext to illustrate the capacity for forgiveness and reconciliation: human unpredictability, in other words, rather than animal-like embeddedness in natural cycles. Flaherty notoriously declared that one could not "make a very good film of the love affairs of the Eskimo . . . because they never show much feeling in their faces, but [one] can make a very good film of Eskimos spearing walrus" (qtd. in Rony 104). Fatimah Tobing Rony provides broader context for Flaherty's now-outrageous comment by explaining that for early twentieth-century filmmakers "the Ethnographic is without an intellect: he or she is best represented as merely existing. It is the camera of the explorer/artist who will capture the reality of their 'simply lived' lives" (104).[19] In response, Isuma filmmakers rewrite some of the classic scenes from Flaherty's film by evoking all the psychological and emotional complexity they can muster. In this context the outtakes of *Atanarjuat* not only celebrate the artfulness of the Inuit actors but also remind the settler audience that indigenous art is a reconstruction of an indigenous past, not that past itself. Thus they shift the attention to strategic deployments of such representations, their successes and failures, their possibilities and limitations, and away from the simplistic assertions or denials of indigenous authenticity.

In a related rhetorical gesture, *Atanarjuat*'s filmmakers eschew re-creating the scenes of contact so prominent in *Nanook*: the trading-post scenes and, most conspicuously, the indigenous encounter with settler technology. In Flaherty's film, the trading-post scene, in which an Inuit child gets sick after gorging on biscuits and lard offered by the trader, only to be cured by the medicine administered by that same trader,[20] works almost at cross-purposes. On the one hand, it offers an early version of what has later become the dominant Canadian official discourse on the Inuit: an illustration of the Inuit as hapless victims of the processes of modernization that put an end to their self-sustaining nomadic life, a people in need of governmental care to manage the successive waves of starvation and disease that are decimating them. But, on the other hand, it illustrates as well the dynamic that gave rise to that discourse and exposes it as self-serving. After all, the trader functions as a solution to a problem that he has precipitated in the first place, just as the Canadian state's move into the Eastern Arctic in the 1950s and 1960s, nominally to deal with mounting epidemics, was only the latest stage in the ongoing process of drawing these not-yet-colonized lands and their populations into the settler administrative networks.[21] The notorious gramophone scene in *Nanook of the North*, in which Nanook pretends to see the gramophone for the first time, biting the gramophone record not once but three times, functions in the same manner as similar scenes in other films resorting to ethnographic conventions.[22] It establishes another staple of ethnographic thinking about the indigenous: their fundamental state of authentic separateness (the naïveté of the freshly discovered) combined with a natural curiosity about and openness to the wonders of settler technology. Isuma's decision to construct a precontact narrative makes it possible to believably omit such scenes and break away, even if only for an imaginative moment, from the political discourses they sustain. The point of these omissions, again, is not so much to arrive at a story of uncontaminated indigenous culture—the final outtakes decisively shut down that possibility—not, that is, to indulge in what rightly can be named a fantasy of disentanglement with the South, but rather to assert rhetorical sovereignty, to tell a story of the indigenous past without appropriating all the structural elements of the North-South narrative. *Atanarjuat* takes up some forms of mainstream ethnographic representation but then emphatically refuses others to clear the space for imaginative alternatives to the paternalistic discourse about the Inuit that has dominated Canadian public imagination in the twentieth century.[23]

The other settler convention deployed in *Atanarjuat* is the epic, a narrative form typically chronicling the emergence and development of major social formations such as nations and empires through the heroic deeds of individual leaders. Easily recognizable in the narrative arc of the film, the conventions of the epic allow settler viewers to collapse the distinction between "us" and "them" and indulge in the cherished fantasy of adoption into the tribe. The success of that tactic is evident in the critical reception of *Atanarjuat*. Here's a representative example from Kenneth Turan, writing for the *Los Angeles Times*: "Everything in *The Fast Runner* combines to create a film that does not feel acted, but rather like it is simply happening in front of our eyes. This is so much the case that, when the closing credits are run next to documentary shots of the film's crew at work, it comes as a shock to see how the artifice was put together. At the film's beginning, one of the tellers of this tale says, 'I can only sing this song to someone who understands it.' What's special about *The Fast Runner* is that by its epic close, the select group includes us." The same effect is conceived of quite differently by the filmmakers themselves: "The goal of *Atanarjuat* is to make the viewer feel inside the action looking out, rather than outside looking in. This lets people forget how far away they really are, and to identify with the story and characters as if they were just like us" (Isuma website). If we pay attention to the language in this quotation and grant the filmmakers automatic authority, the film creates an illusion: "*make* the viewer feel inside the action," "let people *forget* how far away they really are," and the telling subjunctive of "*as if* they were just like us." It does not disregard real differences even as it unfolds a fantasy of their erasure. The *Los Angeles Times* reviewer, however, understands the film as just such a fantasy made real: "the select group includes us." It appears that the settler public would like to have it both ways, a film that plays up the exotic otherness of the Inuit and, at the same time, reveals a reassuring universality at the core of their particular experience, a universality that becomes the passport required for Inuit entry to the rest of Canada and the world.

The epic conventions deployed in *Atanarjuat* play to this desire for inclusion on the part of the non-Inuit viewer but at the same time illustrate the rhetorical dilemma of the indigenous artist's engagement with settler culture's representational conventions. Historically, the epic has been bound up with the cultural work of nation-building, and it has traditionally been used to underwrite a people's claim to nationhood and sovereignty. Because it was released in 2001, two years after Canada's Northern Territory was divided to give Nunavut administrative independence, *Atanarjuat* registers as a claim to cultural distinctiveness bolstering the emergence of the first self-governing province with an Inuit voting majority in Canada. It thus functions as an expression of both a universalist and a nationalist impulse; it is the Inuit claim to global visibility and to their status as a distinct culture and society, in a move that turns what I identified earlier as the settler viewers' contradictory expectation of simultaneous exotic particularity and universality into the filmmakers' conscious strategy, even a kind of pact made with the settler viewer, that allows each to have it both ways. What the film stages for us, then, is the inseparability of the claims on behalf of universalism and particularity within the specific rhetorical conditions of multicultural misrecognition. Because ultimately multicultural misrecognition is a strategy of national integration, it understands cultural difference as a form of universality: we all have our particular cultures, and that very quality testifies to our shared Americanness.

The Cunning of Recognition

In accordance with the multiculturalist paradigm that has also pervaded the US public discourse, the ability to construct a narrative of cultural distinctiveness becomes a condition for belonging within a nation. In Canada, this dynamic was institutionalized in the 1982 Constitution, which proclaimed Canada a multicultural nation of distinct societies. The Inuit produce a cinematographic epic in order to establish their prior distinctiveness, but this epic also evidences a kind of generic integration, roughly analogous to the political incorporation generally demanded of North America's indigenous peoples. As Hugh Brody has been arguing since the early 1970s, the discourse of self-government deployed to open up the Eastern Arctic to the central government's administrative takeover actually increased dependence on the political structures established for the Inuit by Ottawa, even when the Inuit themselves assumed the leading positions within these regional structures. Similarly, *Atanarjuat* is intelligible as authentically Inuit to settler audiences only via its recourse to the dominant epic and ethnographic conventions. The three-hour narrative of the Inuit premodern past ultimately underwrites the claim of participation in the Canadian present staked out by the closing sequences of the film. In this context, the film and the outtakes are fundamentally of a piece, two separate parts of the same rhetorical strategy. Kunuk's film thus exemplifies the insight that there is no eluding "the South," "the West," or whatever we choose to call political and cultural formations brought to the Americas by the settler communities. As political scientist Will Kymlicka has repeatedly argued, minority nationalism is properly understood as a conscious response to the dominant culture's nation-building strategies. Rhetorical sovereignty thus functions only within the horizon of multiculturalism and its politics of recognition. And perhaps this is precisely why some contemporary indigenous intellectuals want nothing less than "to delete sovereignty from [their] vocabulary once and for all."[24]

To say as much, though, is already to insist on a different perspective. But first, let me sum up the insights of the line of reasoning that is invested in the concept of indigenous sovereignty. The interpretive framework that relies on the conception of indigenous rhetorical sovereignty allows us to say that *Atanarjuat* resorts to settler ethnographic and epic conventions in the service of a fantasy of cultural authenticity and distinctiveness and, at the same time, transparent universality, ultimately all in order to assert indigenous cultural agency in the present within existing political conditions, rather than against or outside of them. Between the precontact narrative and the insistence on joyous participation in the present in the outtakes, *Atanarjuat* creates a new kind of indigeneity, one that allows the Inuit filmmakers to "maintain their difference in the very space that the occupier has organized" (Powell 405). The film producers rearticulate dominant beliefs about indigenous peoples in order to offer a version of their own usable past, not to re-create nostalgically the past lost, but to imagine new possibilities of asserting their presence and agency now and in the future. Thus *Atanarjuat (The Fast Runner)* depicts contemporary sovereign indigenous agency precisely by engaging with dominant discourses rather than as a result of carefully purging them. Such engagement is the gist of cultural authenticity advertised by the film's producers. *Atanarjuat* is thus not about a flight from the present moment in search of authentic origins but rather about contemporary indigeneity deployed most authentically in its engagement with its immediate discursive, cultural, and political interlocutor.

We could assert, then, that through the addition of the self-reflexive outtakes and the film's persistent autoethnographic strategy, *Atanarjuat* depicts a contemporary indigenous people representing its past not in a mode of nostalgia and mourning but as an assertion of rhetorical sovereignty. With its explicitly stated commitment "to preserve and enhance Inuit culture, and to create jobs and needed economic development in Igloolik and Nunavut" (Isuma Productions website), *Atanarjuat* not only contests dominant representations of indigenous peoples but also transforms the material reality of contemporary First Nations communities, an uncompromisable concomitant to all claims to sovereignty and an important aspect of contemporary indigenous filmmaking and its embedded aesthetics. Rather than a testimony to unwitting and ironic contamination by settler modes of cultural expression, Isuma's film is an example of a conscious engagement with those very representational strategies in the service of a specific political project: to proclaim the Eastern Arctic Inuit as a "distinct society" on the model of Québec and to gather support for the unfolding process of achieving a measured self-governance, as the Nunavut Agreement moves from an "Agreement in Principle" in 1990 to its implementation in 1999, an almost paradigmatic instance of rhetorical sovereignty.

And yet, the rhetorical sovereignty argument does not tell the entire story of the film's ideological functions. If rhetorical sovereignty hinges on an emphatic engagement with the present to clear space for discursive, social, political, and economic autonomy for indigenous people, serious investment in narratives of the past that rely on representational strategies borrowed from settler culture, even as they work to contest settler fantasies, must seem like a displacement of useful energy. Why not make films such as Shelley Niro's *Honey Mocassins*, which thematizes up front the issues that *Atanarjuat* deals with in the brief sixty seconds of the outtakes? Why edit out altogether the narrative of the colonization and gradual disappearance of traditional lifeways and the serious critique of Canada's ongoing exploitation of First Nations' land such a narrative would imply? Why not follow the lead of Alanis Obomsawin's documentary about the Mohawk standoff at Oka, *270 Years of Resistance*, which puts the political questions concerning First Nations first and foremost? These omissions are precisely the key to *Atanarjuat*'s acclaim among the Canadian film establishment, an acclaim testified to by numerous awards. If the film's primary ideological investment is Inuit sovereignty—rhetorical, cultural, political, and economic—why has the film been so eagerly embraced by the official critical establishment, especially through its connection to the National Film Board of Canada, a government-funded institution interested in Canadian nation-building, in integrative rather than liberatory projects? After all, the story the main film tells is emphatically antimulticulturalist; it is an account of a community reconstituting itself through a forced expulsion of its insubordinate members, an account in which difference is literally demonized—that is, made into a demon. Embodied by the evil shaman from the North stumbling into the Inuit band and precipitating patricide, difference is clearly inimical to the survival of the group; it takes several years and a heroic effort on the part of the protagonist and his collaborators to restore the social balance within the community. The main story hardly functions as a manual about the transformation of social arrangements to accommodate different forms of social organization. If the film embodies an instance of rhetorical sovereignty for the Inuit, what kind of ideological functions does it perform for Canada's establishment multiculturalism, which is unequivocally invested in creating at least the impression of a nation of distinct yet equal societies bound in a single federation and economic system?

The very autoethnographic conventions deployed by the filmmakers to assert rhetorical sovereignty bespeak an entanglement with Canadian politics of recognition and the varied modes of political cooptation such politics necessitate. The film's officially sanctioned popularity can be traced to its complicity with Canada's multiculturalist project and its partial accommodation of multicultural misrecognition. This link, while seemingly inevitable, is also troubling: several scholars, indigenous and non-native alike, have pointed out that this multiculturalist project is, ultimately, inimical to the political and cultural goals associated with indigenous sovereignty.[25] This is so because in practice the project has led to further dependence of contemporary indigenous peoples on the economy and political culture of the capitalist democracy that is Canada, foreclosing any potential for alternate modes of economic, political, and social organization. Multiculturalism has effectively undermined forms of difference that would matter in spheres other than the symbolic: for example, in the United States, while particular ethnic history months proliferate, the structural inequality between different racial groups has not been significantly redressed.

Atanarjuat (The Fast Runner), then, also has to be considered in the context of multicultural misrecognition and its imperatives of national integration. Elizabeth Povinelli, who studied Australian politics of recognition, offers crucial insight about the ideological functions of the concept of the indigenous in multicultural democracies that is helpful in untangling the complicated rhetorical moves deployed in *Atanarjuat*. She explains that "the indigenous does seem to be playing a particular role in debates on multiculturalism. The concept, as opposed to the actual socially embedded persons, seems to be providing the nation an experience of 'before nationalism,' and an experience of a time before the failures and compromises of national projects. But rather than offering a counter-national form, the concept of the indigenous seems to be purifying and redeeming the ideal image of the nation" (26). While facilitating rehabilitation of multicultural nations, this process of national redemption via reference to an indigenous past confronts indigenous people with an impossible task: identification with a putatively authentic past that can only be resurrected performatively. The irony of such resurrection is that some customary indigenous practices are either prohibited by laws or found unacceptable by mainstream public standards of decency, or both (Povinelli 26). What the politics of recognition demands of indigenous people, then, is a performative relationship to their past characterized by open access to and solidarity with the cultural forms that have been effectively wiped out by the encroaching settler communities and that often continue to be perceived as repulsive or immoral. Isuma's filmmakers confront the same demand that their performances of Inuit authenticity function to complement Canada's national reinvention. As Colin Samson has argued in his tellingly titled study, *A Way of Life That Does Not Exist: Canada and the Extinguishment of the Innu*, in Canada the politics of recognition renders the indigenous visible within the nation's political and legal discourses "only long enough to redeem their colonizers and give conscience and meaning to what is in effect a bargain involving the disappearance of real difference and Native sovereignty in exchange for a place in the mosaic of Canadian multiculturalism"(328).[26] A good example of this dynamic is the sedentarization, or gathering into permanent settlements, of the Innu, former hunter-gatherers now separated from the lands that constituted the base for their culture's cosmology as well as everyday practices, and compressed into villages without access to sustainable employment and education, a process similar to that undergone by the Inuit. As in the case of Australia, the multiculturalist discourse of recognition in Canada is really just another attempt at the extinguishment[27] of claims to indigenous sovereignty so that the "historical work of Canadian Federation can continue on what effectively are the purloined ancestral homelands of the indigenous peoples" (9). Multiculturalist rhetoric disguises the continuing usurpation of land no longer protected in theory, and never in practice, by Native title. The nation cedes a space for the indigenous in the national imaginary so that it can continue to have unobstructed access to the land; symbolic recognition ends up enabling continuing material exploitation.

The very language of indigenous political and cultural empowerment, endorsed by the Canadian public media, obscures the history of forced policies of cultural assimilation. This intertwining of discourses of self-determination with integrative mandates seems to be a matter of tradition. Robert Flaherty's comments on *Nanook* are an early example of such colonization through political emancipation, at least for the Arctic. When he suggested that he wanted to show the Inuit "not from the civilized point of view, but as they saw themselves, as 'we, the people'" (qtd. in Rony 18), Flaherty projected a kind of Jeffersonian ideal of self-determination while also falling back on the most hackneyed distinction between the civilized and the barbarians. The Inuit in this logic are radically other but also potentially the same, amenable to the same social and political modes of organization while retaining their fundamentally nonmodern "nature." Contemporary celebration of indigenous agency by Canadian media shifts the responsibility for what in effect are changes desired by and beneficial to the Canadian state, such as handing control over lands protected by Native title to the Canadian federal government, or the move from state administration of indigenous communities to their self-administration via the concept of self-government, onto the indigenous peoples themselves, so that the state cannot be blamed for the adverse effects these transformations often have on indigenous communities. The very notion of sovereignty—political, cultural, rhetorical—ends up completing the historic work of the Canadian federation rather than supporting indigenous nations' efforts toward greater self-determination. The indigenous people thus fully frame the settler culture. First, they provide it with a past to match the European national genealogies; in that sense, the historical narrative of Atanarjuat, in addition to underwriting Canadian claims to an enlightened relationship to its indigenous peoples, also provides Canada with a genealogy, with its own indigenous ancestors, so to speak. But the indigenous people also furnish Canada with a future, a means of marking the new world's difference from the old. As a multicultural democracy fully delivering on its claims of being a nation of distinct yet equal societies, Canada emerges as a viable alternative to the majority of European nations, which continue to insist on the republican integrationist rather than pluralist models of national belonging, despite their rapidly changing populations. What the indigenous people get in exchange is access to Canadian administrative structures, which allow them to participate, now out of political maturity, in the ongoing work of the state's political and economic self-consolidation, all the while, and now without any official obstruction, performing their cultural difference.

In this context, the image projected in *Atanarjuat*'s outtakes—the image of self-empowered Inuits compellingly performing their past—hardly functions as a critique of multiculturalist brands of cultural and political colonization. It is, rather, a necessary corollary to those projects: to Canada's ongoing nation-building and to its reinvention as an internationally conversant economic partner and a peace-making force in world politics in the age of globalization, especially as it continues to confront US economic and cultural domination on the North American continent and in the world.[28] *Atanarjuat* cannot help but become complicit in Canada's nation-building and global self-promotion. This is not an unwitting complicity, of course. Most Inuit-authored political documents beginning in the early 1970s testify to a deliberate deployment of this strategy. The Inuit have typically cast their aspirations for political autonomy in the context of political, economic, and cultural participation in the Canadian nation. This approach has been recognized by Canadian historians as the "genius of Inuit politics" and has been credited with the success of the emergence of Nunavut as a self-governing territory (Miller). It has also been favorably contrasted with more explicitly oppositional tactics of First Nations in Southern Canada. Yet this approach has also been sharply criticized by indigenous governance scholars. Taiaiake Alfred, Mohawk scholar of traditional indigenous governance, for example, has insisted on the wrongheadedness of any political strategy that accommodates the state's founding political framework and its governing assumptions. For Alfred, adoption of settler notions of sovereignty simply works to retrench settler forms of political authority, moving indigenous peoples even farther away from their own traditions of governance.

Atanarjuat (The Fast Runner) plays into the hands of the Canadian multiculturalist project not only through the by now requisite version of contemporary ethnography asserted in the outtakes—where, no longer hindered by the intrusive figure of the settler ethnographers in their participant/observer guise, the self-empowered indigenous peoples represent themselves—but also through the mythical epic narrative of the Inuit past, despite the tale's overtly antimulticulturalist tenor. The cunning of recognition, as Povinelli argues, requires a particular relationship to the past, a foregrounding of authentic indigeneity that is rendered emblematic through identification with a putatively vanished cultural formation. This task is paradoxical because entry into the multicultural present is premised for the indigenous peoples on identification with a past that has been historically both exoticized and suppressed by settler societies. They are called upon to establish clear cultural distinctiveness, and, through this particularly dexterous cultural performance, they earn the right to cultural and political representation within a multicultural democracy. In other words, they earn a right to equivalence, or cultural citizenship, at least in theory.

The marker of authenticity established by ethnographers and the settler public is an impossible ideal, a conception of indigeneity that reaches out for its referent not to contemporary surviving indigenous communities but to the time before conquest.[29] It thus establishes indigeneity as simultaneously visible and irrelevant, necessary but anachronistic—or better, necessarily anachronistic. *Atanarjuat*'s main mythical narrative thus responds to this requirement of contemporary multicultural Canada. In this way, from the Boston Tea Party to North American and Australian multiculturalism, indigeneity as an idea continues to be used for the diverse political and cultural projects of various settler communities in North America and across the globe. The cunning of recognition is such that if in the past the indigenous peoples were overtly compelled to serve these functions, now they appear to *choose* to do so. Their willing participation is deemed an act of self-determination, self-empowerment, and political maturity. In this political context, so wrought with the dangers of cooptation, *Atanarjuat* does not unambiguously furnish an instance of successfully deployed contemporary indigenous sovereignty. Rather, it provides a map of the contradictory forces characterizing the terrain on which exercise of such sovereignty is necessarily undertaken, and it raises the question of indigenous resistance to cultural and political domination within multiculturalist democracies.

Cooptation or Resistance?

This dynamic of resistance and cooptation is played out clearly even when we consider the question of the representational medium. According to Kunuk, digital video technology opened up new possibilities of self-representation for indigenous peoples by allowing them to move directly from the oral to the visual—that is, without mediation through the textual. But it has also inserted indigenous filmmakers into the history of Canadian national cinema and its political economy. While a critic's well-meaning and politically progressive impulse might be to read Isuma's work, or that of any other indigenous filmmaker, as alternatives to Canadian settler representations of indigenous peoples, it is also important to see how much indigenous cinema in Canada shares with Canadian national cinema, how to a large degree it both parallels and complements that ongoing and explicitly Canadian nation-building project. Isuma's film takes on added meaning within the background of a concerted effort in Canada, unfolding over the last thirty years, to establish a national cinema through the creation of festivals, the compilation of "Ten Best" lists (in 1984 and 1993), as well as the securing of financial support through a variety of governmental organizations. At stake in that effort has been a "publicly recognizable body of Canadian [feature] film" (Gittings 3), especially in the context of the strong commitment of early Canadian cinema to documentary projects and relatively late governmental investment in the feature-film industry. This emphatically nationalist project of articulation has unfolded in the context of a threefold dynamic of emergence: 1) the emergence of Canadian cinema against US cultural colonialism; 2) the emergence of Québécois cinema against cultural colonialism emanating from Anglo-Canada; and 3) the emergence of First Nations cinema against Canadian and Québécois settler political and cultural dominance after the 1965 regionalization of governmental structures for the funding and administration of the film industry.

Canada's early film production focused on documentaries and promotional immigration films touting Canada's natural resources and potential for settlement. These early films consistently established whiteness as characteristic of a collective Canadian identity, typically representing the Canadian population as a collection of various immigrant groups from Europe while depicting indigenous peoples as emblems of a vanishing past, as elements of a landscape to be appropriated, or as caricatured testimony to the superiority of European handling of the land (Gittings 82–83). These early productions were funded by a variety of sources, from the private sector to corporate sponsorship to direct state investment, with Canadian Public Radio as a major source of support. Governmental institutions, such as the Exhibits and Publicity Bureau created in 1918 (renamed the Canadian Government Motion Picture Bureau after 1923 and ultimately absorbed by the National Film Board in 1941), with their charge to "promote the production and distribution of films designed to interpret Canada to Canadians and to other nations[,] locked Canada into the production of documentaries promoting tourism and trade" rather than feature films. The effect of this policy was that after World War I, these propaganda films and industrial shorts constituted by far the majority of Canadian cinematographic output (Gittings 76–77). The 1939 National Film Act, which aimed to centralize the oversight, production, distribution, and marketing of Canadian films, ultimately worked to further delay development of a Canadian feature-film industry by focusing on nation-building and immigration-promotion goals. The development of the feature-film industry was also retarded by the growing Hollywood hegemony, by the scattered nature of the Canadian domestic film market, and by Canadian distributors' desire to provide popular cinema inexpensively to Canadian audiences. Attempts to hold back the flood of inexpensive US-produced popular cinema included the ultimately unsuccessful 1948 Canadian Cooperation Project, which aimed to lure American capital to producing films about Canada, as well as the Massey Commission, a federal government inquiry into the state of Canadian arts and culture that recommended "state-sponsored development and protection for the arts in the face of 'a vast and disproportionate amount of material coming from a single alien source'" (qtd. in Gittings 87). It was not until the creation of the Canadian Film Development Corporation in 1967 (renamed Telefilm Canada after 1984), which was charged with developing funding structures for the feature-film industry, that the Canadian state demonstrated a serious investment in Canadian feature film.

At about the same time, starting around 1965, the Canadian film industry began a process of gradual regionalization and decentralization of production. Local and regional offices were established and the National Film Board (NFB) created separate studios. In 1964, a separate French language production unit spurred development of a specifically Québécois cinema, which set out to construct a Francophone community by "representing the Québécois to themselves" (qtd. in Gittings 88). And yet Québécois filmmakers continued to see the NFB as a colonial institution interested not in promoting self-determination for Québec but in promoting its incorporation into a bicultural Canada.[30] In 1974, the NFB established Studio D, the first publicly funded women's production unit in the world.[31] In 1991, the Initiatives in Film Programme was founded, with the mission of promoting "representation of the ethnic and racial diversity of women's culture as a major component of the studio's production" (qtd. in Gittings 92), and Studio One in Edmonton began as an effort to create an aboriginal film community in Canada. Finally, in 1996, the Aboriginal Filmmaking Programme, which decentralized the earlier structure, provided access to funds for indigenous filmmakers across the country. All of these administrative readjustments reflect a larger effort underway in Canada to "reconfigure 'national' as a category by focusing on the local and specific in Canada's diverse regions" (Gittings 89). They are one testimony to a more general movement from a universalist to a multiculturalist perspective on the nation within Canadian public discourse and its constitutional documents. The focus has shifted from the whole to the parts, from the nation to the federation, we could say. Integration has remained the ultimate goal, with the strategy changing to de-emphasize the universal and the national in favor of the particular, the regional, and the diverse.

Atanarjuat (The Fast Runner) is particularly well positioned to serve the needs of the Canadian national cinema developing in the age of multiculturalism. Inuit video and film productions, along with other work by minority filmmakers, are funded by the Canadian cinematographic establishment because they visibly contribute to an ongoing Canadian effort to shape a national cinema that reflects a vision of a multicultural democracy by helping to locate its diverse communities within an imagined Canadian national community. Isuma's video and cinematographic projects, as they have developed over the last two decades, testify to a changing politics of community, of insidership and outsidership. Its early video work in all aspects of its production, distribution, and exhibition was addressed to the Inuktitut-speaking Inuit audience. But *Atanarjuat* explicitly targets settler American and global viewers even as it taunts them with the opening line of demarcation between those who already know the tale and those who do not, with the banishing of English and French to the subtitles, and with the anti-integrationist tenor of the tale. In a way similar to early films in Québec, which were produced by Anglophones and then translated into French, Isuma's first feature also moved between Inuktitut and English at different stages of its production, only to ultimately privilege a minority language rather than a national one. Clearly the effort here has been to overcome the cultural and linguistic split not by instituting a common language—not, in other words, in a patently integrationist mode—but rather by enacting a national cinematic project that embodies the nation as a federation of linguistically and culturally distinct societies. Isuma's film delivers multicultural Canada to Canadians precisely by offering the Inuit the story of their origins and their present told in Inuktitut rather than English (or French).

But it delivers still more. That the political economy of Canadian film production has to be considered in the context of British and American hegemony further informs the success of *Atanarjuat.* Canada's film industry has embraced the film because it could be presented as Canada's indigenous film, solidifying the national canon by offering it a film that in its subject matter, production, and exhibition is unlike standard Hollywood fare. Ironically, no doubt, the film could mark Canadian authenticity, even though it was emphatically intended to mark an alternative cultural sensibility: the Inuit world shown through Inuit eyes. As much as it serves as the Inuit claim to simultaneous cultural distinctiveness and embeddedness in Canada's present, Isuma's film functions also as Canada's claim to Canadian cultural distinctiveness. One kind of difference—that is, Inuit specificity—which is produced with the help of Canada's mainstream institutions but also against them as an alternative to Canadian settler society, is incorporated by these institutions and marketed as another kind of difference, now manifesting Canada's cultural specificity against US hegemony.

That a screening of *Atanarjuat (The Fast Runner)* in Washington, DC, at the First Nations/First Features showcase in May 2005, was funded by and took place in the Canadian Embassy is only one example of the dynamic I describe above. Another is the fact that *Atanarjuat* has entered the canon of world cinema as a representative of not only Inuit but also Canadian national cinema. Here's Edward Buscombe accounting for Isuma's film via full-fledged multicultural misrecognition in *Cinema Today*, an encyclopedic history of world cinema released by Phaidon Press in 2003:

> This is the first film made in the Inuktitut language spoken by the native peoples of the Canadian Arctic. It tells a legend from two thousand years ago about Atanarjuat, who incurs the jealous enmity of Oki when he marries Atuat. Oki kills Atanarjuat's brother, but Atanarjuat escapes in a stunning sequence, running naked across the ice floats, outstripping his pursuers until, his feet torn and bloody, he is taken in by a friendly shaman. Atuat is later raped by Oki. Years later, with the help of the shaman, Atanarjuat outwits Oki, beats him in a fight and expels him from the community.
>
> Shot in digital Betacam, the film makes the most of the immense snowy landscapes. It is also acted with complete conviction by its mostly first-time cast. Director Zacharias Kunuk is the first of his family to live in a permanent settlement, to read, write and make films. Inevitably the film will be compared to *Nanook of the North*, the famous "creative" documentary made in 1922 by Robert Flaherty. *Atanarjuat* concedes nothing in the way of authenticity, with sequences that show in realistic detail the training of the sled dogs, cutting up animal carcasses or making an igloo. But the convincing ethnographic elements only serve to enhance the compelling story and characters, which take on a truly epic dimension.
>
> If the purpose of the national cinema is to represent the culture of the peoples it belongs to, then *Atanarjuat: The Fast Runner* achieves this triumphantly, both the content of the film and the manner of its telling being wholly specific to Canada, yet in the process achieving universal appeal. (466)

Buscombe's appropriation of Isuma's *Atanarjuat* for Canadian nationalism depends on a complete evacuation of the political and historical aspects of the film's context that pertain to the Inuit. We never learn, for example, as a result of what processes Zacharias Kunuk was the first of his family to live in permanent settlements, nor do we see any mention of the 1999 establishment of Nunavut. Buscombe pays attention primarily to the visual aspects ("stunning sequences") and takes serious liberties with the diegesis to fit it more precisely into the convention of the epic. For example, and perhaps most perniciously, he subverts the explicit gender politics of the film by crediting Atanarjuat with the expulsion of Oki and his collaborators. In the film, the ritual of community-cleansing is performed by the Inuit elders, and the sentence of exile is pronounced by Panikpak, the wife of Kumalak. The very claim of *Atanarjuat*'s Canadianness depends, paradoxically, on a simultaneous assertion and dismissal of indigenous authenticity ("ethnographic details only serve to enhance the compelling story") in favor of Canadian national identity, which is understood as unspecified representational adequacy and is already in the next clause reduced to "universal appeal." Although noted as "made in the Inuktitut language" by unspecified "native peoples of the Canadian Arctic," in Buscombe's hasty critical assessment *Atanarjuat* becomes a quintessentially Canadian film, reflecting the diversity of this nation of many cultures.

Christopher Gittings concludes his magisterial history of Canadian cinema by suggesting that contemporary Canadian films are more likely "to represent diasporic identities and race relations in Canada through multicultural fields of vision" (102). The question remains whether within this new national cinematographic landscape there is room for indigenous narratives that cannot be folded back into the Canadian nation-building project, in the way *Atanarjuat* seems to be. Isuma's first feature provides an excellent test case of the limitations and opportunities for the representation of difference within multicultural states and their institutionalized politics of recognition. Gittings, along with Himani Bannerji and E. San Juan Jr., insists on the distinction between "establishment multiculturalism" (E. San Juan Jr.'s term to describe the state-funded and state-benefiting multiculturalist projects of recognition) and "popular multiculturalism" (Bannerji's term to describe the work of indigenous and minority filmmakers and artists in Canada) and suggests that the necessary work of educating Canada into antiracism is more effectively done by the latter. Without drawing any conclusions from the observation, he points out that this work is funded in large part by the political economy of establishment multiculturalism, which continues to reinscribe normative whiteness as a chief characteristic of Canadian national identity and settler modes of political, social, and economic organization as the parameters of contemporary multicultural states. In this context, *Atanarjuat* illustrates the thin line between popular and establishment multiculturalism in Canada. Hardly the only minority-produced cinematographic project supported by the state, Isuma's first feature has enjoyed unprecedented official success, precisely due to its political savvy in articulating its political and cultural emancipatory ambitions safely within the framework of the Canadian political discourse of a multiculturalist federation.

What, then, are the ideological functions of what I singled out at the beginning of this chapter as the film's fundamental formal gesture? Ultimately, the juxtaposition of outtakes and main narrative in *Atanarjuat (The*

Fast Runner) embodies the predicament of indigenous art in contemporary multicultural democracies, including Canada and Australia, where multiculturalism has been constitutionalized, but also the United States, where it governs much of the nation's public imaginary as well as a good share of its institutions. This juxtaposition maps precisely the contradictions inherent in indigenous efforts at self-representation in the pervasive context of multicultural misrecognition. It also offers a formal solution to these otherwise unsurpassable contradictions. This solution is counterintuitive. *Atanarjuat (The Fast Runner)* foregrounds rather than covers up the contradiction between resistance to and cooptation of multicultural misrecognition via its juxtaposition of the outtakes and the main narrative; the outtakes expose rather than dissolve this contradiction. To read the outtakes as a straightforward assertion of rhetorical sovereignty would be to paper over the very contradictions embedded in the exercise of such indigenous agency in North American democracies, which continue to be colonial states with regard to indigenous nations. To appreciate the entire extent of the film's ideological investment and effect, we need to be acutely aware of its deftly orchestrated shifting between the political and cultural meanings of indigeneity and between its simultaneous appeals to particularity (Inuit and Canadian) and universality.

More than a straightforward claim of the Inuit right to represent their usable past in a gesture of asserting rhetorical autonomy, the outtakes underscore the mythical status of the main narrative and by doing so insist on the recreation/reproduction of cultural practices rather than on their unproblematic accessibility to those appropriately located. They expose indigeneity as a performance necessitated by the multiculturalist politics of recognition and intended to secure concrete political and material gains, for example, a voting majority in Nunavut and asserting title to a portion of original Inuit land. The point, of course, is not to suggest a simple cause-and-effect relationship but rather to expose the entire ideological field within the constraints of which the film operates. So we are shown a terribly vicious circle: the need to perform cultural difference in order to gain recognition, which in turns precipitates official incorporation into the state and its capitalist economy, which, in yet another turn, results in the erasure of any meaningful difference (that is, difference in social and economic arrangements) beyond the screen of difference performed. Difference gets transposed solely into the realm of the cultural, and can be experienced only in the realm of representation, while social and economic arrangements become aligned with the homogeneity of capital. Such is the mandate and effect of multicultural misrecognition. It is noteworthy how often in historical and other writings (Gittings, Miller) the Nunavut agreement is contrasted to other forms of negotiating nation-within-a-nation status in Canada—for example, the armed conflict between Mohawk warriors and the Canadian army in Oka, documented in Alanis Obomsawin's *Kanehsatake: 270 Years of Resistance.* The political and nonviolent strategy of the Inuit is hailed as more successful at yielding a potentially self-governing territory. But it is worth pointing out that it is successful for Canada as well: it effectively integrates Nunavut further into Canada's administrative, economic, and political structures. In the end it is also an assimilative strategy that reduces the contest over difference to the field of culture only, bearing out Slavoj Žižek's point, in "*Multiculturalism, or the Cultural Logic of Multinational Capitalism,*" about multiculturalism and its compulsion to mark and represent cultural differences as a smokescreen for the ongoing process of global homogenization characteristic of the age of multinational capital.

My point is not, let me insist, that *Atanarjuat* fails as a gesture of rhetorical sovereignty and that this is a bad thing. Rather, my point is that by inscribing the entire extent of its contradictory ideological investments, Isuma's first feature specifies the possibilities and constraints of indigenous self-representation under the current multiculturalist regime. It actively invites fantasies of the return to an uncontaminated indigenous past, only to dispel them. That possibility has irrevocably disappeared with the historical fact of colonialism. Instead, *Atanarjuat (The Fast Runner)* clearly posits indigeneity as a cultural performance in the name of specific cultural projects, which in turn fulfill multiple ideological functions for indigenous nations as well as for the nation-states within which these nations cannot help but be embedded. It also makes clear, though, that simply acknowledging this implication is only the beginning of our critical work. Resistance and cooptation: How do we tell the difference between the two? Do we need to? After all, Sitting Bull spent a season riding in Buffalo Bill's Wild West.

3
Palimpsestic Images

Contemporary American Indian Digital Fine Art and the Ethnographic Photo Archive

History decomposes into images not into narratives.
Walter Benjamin, *The Arcades Project*

The Indian with a camera announces the twilight of Eurocentric America.
Leslie Marmon Silko, *Yellow Woman and the Beauty of the Spirit*

Consider the following pieces of digital fine art by three contemporary American Indian artists: *Damn! I Keep Dreaming of Three Cherries!* by Hulleah Tsinhnahjinnie, a photographer of Taskigi/Diné ancestry (fig. 3.1); *Kainawa*, by Pamela Shields, a Blackfoot (Blood Band) artist (fig. 3.2); and *Alana Spencer and Baby Tecellah (Pit River and Maidu), Chaw'se, 24 September 1995*, by Dugan Aguilar, a Paiute, Pit River, and Maidu photographer (fig. 3.3). Albeit in markedly different ways, all three artworks evoke early photography. Their specific point of reference is the vast photographic archive of North America's indigenous peoples assembled from the mid-nineteenth through the early twentieth century, an archive produced by an army of photographers working for the US military and diplomatic corps, federal and private surveyor companies, ethnological institutes, and Indian boarding schools, as well as, perhaps most famously, by individual photographers such as Adam Clark Vroman, John K. Hillers, Edward Sheriff Curtis, and many, often unnamed, others. All three artists mine this archive for usable material ranging from fragments of historic photographs, to old photographic technologies, to aesthetic conventions characteristic of this particular subset of early photography.

Hulleah Tsinhnahjinnie's digital print appears to be the most straightforward of the three. All Tsinhnahjinnie seems to have done is take a nineteenth-century photograph, crop and enlarge it to exaggerate the grain along with traces of damage wrought by time and use, and append it with a digitally superimposed caption, all the while preserving the original black-and-white coloring. The enlargement underscores the photograph's archival quality, the importance of detail, and the image's documentary authority. This documen-

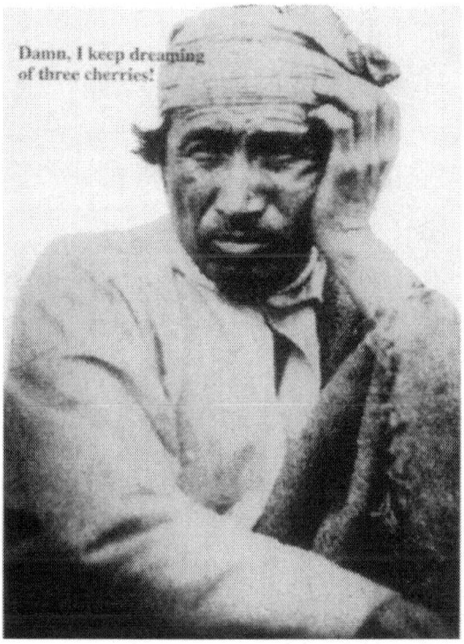

Fig. 3.1. *Damn! I Keep Dreaming of Three Cherries!,* Hulleah Tsinhnahjinnie, 1998.

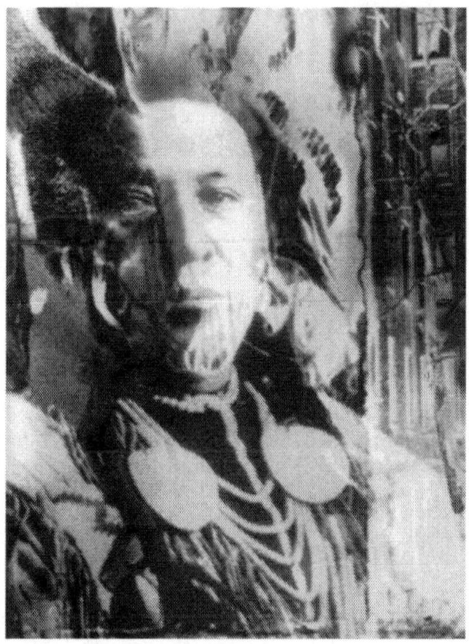

Fig. 3.2. *Kainawa*, Pamela Shields, 1997.

tary authority stems from what scholars call photography's indexical relationship to reality.[1] Photography is an index of reality not because it reveals the truth about its subjects but because it testifies undeniably to the fact of the subject being there in front of the camera at one point in time, that fact being registered through a chemical process that reproduces the play of light and shadow on the photographic plate. We are drawn in to pore over

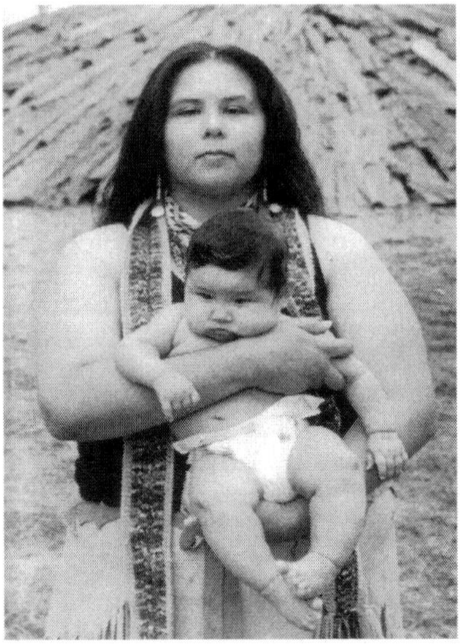

Fig. 3.3. *Alana Spencer and Baby Tecellah (Pit River and Maidu), Chaw'se, 24 September 1995)*, Dugan Aguilar, 1995.

the details like detectives or historians examining ever-larger close-ups of visual evidence, because seeing more closely, with more detail, is seeing *better*, especially in the case of photographic indexes, which testify to the factual existence of persons and objects depicted. The image Tsinhnahjinnie reproduces here is one among many photographs of American Indian men who were captured during the military conflicts between indigenous nations and the US army in the second half of the nineteenth century and photographed while imprisoned in various military forts across the country. Taken to publicize US military successes in Indian Territory, these photographs circulated widely as postcards or stereographs, sometimes in the wake of their subjects' executions.

Tsinhnahjinnie's enlargement zooms in on an older man wearing a canvas shirt, a cloth head wrap, and a frayed, woolen government-issue blanket.[2] Although his body faces the camera, the man looks to the side, away from the lens. He rests his head in the palm of his hand, which is propped against his raised knee, an expression of dismay, worry, or pain on his face. No discernible detail is present in the light, washed-out background, so by default we focus our attention on the man depicted: the details of his clothing, the particular arrangement of his body, and the features of his face. We are also drawn to the words inscribed on the image. As if to evoke comic book conventions minus the requisite speech or thought balloon, the written text appears in the left corner, slightly overlapping the top of the man's head. Its emphatically modern typeset makes clear that the caption is a contemporary addition rather than original to the photograph, further underscoring the image's age as well as the fact of the artist's intervention. There's no accompanying information dating the reproduced photograph, disclosing its origin or the man's identity. The caption proper simply names the author of the piece, details her mixed ancestry, and repeats the phrase inscribed on the image itself for the title of the piece. The first overall impression is that of looking at an old photograph rescued from further damage by contemporary technology—the print's glossy surface juxtaposed against the exaggerated grain and creases of the original. If we sense irony at work at all rather than simply experiencing puzzlement, chances are that beyond realizing it has something to do with Indians, casinos, and the American Dream,[3] we will not be quite able to grasp how it plays out or who we are supposed to be laughing at.

In *Kainawa*, also a digitally manipulated print, Pamela Shields resorts to a similar strategy of reproducing fragments of the historic photographic archive. Again an upper-body close-up of an Indian man—this time wearing traditional clothing along with abundant adornments and looking straight into the camera's lens—takes up the majority of the image's frame. Even though we might not recognize the person depicted, we are familiar with the convention: portraits of dignified Indian warriors or of tribal elders have graced the pages of American family photo albums,[4] coffee-table books, and the mantelpieces and walls of American homes—indigenous and nonnative alike—for well over a century. If Tsinhnahjinnie borrows from the carceral subset of the photographic archive assembled to document the military defeat of American Indians in the West, Shields mines a different, unabashedly more sentimental and nostalgic, kind of portraiture, one more familiar (because more widely circulated) to the contemporary general public and therefore responsible for a host of representational stereotypes of American Indians.

Unlike *Three Cherries!*, which consists of a single reproduced image, *Kainawa* is crowded with fragments of old photographs, all superimposed one upon another as if Shields's composition were a visual equivalent of medieval palimpsests. The left side of the man's face is partially obscured by images of a brick wall, a section of tree trunk, and what looks like a piece of an animal-skin garment. From the left intrudes an old photograph of a courtyard with denuded trees, which also seem partially stripped of bark, outlined against four floors of a brownstone. At the bottom of the frame, across the man's chest, extends a fragment of an old photograph showing a long horizontal crack in a cement wall or foundation, simultaneously turning the man's photograph into an image of a cast bust and suggesting its impending toppling. The area around the right side of the man's face appears overexposed, as if the image has faded from excessive exposure to light or was damaged by fire. The entire sepia-toned composition overflows with fragments of separate photographs, all digitally manipulated into copresence by the artist. The result is akin to a montage, a visual rhetorical strategy of juxtaposition that is typically imbued with aesthetic and political avant-garde potential, but it is better described as a palimpsest, a form that introduces an element of time and of historical struggle over surviving meanings in a given picture. Medieval palimpsests, in the form of clay tablets, velum, and occasionally papyrus, resulted from the repeated scraping away of previous text so the material could be used again to record new accounts; they testified, on the one hand, to the scarcity of durable writing materials, and, on the other, to the vicissitudes of power and fragility of dominant historical formations. As the traces of the obliterated text keep reappearing from underneath new inscriptions, the palimpsest makes visible the historical processes of emergence, disappearance, or forceful erasure, as well as the stubborn residual persistence of rhetorical meanings and their corresponding political conditions.

Shields takes full advantage of the symbolic potential of the palimpsest in *Kainawa*. The visual fragments she brings together within the artwork's frame compete for our attention—translucent photographic layers both obscuring and showing through each other—replaying the historical contest of the disparate material realities they depict. As it multiplies these photographic layers, *Kainawa* poses numerous questions: What people and places are represented here? How are they related to each other? What larger representational landscapes are these fragments replacing? What is the logic underlying these particular selections? The entire artwork would appear more intent on mystification than elucidation, if it weren't for the insistence on careful looking it projects at its focal point. The only area of the image that has not been tampered with, that has been left intact in its documentary or indexical authority, it seems, is the upper-left corner of the man's face, his left eye fixing that of the viewer, admonishing her to look intently and at length or perhaps inviting her to a kind of perceptual duel—an eye *against* an eye, this time. The captioning does not appear particularly helpful in this case either, beyond identifying the author and dating the artwork. The title eschews the English language and deepens the image's multiplying enigmas to viewers unfamiliar with the historic or contemporary Blackfoot.[5] If *Three Cherries!* restores an old photograph and honors its evident documentary authority, *Kainawa* simultaneously preserves such photographs and damages them by distortion; it evokes their indexical authority only to put it into question by exposing the photographs' fragility and their susceptibility to framing or manipulation, all the while exhorting us to critical examination with potentially high stakes.

Unlike Shields and Tsinhnahjinnie, Dugan Aguilar does not use any archival material in *Alana Spencer and Baby Tecellah (Pit River and Maidu), Chaw'se, 24 September 1995*, yet this piece too functions as a palimpsest of indigenous representation in North America. By including the date in the photograph's title, the photographer emphasizes that his subjects belong in the contemporary world. He does so, of course, because we could easily assume otherwise. Were it not for the disposable diaper sported by baby Tecellah, the photograph could pass for one of the many portraits included in the monumental *North American Indian*, a twenty-volume collection of photographs assembled over a forty-year period by Edward S. Curtis and published beginning in 1907. Aguilar composed his selenium-toned print in a way that unmistakably evokes old American Indian portraiture, and the work of Curtis in particular.[6] While he does not reproduce actual archival images, he certainly recycles earlier photographic techniques and conventions. His subjects, a mother and child, a grouping popular in early photographs of American Indians, pose facing the camera. They take up the center of the frame of the black-and-white photograph, focusing the viewer's attention away from any details that the background might contain. Alana Spencer wears a fringed leather skirt, twine-woven scarf, beaded earrings, and necklaces abundant enough to nearly obscure her black tank top; she keeps her hair dark, straight, and long, falling down her back—all details the settler public has typically associated with a kind of general Indianness. Spencer even attempts to perform the stoic look, however unsuccessfully—a smile, if not a smirk, appears to lurk around the corners of her lips—as if she is playing Indian especially for the camera. The black-and-white color scheme, along with the softened focus, evokes Curtis's photographic techniques as well. Whether we understand it as an homage to or a parody of Curtis, Aguilar's photograph depends for at least some of its meanings on viewers' exposure to this most widely circulated set of historic photographs of North American Indians. Along with the works by Shields and Tsinhnahjinnie, it appears to bear out a claim by a Tuscarora photographer and writer, Rick Hill, that in the late twentieth century, photography by American Indians still did not reflect indigenous values or traditional philosophy and was, instead, "an artistic movement within photography itself—a reaction to photography" (126).

Tsinhnahjinnie's, Auguilar's, and Shields's pieces exemplify a persistent trend in contemporary American Indian art. Archival visual materials show up insistently, not only in digital fine art but also in mixed-media art and in film by contemporary indigenous artists in North America. To offer a few additional examples, one might mention the work of photographers such as Jolene Rickard (Tuscarora) and Zig Jackson (Hidatsa); painters such as George Longfish (Seneca/Tuscarora), Jaune Quick-to-See Smith (Flathead Salish/French-Cree/Shoshone), Gerald McMaster (Cree), and Arthur Amiotte (Lakota); and filmmakers such as Alanis Obomsawin (Abenaki), George Burdeau (Blackfoot), Shelley Niro (Mohawk), and Victor Masayesva Jr. (Hopi). All of these artists insert settler archival images into their works not only to complement other visual materials but also to disaggregate the entire settler photo archive and put the resulting fragments to new rhetorical uses. I argue in this chapter that settler archival photographs of vanishing Indians show up in contemporary indigenous art in palimpsestic images, which testify to recovered indigenous histories and centuries of endurance against colonial pressures in North America. Through their layering of archival fragments and multiple historical contexts and in their mimicry of settler photographic conventions, these digital palimpsests successfully subvert the interpretive imperatives of multicultural misrecognition. In place of static images of supposed Indian cultural authenticity, they offer complex narratives of historical struggles over lands, lives, and their enduring meanings.

Arthur Amiotte's 1995 *The Visit* (fig. 3.4) is perhaps the most explicit in its use of this strategy, which I'm going to trace in more examples below. Amiotte superimposes an old photograph of an early-model car[7] onto a ledger-book drawing featuring a series of scenes—a Ghost Dance performance, a Lakota couple riding horses, an honorific portrait of a Lakota elder, a log cabin—and two fragments of handwritten text. However, the photo of the car has been cut in half and in the gap Amiotte inserts an old photograph of a Lakota family—Standing Bear and his wife in full traditional dress, a child by their side—an image that is in turn superimposed on a drawing of a log cabin, so that the photographed figures stand in the cabin's door. Additionally, the photograph of the car is appended, graffiti-like, by a colored-pencil drawing of two Lakota figures at the wheel, a man and a woman, who are also depicted riding horses in the image's bottom right corner. Going back and forth between different visual media, sliding them one upon or underneath the other, is the main formal strategy here. We see a modern/settler representational technology (the photograph) replacing an older one (ledger-book drawings) at the same time as the concept of mobility associated with progress and modernity (the car) is deconstructed by that of settlement (the cabin). Amiotte's piece adds further ironies: the log cabin is most famously an emblem of American Manifest Destiny, of pio-

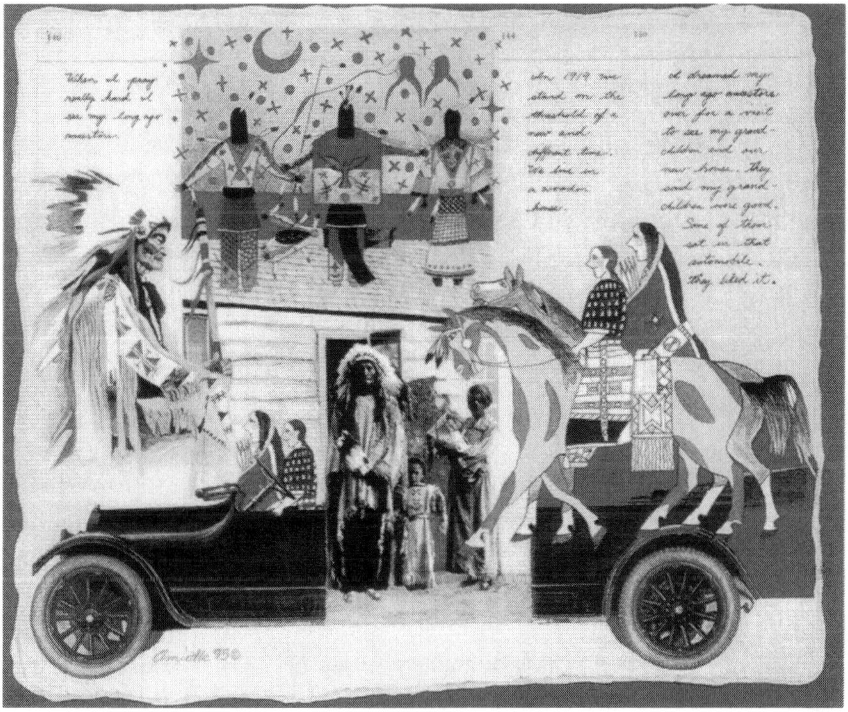

Fig. 3.4. *The Visit*, Arthur Amiotte, 1995.

neer expansion into the American West. The image of the Indian family in a log cabin turns the indigenous people into pioneers, if not outright immigrants, by virtue not of their voluntary migration but of their prior uprooting, their forced removal onto reservations. The ledger-book drawings, too, are an ambivalent emblem of indigenous traditionalism. Although evocative of the paintings on the animal-skin lodges of Plains Indians, the drawings are a testimony to the integration of settler representational technology in traditional communities: ledger books were used at trading posts and on reservations to keep accounts of the delivery of commodities due indigenous nations as a result of treaties ceding their territories to the US government. The ledger books were also repurposed for use by Indian prisoners of war in the late nineteenth century, most famously at Fort Marion in St. Augustine, Florida. Henry Richard Pratt, the mastermind behind the Indian boarding schools, distributed such books among the Cheyenne, Arapaho, and Kiowa survivors of the Red River War, encouraging them to record their recent experiences. The result of Amiotte's experiment with these diverse materials and contexts is a jumble of diverse representational archives recording complex historical developments and testifying to multiple recoding agents, settler and indigenous, a far cry from the typical Curtis photograph attempting to capture a vanishing Indian.

The settler photographic archive of America's indigenous peoples might have provided viewers, past and present, with ready visual evidence to fuel multicultural misrecognition. But, as contemporary indigenous art amply testifies, it can also be a valuable resource: a vast store of material evidence of past encounters and historical realities that continues to intrude on, but also illuminate and ultimately transform, the contemporary scene of indigenous self-representation. In what follows, I explore how in the hands of contemporary indigenous artists, fragments of the settler photographic archive are deployed to construct digital palimpsests that effectively jam the mechanisms of multicultural misrecognition. They do so by reinvesting the flat portraits of indigenous cultural difference with multidimensional narratives of contemporary indigenous realities as thoroughly saturated with suppressed political histories.

Critiques of the Settler Photographic Archive

Considering the nearly unanimous condemnation of the ideological functions of historic settler photographs of American Indians among both indigenous and non-native critics in late-twentieth-century North America, the insistent presence of this archive in the work of contemporary artists requires some explanation. When images by contemporary indigenous photographers first began to gain broader visibility in the early 1990s, they were often emphatically juxtaposed to the historical photographs of Indians taken by settler photographers, explicitly offered as a remedy for a century and a half of representational mystification. In the programmatic vein of classic manifestos, exhibition catalogues and special issues of relevant journals celebrated the emergence of contemporary indigenous photography while denouncing historic settler photography as complicit with the US colonial project in North America and as responsible for a host of pernicious Indian representational stereotypes. This emphatic condemnation was accompanied by proclamations that indigenous photographers had finally begun to reappropriate the medium. Exposed as a weapon used against indigenous peoples in the ongoing American wars of representation, photography was finally being reclaimed, still as a weapon, by indigenous photographers themselves to confront what Jolene Rickard, a Tuscarora photographer, art historian, and museum curator, called the "representational ruins of indigenous America."[8]

Art historian Lucy Lippard's 1992 collection *Partial Recall: Photographs of Native North Americans* and a 1993 special issue on contemporary Native American photography in *Exposure*, a journal of photography, serve as good examples of the simultaneous indictment of historic photography and celebration of indigenous appropriation of this supposedly compromised medium. In Lippard's collection, the historic photographs remain largely the focus,[9] but the editor hands the task of interpretation and commentary to contemporary indigenous photographers, art historians, museum curators, and scholars. If the majority of the photographs reproduced in the volume originally posited indigenous peoples as objects of representation in the service of settler nationalist narratives, the accompanying texts testify to contemporary indigenous artists' newly won position as subjects in the critical conversation, if not argument, about the lasting pernicious effects of the settler photographic enterprise as well as the potential redeeming qualities of the archive itself. *Exposure*, while providing historical and critical commentary, also almost exclusively by indigenous writers, on indigenous people's long and troubled relationship with photography, showcased the work of contemporary indigenous photographers, along with their programmatic statements.[10] Although evoked in the critical commentary, the old photographs are visually absent from the journal's issue; tellingly, they are not reproduced at all, not even as a reference for the historical and critical essays or as a foil to contemporary work. Remembered and dissected in the essays, the archive is bypassed in the visual sections of the special issue to clear space for indigenous photographic self-representation.

Other publications assessing the historic functions of the photographic archive and showcasing contemporary work by American Indian photographers quickly followed. *Strong Hearts: Native American Visions and Voices*, published by Aperture in 1995, offered a collection of photographs and essays by contemporary indigenous photographers, historians, museum curators, and scholars. *Native Nations: Journeys in American Photography,* a catalogue issued by Barbican Art Gallery and Booth-Clibborn Editions in 1998 on the occasion of a major exhibition in London, England, featured nineteenth- and early twentieth-century photographs of North American Indians by settler photographers along with a very comprehensive selection of work by contemporary indigenous photographers in North America, all accompanied by critical commentary on the archive and extensive introductions to the contemporary artist-photographers. The last decade of the twentieth century and the beginning of the twenty-first witnessed new interest in scholarly assessments of the historic photographic archive: studies appeared featuring new interpretations of Edward Curtis's monumental body of work,[11] along with histories of photography in the American West, of photography's impact on particular indigenous nations, of specific historical Indian figures' engagement with the medium, and of American women photographers of Native Americans.[12]

Taken together, this body of work—both commentary occasioned by exhibitions and scholarly writing by historians—has added up to a scathing critique of the ideological functions of settler photography of North America's indigenous peoples. Early historic photography was "exclusively a white man's propaganda weapon and toy" (Harlan, "Creating a Visual History: A Question of Ownership," 22), "a tool of the apparatus of the [US colonizing] 'State'" (Rickard, "Occupation" 58), and "a weapon in the final skirmishes of cultural warfare in which the Natives of North America could be properly and finally embedded in their places in the cultural evolutionary incline" (Vine Deloria, qtd. in Lippard 20). Early photographs of American Indians, such as those of Curtis, for example, compressed multiple realities of their lives into iconic images of a vanishing race in an attempt at salvage ethnography (Rickard 71), a discourse and practice readily testifying to the settler belief in the disappearance of America's indigenous populations. They colluded with "the desire of the US government to undermine Native authority and autonomy" (Rickard 58) in a larger effort to clear literal and imaginative space for colonial settlement. Settler photography of American Indians did not simply depict the unequal relations between indigenous people and the members of settler society but outright "solidified the racial and gender hierarchies that produced" this inequality in the first place (Faris, qtd. in Bernadin et al. 25). Curtis's success in creating Indian authenticity, for example, was so pervasive that some contemporary indigenous critics have occasionally conceded that his photographs conveyed a kind of truth even to them: "For years, partly out of blind faith, I believed that the Edward Curtis type of photograph—portraying the classic, majestic beauty of the Native North American—was the truth," confessed Gerald McMaster (Lippard 77). Because of their sheer mass and popularity, combined with the absence of self-generated indigenous photographic representations, these images wrenched Indian eyes "from the command of [their] own realities" (Green, qtd. in Lippard 48). Contemporary indigenous critics at times register surprise at the apparent modernity of the late nineteenth- and early twentieth-century indigenous subjects encountered in the historic archive,[13] not because indigenous people did not encounter modernity at the time but because Curtis's and others' photographic work managed to convince everybody that those who were *authentically* indigenous did not. In settler hands, cameras helped to turn the peoples who prior to the Wounded

Knee Massacre in 1890—an event that came to mark the end of the Indian wars in the West—were allied into a complex network of separate nations and confederacies still resisting settler encroachments onto their lands, into Indians, the homogenized other of settler North America. Cheyenne, Lakota, Diné, Shoshone, and many other indigenous peoples who "didn't know a damn thing about being Indian [because] this information was missing from [their] Original Instructions . . . had to figure it out as [they] went along" (Paul Chaat Smith, qtd. in Lippard 97–98), and in that effort they often turned to the existing visual archive. Ironically, then, settler photography—and this is perhaps its greatest sin—served to teach indigenous peoples how to be Indians, by instilling representational stereotypes of the dominant culture so successfully that they were no longer recognizable as such.

Noting that the US federal government was the biggest publisher of photographs of American Indian subjects in the second half of the nineteenth century and first decades of the twentieth century (Sandweiss 244), historians zeroed in on the specific functions that each subset of this photographic archive, compiled on behalf of the state, played in American efforts at nation-building and westward expansion. For example, the largest and most varied among those, portraiture, contributed in myriad ways to the gradual development of the vanishing-race narrative[14]—a belief that indigenous life was bound to disappear in the face of encroaching settler modernity and a discursive formation that converged uncannily with the earlier American belief in the nation's Manifest Destiny. Some of the earliest photographs of American Indians ever taken, the collective and individual portraits of Indian diplomats visiting the country's capital to negotiate the ever-increasing territorial cessions and to persuade the US government to deliver on existing treaty provisions, cast their indigenous subjects as surreal figures belonging in a reality different from the American modern present. Inevitably wearing their regalia, tribal leaders appeared as nearly exotic creatures, incongruous against the backdrop of Western emblems of civilization and diplomacy: framed portraits of national leaders on the walls, period furniture, and be-suited officials of the US government. Prisoner or preexecution photographs of captured Indian warriors—some of whom, astonishingly, were the same people earlier featured in the diplomatic photographs—testified to increasing US military gains in late nineteenth-century Indian wars. These images of defeated military leaders worked to debunk the other photographic staple of the representational wars: the dignified Indian warrior. Commissioned by ethnological institutes, portraits of individual "tribal types" depicted their subjects in their "natural" environments or against standardized studio backgrounds. They represented indigenous people as either ahistorical—elements of the natural landscape rather than members of functioning societies[15]—or anachronistic—stubborn relics surprisingly, if only momentarily, enduring on ever-shrinking islands of indigeneity in a sea of civilization, the proper objects of salvage ethnography. One subset of these are the individual and group "before" and "after" portraits of Indian boarding school students, which, as Susan Bernadin has argued, "implied that exposure to Euro-American culture through 'benevolent' pedagogies would transform 'wild' Indians into 'civilized' citizens." The images pairing a parent, usually in traditional attire, with a child wearing settler clothing further testified to the success of such processes of assimilation and the gradual but inevitable disappearance of traditional tribal social forms (9). If the images taken for the ethnological institutes linked Indians' disappearance to their stubborn adherence to traditionalism, the latter sets of portraits exemplified Indians' vanishing into settler modernity through assimilation.

In addition to the vanishing race narrative, early photographs facilitated the telling of two other related national stories. One was the photographic equivalent of the virgin-land myth popular in North American mythmaking at various times since the continent's "discovery," the other the story of European America's own ancient origins. Carried out primarily in landscape photographs produced by federal and private surveyors, and in images documenting the construction of the transcontinental railroad in particular, the virgin-land idea turned the West into an empty space awaiting settler husbandry. As Western landscape photographs removed indigenous peoples from their land, the equally popular and widely disseminated images of cliff-dwelling ruins in the Southwest and burial mounds in the Mississippi region separated indigenous peoples from their history so that it could, in turn, become available for a specific US nationalist discourse.[16] In a particularly ironic twist of cultural discourse, material evidence of indigenous antiquity served to bolster genealogical and ownership claims by the new American nation; it supplied it—ironically, considering the emphasis on newness—with its own ancient origins to match those of European nation-states.[17] As historian of American photography Martha Sandweiss points out, though seemingly contradictory at first—one set of images acknowledging indigenous presence in the American West, the other denying this presence—both kinds of photographs diverted attention from then-contemporary indigenous societies, many of which were at the time still resisting the military and cultural assaults of the US government and the growing influx of American settlers (250–53). As Susan Bernadin further argues, both sets of images displaced the nineteenth-century indigenous peoples living in those "empty" spaces from the American public imagination in advance of the actual conclusion of the Indian wars, development of the reservation system, and removal from ancestral lands into Indian Territory (59).

The early photographs make clear that the supposedly vanishing race received ample assistance in their disappearing act from those apparently most eager to commemorate it. Suffering from an early version of imperialist nostalgia, settler photographers strove to depict realities that they understood to be perishing through the progress of their modern society. The booming market in visual materials helped disseminate such images. All the kinds of photographs I mention above—Western landscapes; photos of archeological ruins; diplomat, prisoner, and ethnographic portraits—though originally taken for official purposes, often ended up as stereographs and postcards (or cartes de visite as they were called at the time), which were very popular across the country in the second half of the nineteenth century. As such, suggests Lucy Lippard, they were no different from the postcards sent by the French soldiers during their tours of duty in the French colonies. Drawing on Malek Alloula's work on the French postcards of the colonies in North Africa, Lippard points out that such commercialized images "produce[d] stereotypes in the manner of the great seabirds producing guano"; they provided "the fertilizer of the colonial vision" in North America as successfully as their equivalents had done in Europe (32).

This damning assessment of the ideological functions of historic photographs of indigenous peoples was, to be sure, informed by the history of colonization in North America. But it also drew on new developments in the criticism of photography as a unique representational system that took place in the second half of the twentieth century. Although from the moment of its invention in 1839, photography has generated a sizable body of theoretical commentary,[18] it was not until relatively recently that criticism by such Michel Foucault–inspired students of photography as Susan Sontag, Allan Sekula, John Tagg, and John Berger revealed at the very heart of the medium a complicity with administrative imperatives of the modern nation-state, on the one hand, and with the logic of free market, on the other. Rather than the specific uses to which the supposedly objective medium was historically put, it was photography's very generic uniqueness, its *photographiness*, so to speak, that came under scrutiny and indictment.

For example, in the early 1970s, in her famous and still widely referenced collection of essays *On Photography*, Sontag argued that "to photograph is to appropriate the thing photographed," to put "oneself into a certain relation to the world that feels like knowledge—and, therefore, like power"

(4). Photography has always been imperial in its scope, attempting to map vast territories and represent all subjects (7). It served to "give people an imaginary possession of space in which they are insecure" (9).[19] The idea of the camera as a weapon, so readily embraced by historians and critics of the settler photography of American Indians, also comes from Sontag: "Just as the camera is a sublimation of the gun, to photograph someone is sublimated murder" (15). Perhaps most damagingly, since the camera "reinforces a nominalist view of social reality as consisting of small units of an apparently infinite number," in photographic representation "the world becomes a series of unrelated, freestanding particles, and history, past and present, a set of anecdotes and *faits divers*" (23), narrative bits easily turned into lucrative commodities on the fast-developing public market for images.[20] If, as Sontag suggests, "the camera makes reality atomic, manageable, and opaque" and presents "a view of the world which denies interconnectedness and continuity" (23), then by definition as a representational system, photography is at odds with indigenous cosmologies that historically have tended to emphasize connection, continuity, and totality: the "all my relations" view of the universe. It is particularly well suited to misrepresenting the indigenous world, by disaggregating it into unrelated units and facilitating its commodification.[21] Sontag's criticism reveals the camera and its products, photographs, as effectively transforming indigeneity into purchasable goods and ideologically expedient visual "talking points."

Photography not only cannot help but disaggregate the social worlds it represents, it also suppresses speech and by implication the potential of making realities intelligible by telling. In his widely influential 1986 essay on photographic practices in mid-nineteenth-century French state institutions, "The Body and the Archive," Allan Sekula argued that the photograph replaces the potential speech of subjects it depicts with their images. In place of the oral accounts that the photographed subjects might have offered about their worlds and lives, photography substitutes the "denotative univocality" of an image, its easily readable realism.[22] In the specific archive that Sekula studied, instead of the depositions of the accused, we get their faces, scientifically depicted en face and in profile and made meaningful by the newly developing "science" of craniology. In a culture that increasingly puts a premium on visuality,[23] image becomes a more reliable testimony than speech, at least as far as institutions such as the police, the government, and the museum are concerned. Against the belief of Zacharias Kunuk that access to modern visual technologies allows indigenous artists to bypass the entire thorny issue of a move from orally based to textually based cultural formations[24]—a process often welcomed by the colonial administration as a testimony to successful civilization and denounced by some indigenous intellectuals as capitulation to settler modernity—Sekula's insight reminds us about the inherent silencing potential of the first reproducible medium of representation.

Photographic portraiture in particular presents dangers here because as Sekula explains, it is a "double system of representation," which functions "honorifically and repressively" at the same time (5). Since the seventeenth century, portraiture in painting has facilitated the "ceremonial presentation of the bourgeois self" (5). Because of its accessibility to the members of a broader socioeconomic spectrum and its potential for reproducibility, photography extended these privileges of portraiture beyond the aristocracy and the newly emerged bourgeoisie. However, in the absence of radical changes to existing social relations (and not for lack of trying: in Europe, the mid- and late nineteenth century witnessed an unprecedented string of attempts at social revolution) photography simply facilitated the reinscription of these representational privileges and their "trickling down" the socioeconomic ladder (5). This proliferation downward, though, did not result in any kind of social equalization. On the contrary, portraiture, now regularly depicting lower and criminal classes, "served the imperatives of the medical and anatomical illustration," and thus helped to "delimit the terrain of *the other*" by defining "both the generalized look—the typology—and *contingent instance* of deviance and social pathology" (6).[25] That is, it subtended the scientific discourse of the normative. Sekula's insights are illuminating here, because in addition to the numerous ideological functions I describe above, settler photography, and portraiture in particular, aimed to depict the ethnological types of the indigenous.[26] In the process of doing so, it constructed their radical difference, by marking them not as deviant, as was the case in the archive Sekula studied, but as underdeveloped. That is, they were not viewed as having regressed from a supposedly universal norm but as having never attained the norm of modernity.[27] By depicting indigenous peoples as specimens,[28] early photography established them as relics of an earlier time.

Taken together, these critical insights suggest that with the exception of those among its subjects who could testify—primarily by donning settler dress—to their assimilatory potential, early photography captures indigenous peoples as settler America's paradigmatic other. It makes them the anachronism taken over by the progress of history and reserved for museum exhibition (the famous cases of Ishi in California and Minik in New York City come to mind here); the other restricted to reservations, which become social laboratories for further cultural engineering in search of viable modes of assimilation; the other displayed as exotic tourist attraction in printed visual media or admired nostalgically as an emblem of a nobler, more natural time, unspoiled by the indignities of modernity. The important point here is the uncanny convergence of the photographic medium's uniqueness as a system of representation, its structural ability to depict peoples, landscapes, and events in a particular way, with the colonial imperatives of the United States in the late nineteenth and early twentieth centuries—that is, at the height of photography's primacy as a mode of representation.

Recuperating the Medium and the Archive

What happens, then, when instead of governmental officials, missionaries, surveyors, ethnologists, and tourists, indigenous peoples themselves take up the camera?[29] If photography is inherently complicit with the nationalist and colonialist imperatives of North American democracies, if it is by design incompatible with indigenous cosmologies and epistemologies, then how successful can its appropriation by indigenous peoples be? Aren't American Indian photographers, in the end, using the master's tools to strengthen rather than undermine the master's house? Some indigenous critics have acknowledged, and celebrated, photography's ideological potential. Theresa Harlan, for example, argues that "although the medium of photography was a dutiful servant to the nation-building and myth churning of a young America, it now equally serves the interests of Native photographers as they dismantle Eurocentric representations of indigenous people and make way for representation of indigenous sovereign nations" (qtd. in Squiers 138). Jolene Rickard, too, emphasizes photography's usefulness for articulating indigenous claims to sovereignty ("Sovereignty" 51). Others have been more cautious about the medium's representational effects. A Hopi photographer and filmmaker, Victor Masayesva Jr., for example, argues that "since the camera's function doesn't change so drastically when it moves from white to brown hands," indigenous photographers have to be judicious in its use and at times altogether refrain from photographing sacred, or otherwise restricted, objects or events (qtd. in Lippard 21). But Masayesva also suggests that in indigenous hands and inspired by cultural conscience and tradition, photography can serve "as ceremony, as ritual, something that sustains, enriches, and adds to [Hopi] spiritual well-being" (qtd. in Lippard 21). For Masayesva, photography's historically pernicious effects could be lessened by the medium itself, as long as the camera is wielded by indigenous hands and deployed on behalf of indigenous communal needs.

And so one is tempted to ask: If the ideological functions of photographic images of American Indians are so categorically tied to the social location of their authors, why then not abandon the necessarily compromised settler historical photo archive altogether? Why not leave it forgotten in the dustbin of history and move on to contemporary, self-authored representations of indigenous worlds? Rick Hill, who condemned indigenous appropriations of settler photography as a reiteration of Indian stereotypes and who doesn't use it in his own work, suggests as much ("In Our Image" 9). However, the frequency with which the old photographic materials reappear in contemporary art suggests that this vast archive continues to be of use to indigenous photographers, that perhaps it is necessary to their efforts to take control over the contemporary scene of indigenous photographic representation by confronting multicultural misrecognition. If one of the main effects of multicultural misrecognition is to flatten indigenous history into innocuous representations of American Indian cultural difference, then the settler photographic archive, via the indexical nature of analog photography and the documentary force of images the photographic index implies, serves as a potential mine of viable anchors by which to moor the contemporary indigenous experience to its historical origins.

Redemptive readings of the settler photographic archive have taken two discernible paths: while neither denies the collusion of settler photography with North American colonial projects, one focuses on explaining the contemporary uses of that archive by indigenous communities, and the other searches it for signs of consent and intentional collaboration—for evidence, that is, of indigenous agency in these early Indian-settler photographic encounters. In an example of the first approach, contemporary American Indian communities have turned to the ethnographic archive on numerous occasions in efforts to bolster their claims for federal or state recognition (for example, Micmac in Maine,[30] Inuit in Nunavut,[31] or Abenaki in Vermont). In those cases the photographs provided documentary evidence of an indigenous presence in particular geographic regions, the continuity of traditional practices, and the emblems of cultural distinctiveness. Photographs of ritual objects and other examples of material culture have been used in repatriation claims by the Tlingit, Karok, and Kwakwaka'wakw. The Hopi hang the photographs by Kate Cory, who lived among and photographed them in the 1930s, in their Cultural Center (Bernadin et al. 30). And many other indigenous communities and individuals have turned to historic photographs to recapture communal as well as familial histories and genealogies.[32]

The following passage from an essay by Louis Owens exemplifies the logic subtending this kind of redemptive recuperation of archival photographs:

> This is perhaps the greatest paradox of colonial photography. The hand on the shutter and the eye behind the aperture may belong to the colonial acquisitor, and the purpose may well be to document a vanishing culture and in doing so participate deeply in that project of cul-

> tural erasure, but the artifact has the power ultimately to help ensure a cultural coherence, to play a crucial role in giving a people a picture of themselves. Admittedly, the picture Native people inherit in such instances is filtered through the lens of the dominant, invasive culture, and the frame that defines can obfuscate greatly, but nonetheless what adheres is the living air of a people and a culture, an air visible to those looking from within rather than without. My Yurok friend sees her Yurok family, not vanishing Americans. (qtd. in Bernadin et al. 192)

In an interpretive gesture evocative of Walter Benjamin's demand for the name of the fishwife from Newhaven who in a nineteenth-century photograph "looks at the ground with such relaxed and seductive shame" that "even now" she "is still real and will never perish into *art*" (qtd. in Trachtenberg *Classic Essays* 30), Owens depends on photography's indexical relationship to reality to recuperate the historic archive for contemporary indigenous viewers. However, unlike Benjamin, who believed that photography's optical unconscious spoke to anybody willing to listen, Owens, like the critics mentioned above, puts a premium on the ontology of positionality that gives the epistemological edge to indigenous viewers. The same logic informs Lucy Lippard's groundbreaking collection, which enacts handing over the critical assessment of settler photography to those who might be better equipped to listen to its optical unconscious and apprehend the "living air of people and culture" who left their traces on the photographic plate.

Recuperative readings of the historic archive that stress indigenous agency owe something to Benjamin's thinking about photography's structural imperatives as well. By suggesting in her introduction to *Partial Recall* that in the old photographs "we can at least sense vicariously the intersections of, and the differences between, the mythic West of white culture and of Native cultures" (14), Lippard approached these archival photos in a Benjaminian mode, as intelligible material traces of contradictions pervading the historical moment of their creation and efforts to represent it. Thus many of the essays included in the collection attempt to recover indigenous agency in the supposedly compromised scene of photographic representation, following Lippard's call for readings attuned to historical complexity. Jimmie Durham's reading of *Geronimo at the Wheel*, the 1904 photograph of the famed Mescalero Apache leader taken by Walter Ferguson when Geronimo was a prisoner at Fort Sill in Oklahoma,[33] is perhaps the most telling example of this approach to the historic archive. The photograph depicts Geronimo, who sports a settler suit and top hat, in the company of three other Indian men decked out in traditional dress, behind a wheel of a Cadillac, which is parked in the middle of a grass field. The photo is structured around a set of supposed incongruities: the symbol of indigenous resistance appears here in conventional sartorial emblems of settler culture, testifying to his assimilation; and instead of brandishing a gun as he does in most surviving photographs of him, Geronimo drives the car, the symbol of settler mobility and progress. But his command of the car and all it implies is undermined: Geronimo does not drive the car; he only poses, playing assimilated Indian, stranded on an island of modern technology in the sea of American nature.[34] Yet for Durham, who focuses on Geronimo's eyes gazing right into the camera lens, the photo represents Geronimo's successful efforts at seizing the rhetorical opportunities presented by the photographic exchange: "Look at his face getting in your face. . . . He is trying to photograph himself, but from within. He is taking a photograph of his thoughts. It is as though he was using his personal integrity, no matter what the situation, to reach, to challenge our own personal integrity. That implied a profound trust. He was not saying, 'I am a human being'; he was saying, 'I know *you* are human beings'" (246). Durham's reading emphasizes Geronimo's intent and his agency in carrying it through. It turns the established wisdom regarding the power relations structuring these early photographing encounters inside out: no longer just an object of representation, Geronimo becomes the photographer, one who instead of reducing an indigenous voice to a silent face manages to narrate indigenous interiority and to challenge rather than confirm settler society's received notions regarding the indigenous. In place of emphasizing cultural distinctiveness, he makes claims about universal humanity—not, as we might expect, on behalf of American Indians but on behalf of settler viewers. Interpretive coup that it is, Durham's reading could be, of course, dismissed as the wishful thinking of a contemporary Cherokee artist deeply invested in indigenous agency. James Faris, for example, who has written extensively on Navajo photography, insists "that reading sympathy, empathy, resistance, or collaboration into the relationship between a Euro-American photographer and her subjects constitutes sentimental wish fulfillment on the part of the critic" (qtd. in Bernadin et al. 25). And yet, the growing body of new historical work on colonial photography appears to bolster the belief that, far from being bemused into silence by their wonder over the very idea, indigenous subjects of early photography participated, knowingly and intentionally, in early photographic encounters.

Martha Sandweiss, for example, focuses on photography's earliest period—from the invention of the daguerreotype in 1839 to that of the Kodak box camera in 1888—to argue that the technical demands of the early photographic processes, which required lengthy sitting periods, necessitated consent by the subjects and their willing, prolonged participation. Sandweiss presses the point that these portraits "confound prevailing notions about the photography of Native Americans as an inherently inequitable encounter, designed to fix their subject in a world of unassailable 'otherness' unsullied by contact with Euro-American civilization" (212) by pointing out the earliest photographs of North American indigenous people ever taken: an 1843 daguerreotype of Timoteo Ha'alolio, a Hawaiian diplomat traveling in Paris at the time; 1845 daguerreotypes of the Cherokee Reverend Peter Jones and of his family; and 1847 daguerreotypes of the Sauk and Fox chief Keokuk, his wife, and grandson taken in a St. Louis studio during his journey for tribal business. In the context of historical and political circumstances, the technological limitations of early photographic process, and their formal and thematic features, these early images reveal subjects engaging in photographic encounters with an understanding of the process and of the images' potential political effects. Sandweiss goes further and insists, against the predatory notions of photography developed by Sontag or its generic potential to silence the subject, as pointed out by Sekula, that even though colonial photography was often used to endorse political agendas inimical to the survival of indigenous peoples in North America, "nothing embedded in the very concept of photography itself dictated such a use of the pictures. Indeed, to imagine that every photograph of an indigenous person represents an act of cultural imperialism is to deny the ambitions of the sitter, the capacity of that sitter to understand the collaborative process of portrait making, and the cultural malleability and contingency of any photographic image" (215). Sandweiss's argument, then, as much as it relies on the changing technical possibilities of the medium and the radical shift in photographic encounters between indigenous peoples and European settlers or tourists in the American West following the popularization of photography after Kodak's momentous invention, attempts to recuperate the idea of indigenous control over photographic representation. The developing photographic technology did change indigenous peoples' relationship to the photographic encounter and diminished their ability to use photography for their own ends and to determine the photographic messages they helped produce. But even after the mass popularization of the camera, indigenous peoples exerted a degree of control by restricting settler photographers' access to their communities: Zuni, Hopi, and Lakota banned photography during ceremonials as early as 1910; Crazy Horse never sat for a photographer; and Red Cloud, Geronimo, and Sitting Bull intentionally exploited the medium for a variety of political and material gains.

This point about indigenous intentional agency in photographic encounters is also made in a recent book by Frank Goodyear III, who suggests that the Oglala leader Red Cloud, arguably the most photographed American Indian ever, fashioned himself as a kind of early celebrity, and counted on this status to remain visible as a concrete leader of a concrete people rather than as a type, an ethnological specimen of a dying race. He insistently inserted his photographic images, in traditional and in modern dress by turns, into the photographic archive to complicate this archive's ideological messages. Red Cloud's example suggests that indigenous peoples "embraced photography as an alternative means of communication," testifying to the Lakotas', and by implication other indigenous nations', adaptability to changing political circumstances and new technologies of representation (185–86). Goodyear goes as far as to claim that "in the context of Native American political culture, the photographer's studio in which Red Cloud sits represents an important battleground on which the historic fight for Native rights and respect has been and continues to be fought" (189). In a similar recuperative effort, Carol Williams concludes her study of the settler photography of the American Northwest in the late nineteenth and early twentieth centuries, *Framing the West*, with a chapter chronicling the variety of uses to which the region's American Indians put the new and quickly popularizing medium. Such uses included commissioned individual and family portraits to testify to both the middle-class status by settler standards and to alternative visions of modern indigenous self and family, as well as ritual uses of images in tribal commemoration and naming ceremonies (26–27).

As the various studies of the settler ethnographic archive I describe above suggest, the assessment of the historic photography of American Indians has undergone a radical change in the last two decades: moving away from indictments of the predatory nature of colonial photography and its service to US colonial imperatives to assertions of indigenous agency in settler-Indian photographic encounters, and even of indigenous savvy in exploiting the medium to further tribal political and materials needs. The ideological implications of this shift are worth pondering, because they reflect a larger contradiction in the politics of indigenous representation at the turn of the twenty-first century. Like the National Museum of the American Indian and indigenous cinema such as Isuma's *Atanarjuat*, the historic photo archive is also caught up in the dialectic of recognition. As evidence of the ongoing colonial nature of indigenous-settler relations in North America, it is available to bolster arguments for indigenous sovereignty. As testimony to the transcultured contact zone in which indigenous subjects could, and chose to, deploy their agency, it subtends multiculturalist readings of North American history. The fact that readings of the archive that rely on arguments about indigenous agency coincide with the advent and mainstreaming of multiculturalism should not come as a surprise. Unlike nearly a hundred years earlier, when American Indian federal policy stressed the economic, social, and cultural assimilation of indigenous communities into the settler society, at the turn of the twenty-first century the US nationalist project depends on multicultural misrecognition and the textual and visual testimony it furnishes to American Indian prior and continued cultural distinctiveness.

Contemporary Digital Fine Art and the Settler Photographic Archive

As if they were not perplexing enough to start with, the photographs I describe at the beginning of this chapter take on added complexity in the context of this longer history of photographing Indians in North America—and, increasingly, in the context of debates over the value of the resulting body of images. Drawing on the historic photo archive is weighted with aesthetic and political consequences. Its presence in the work of contemporary artists speaks not only to issues that usually get summarized under the now troubled heading of cultural sovereignty but also to the politics of representation under multiculturalism, as well as to the very nature of the photographic medium and its political potential. Given the fraught terrain of indigenous photography, old and new, the specific interpretive consequences of Dugan Aguilar's aesthetic referencing of Curtis, Hulleah Tsinhnajinnie's potentially risky satirizing of prison photographs, or Pamela Shields's archeological palimpsests are worth further examination. Their shared strategy of layering archival images, aesthetic conventions, and historical contexts proves particularly fruitful in confronting multicultural misrecognition in the specific ways I describe below.

Dugan Aguilar's *Alana Spencer and Baby Tecellah* comes from a series of portraits shot during the same photographic session on September 24, 1995, at Chaw'se, California, during a ceremony in and around the Chaw'se roundhouse. All portraits in the series are structurally identical: upper-body close-ups centered in the frame, subjects facing the camera, the same roundhouse in the background. All are titled by the subject's name and tribal affiliation: *Andrea Vera (Miwok), Amanda Few (Maidu), Rocky Jim (Washoe), Sarah Keller (Seneca)*. All emphatically omit explanatory captions. The series is somewhat unusual in the context of Aguilar's entire body of work, which tends to capture communal events in long shots. *Pomo Dancers Preparing to Dance at Chaw'se*, from the same photographic session as *Alana Spen-*

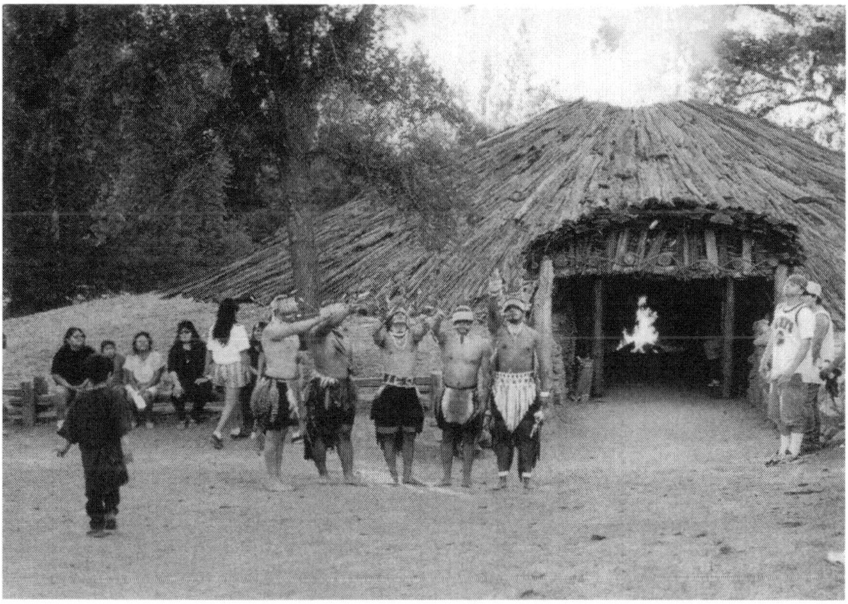

Fig. 3.5. *Pomo Dancers Preparing to Dance at Chaw'se*, Dugan Aguilar, 1995.

cer (fig. 3.5), is a more typical example of Aguilar's subject matter, editing strategies, and his stated goal of "documenting the native peoples of California and Nevada" in a genre he names "environmental portraiture" (Aguilar).[35] Styled more as posed photographs and playing less with documentary conventions—more portraiture than environment, one might say—Aguilar's images participate in a broader effort among contemporary indigenous photographers to redo the American Indian portrait, to rephotograph American Indian subjects by openly confronting the weighty legacy of Curtis's portraiture.[36]

Much of that effort is focused on reversing the ideological functions of Curtis's portraits—their representation of indigenous subjects as emblems of moribund though dignified traditionalism—by playing Curtis, that is by mimicking Curtis's aesthetic conventions. Curtis has been repeatedly lambasted for retouching his photographs to remove any signs of his subjects' contact with settler modernity. The story of an alarm clock, present in the original photographic plate but missing from published copies of his *Lodge Interior—Piegan, 1911* is well known among scholars as well as lay enthusiasts of Curtis's work. Baby Tecellah's diaper, then, drawing the viewer's attention like a proper Barthesian punctum, stands in metaphorically for the missing Piegan-owned grandfather clock; it functions to evoke, and indict, Curtis's notorious attempts at erasing indigenous modernity from the photographic record.[37]

But *Alana Spencer* does more than that, and in rhetorically more complex ways. It lays bare what we could call the politics of the background, on the one hand, and of intergenerational relations, on the other, in American Indian portraiture. Both speak to the changing relationship between traditionalism and modernity in American cultural discourse. Because of the medium's accessibility to the nineteenth-century middle classes, the backgrounds of early portraiture constructed in photographic studios featured emblems of capitalist acquisition and the individualist self—sumptuous furniture, antiques, art, books.[38] Against photography's generic impulse to disaggregate the totality of the social world into discrete aesthetic moments, backdrops served to provide the subjects depicted with the social contexts they (or the photographers) desired. Historic portraits of indigenous people by Curtis and other settler photographers tended to depict their subjects either against standardized backgrounds signifying Nativeness (such as woven grass mats or blankets) or the blankness of the photographic studio wall. In the ethnographic version of the vanishing-race discourse, emblems of traditionalism visible in the background testified to American Indians' stubborn primitivism and therefore their impending and inevitable departure from the historical stage. But the assimilationist version of this discourse needed to eliminate any such emblems because they undermined the belief in Indians' adaptability to settler modernity. For this reason, the boarding school "after" photographs, for example, featured the school buildings and grounds, to imply the institution's centrality to Indian reformation, or they eschewed specific backdrops altogether in favor of studio interiors, to posit Indian children as properly assimilated individual subjects. And yet, while ethnographic portraiture tended to favor single individuals, boarding-school photographs depicted their subjects both singly and in groups. By reasserting their subjects' tribalism, group portraits mitigated settler society's worry about the necessity of social interaction with reformed Indians on equal terms. Despite the evidence of civilizing progress represented in the photographs by settler dress and hairstyles, the "after" group photos could not help but evoke their "before" counterparts, which represented Indian children in their supposed wild tribal state.[39] With this rhetorical maneuver, the group photographs let the settler imaginary have it both ways: imagine Indians as susceptible to reformation and represent them as separated irrevocably from their white social betters.[40] In any case, this body of portraiture symbolically removed American Indian subjects from their social worlds by framing them as isolated individuals or as victims of primordial tribalism, vestiges floating ungrounded in settler modernity, without any background or photographic backdrop whatsoever. It is easier to imagine the defeat of a single person or a displaced group than the defeat of a nation firmly rooted in its material and social world (Rickard "Occupation," 63).

Already established in Aguilar's other photographs as a viable place where collective tribal life unfolds, the roundhouse in the background in *Alana Spencer* and other portraits in the series serves to restore American Indian subjects to their proper social world; it reinserts them into indigenous communities and those communities' sustaining cultural practices. It asserts a collective-oriented indigenous worldview against the individualism of settler society and the generic imperatives of photographic portraiture. *Alana Spencer* depicts a particular individual rather than an ethnological type, but it also links her to a culturally specific group. The subjects of Aguilar's photographs are California's Pit River and Maidu communities as much as Alana Spencer herself. This is how portraiture becomes environmental again.

As it revises Curtis's ideological project by mimicking his representational strategies, Aguilar's portraiture reveals the changed symbolic value of indigenous traditionalism in the late twentieth century. No longer a testimony to primitivism and an inability to adapt to changing historical conditions, traditionalism embodied in the ceremonial roundhouse demonstrates cultural staying power; it stands for indigenous authenticity in late settler modernity. Aguilar's backgrounds dovetail here with the representational needs of contemporary North American multiculturalism. In the early twentieth century, indigenous traditionalism was a roadblock to American national expansion and consolidation. In the late twentieth century, with the advent of the politics of recognition, the very fact of their distinct culture, embodied in concrete material symbols of collective practice such as the roundhouse, asserts the Americanness of indigenous societies, their place in the multicultural nation. In this version of multicultural misrecognition's integrative logic, the roundhouse is not a sign of California Indians' national difference, of their sovereignty as nations, but merely of their cultural difference. In the context of a single photograph the roundhouse readily serves as an assertion of indigenous persistence against the earlier narrative of a vanishing race. However, once repeated unchanged across the entire series of portraits, it becomes a kind of expected prop, a standardized backdrop required by US ideological imperatives. Just as Isuma's *Atanarjuat (The Fast Runner)* delivered multicultural Canada to Canadians by presenting the Inuit in a traditional epic narrated in Inuktitut, Dugan Aguilar's portraits mirror multicultural America to the settler society by depicting California

Indians as adhering to their culturally distinct practices. *Alana Spencer* is both—a revisionist gesture and hegemonic discourse. Which of its ideological functions takes precedence, if at all and ever, depends to a large measure on how we choose to read its background: whether we understand the roundhouse as a place of collective cultural practice equivalent to churches, temples, mosques, or meeting houses, or as a claim to land, a symbol of indigeneity in its proper sense—as belonging to the place—and therefore an emblem of national separateness. Although technically a single image, *Alana Spencer*, too, palimpsestically layers diverse historical meanings as its subject plays Indian for the camera and its author plays Curtis for the spectators.

This contradictory and context-dependent engagement of photographic history is also reflected in the ways Aguilar takes up in *Alana Spencer* another staple of settler representation of American Indians: the mother and child portrait. Historically, intergenerational pairings in American Indian portraiture served to represent the widening gap between assimilating children and their tradition-bound parents, a process unsurprisingly symbolized in their culturally evocative dress.[41] Depending on the point of view, one or the other represented the lost, or stolen, generation in early photography: parents lost to anachronistic traditionalism, children stolen (or "saved") by the civilizing efforts of the colonial state. Aguilar's take on intergenerational relations in the contemporary Indian Country leaves the narratives of generational gap and cultural loss behind. Alana Spencer's sartorial traditionalism does not confine her to a dying world of indigenous collective traditional practices. On the contrary, like the ceremonial roundhouse featured in the background, it testifies to cultural revitalization, regardless of whether it might dovetail with the multiculturalist appetite for the performance of difference. The baby's diaper, unlike the settler clothing worn by American Indian children in the early photographs, which evoked the assimilatory programs of the boarding schools and symbolically separated the children from their parents, depicts a different relationship between generations, that is, between traditionalism and modernity in the late twentieth century. It speaks to an openness to modernity, to an untroubled participation in it. Excised from Curtis's visual testimony to the vanishing of American Indians, modernity in contemporary indigenous photography coexists with indigeneity in obvious ways, without compromising claims to cultural authenticity. Although evoked referentially rather than materially, the historic photography in Aguilar's work functions as a necessary context in which his environmental portraiture can successfully claim modernity for American Indians even, or precisely, as it reasserts their cultural and social difference through adherence to traditionalism.

Hulleah Tsinhnahjinnie's work evidences a career-long interest in ideological reappropriations of colonial photography, fragments of which combine in her digital palimpsests with contemporary materials to satirical effects. All of her major photographic exhibitions—1995 *Notes from a Diary of an Aboriginal Savant*, 1998 *Damn! Stories*, and 2003 *Against Amnesia*[42]—consist almost exclusively of images focused, in a variety of different ways, on the historic photo archive. The pieces in the first two collections feature old photographs of American Indians appended by captions with a satirical edge. For example, *Notes from a Diary of an Aboriginal Savant* includes *Geronimo in Florida,* an "after capture" portrait of the Apache leader in cropped hair and settler dress framed by slogans advertising Florida as the retirement haven ("palm trees, beaches, gators, everglades, art deco, Seminoles, egrets, geritol, Disney world, manatees"). Looking straight at the viewer, Geronimo, who before living out the rest of his life in Fort Sill in Oklahoma, was initially imprisoned in Florida's Fort Pickens, declares that "It's time to go home." *Don't Leave the Rez without It!*, from the same collection, presents six Certificate of Degree of Indian Blood (CDIB) cards, the US government-issued contemporary Indian identification cards,[43] five of them "belonging" to such historic indigenous figures as Wovoka, a Paiute Ghost Dance prophet; Sara Winnemucca, a Paiute writer; Ayyini, a Cherokee religious leader; Arapaho Zah-e-cha/Hur-ke-i; and Geronimo, all captioned as "Activist" across the bottoms of their photographs. The sixth is Tsinhnahjinnie's own CDIB card, which tags her, in turn, as a photographer. By using for the captions old-fashioned typeset evocative of the documentary authority of official archives—the kind we still see in the intertitle cards on *Law and Order*, for example, as the white words appear on the black screen to the sounds of a typewriter at work—*Don't Leave the Rez without It!* indicts settler portraiture as a system of administrative surveillance of indigenous subjects and a precursor to contemporary efforts at governmental regulation of indigenous identity. Meanwhile, it also suggests, through the allusion to the American Express card slogan, that Indian identity serves as capital in the contemporary world, that it is a matter of debt, interest, and credit. At the same time, by equating photographers with activists, Tsinhnahjinnie's piece announces the political nature of her art and reconstructs a long historical genealogy of indigenous activism.

Damn! I Keep Thinking of Three Cherries!, from the *Damn! Stories* series, provides perhaps the best example of Tsinhnahjinnie's investment in laying bare the ideological functions not only of the government-sponsored photo archive of American Indians but also of its amateur counterparts, which, like Curtis's work, for example, have often been extolled as art. *Three*

Cherries! removes a document from the government's archive and attempts to transform it into a Curtis-like portrait and to have it literally exhibited like art, or circulated like a contemporary equivalent of nineteenth-century stereographs (this piece has solicited more requests for permission to reproduce than any other from her body of work). But a prison photograph does not easily translate into a portrait of a dignified but vanishing Indian warrior. Instead of sepia-toned soft-focus, we get exaggerated grain, creases, and other imperfections wrought by time and circulation. It takes photographic manipulation well beyond simple enlargement to glorify the grim realities of indigenous life in late nineteenth-century North America, suggests Tsinhnahjinnie. And then, to complicate matters further, she hurtles this already compromised image into modernity through the added caption.

Settler photography was often accompanied by extensive captioning, which fixed the potentially ambiguous meaning of the photographic image and harnessed it to the ideological needs of settler society.[44] As Theresa Harlan has suggested, Tsinhnahjinnie's recaptioning of archival photos is certainly aimed, both humorously and critically, at the condescending captions attached to colonial photography ("Indigenous Photographies," 241). But the effects of her play with the historic image's textual framing are not immediately obvious. The relationship between image and text has historically been a slippery thing indeed. For example, Walter Benjamin argued that since photographs were generically reactionary in the way they aestheticized suffering and thus inoculated viewers against outrage at injustice, captions had a progressive, if not outright revolutionary, role to play. Proper captions could wrench viewers away from what Susan Sontag described as an amorous relation to the image—their enthrallment with the image's beauty—into one of understanding by narrating the network of historical relations that had led to and illuminated the particular moment now frozen in time by the camera's lens; they could restore the very continuum out of which the photograph removed the objects and people it depicted (Berger, "Understanding Photography," 293). Because it exposes the aestheticization of American Indian suffering in settler photography by intentionally failing to mimic it, *Three Cherries!* appears to align with Benjamin's critique of the medium's inherent conservatism. But its caption seems to function both to thwart understanding in some viewers while reasserting the authority of others; it plays, in other words, at the insider/outsider politics of knowledge.

Tsinhnahjinnie's captions certainly set out to improve on their historical precedents, but they are not obviously explanatory. They do not aim to educate the uninformed. On the contrary, often they function as insider jokes. Unlike in her earlier work, in *Damn! Stories* Tsinhnahjinnie does not identify the historical figures portrayed in the photographs she filches from the archive. Because the archival nature of the images implies the historical importance of the represented subjects, when the viewer fails to identify them, she is potentially confronted with her historical ignorance: *if these people were important enough to be photographed way back then and if their images survived for so long, why don't I know about them?* If she recognizes some of the figures but not others—for example Albert Einstein in *E+mc2*, but not the Ute leader Shavano in *This Is My Homeland*—she recognizes her selective historical and cultural literacy. On the other hand, the viewer who *is* able to recover the implied historical context is rewarded with a sense of cultural authority and mastery over the visual archive as well as its contemporary appropriations. And so, we miss the irony of *Three Cherries!* if we fail to recognize the man in the photograph—Shakpee (or Little Six), a Mdekwanton Dakota tribal leader executed for participation in the 1863 Minnesota Uprising—or are not familiar with the complex history behind this event, on the one hand, and the contemporary debates over casinos as emblems of indigenous sovereignty, on the other. But the image appears enigmatic only to the uninformed viewer; it pokes fun at her while winking knowingly at those who are in on the joke.

If we already know, or care to research, the relevant history, *Three Cherries!* takes on complex resonance. It also becomes less funny. The 1863 uprising, in which Mdekwanton Dakota killed about three hundred Minnesota settlers and displaced hundreds of others,[45] erupted following several years of disrupted social and economic cycles, failed crops, and increasing hunger among the Dakota. Shakpee, along with Little Crow and other tribal leaders, attempted to mitigate the increasing instability by traveling to Washington to persuade the US government to deliver on treaty provisions, including delivery of food to the Dakota communities. Incidentally, while there he was photographed in the McCleese studio, and several copies of his diplomatic portraits survive. Detained for months in the city when governmental officials refused to see them, and ultimately forced to negotiate a treaty exacting further land cessions and forfeiture of earlier provisions, Little Crow and Shakpee returned to a nation that had reached a breaking point. They could not stem the growing impetus for rebellion, so instead they led it. Having fled to Canada in the wake of the violence, Shakpee was eventually captured, imprisoned, and executed in 1865 along with thirty-seven other Dakota men in what is the largest public hanging in US history. Several of his prison photographs, which quickly circulated as postcards, also survive. In 1995, when Mdekwanton Dakota opened their first casino, they named it after Shakpee, the diplomat, the rebellion leader, the prisoner, and the martyr.

Tsinhnahjinnie's caption, then, makes a striking historical connection. As Harlan points out, Shakpee's apparent obsession in *Three Cherries!* with success at the slot machine does satirize the US mainstream public's insistence on reducing the issue of indigenous sovereignty to access to untaxed income. But, especially in view of his impending death, it might also appear frivolous, misguided. In that sense, in Shakpee, Tsinhnahjinnie gives contemporary opponents of Indian-run casinos the obsessively greedy Indian they imagine and evoke in public arguments over the issue. At the same time, however, Shakpee's supposed belated realization that national interest is bound up with economic self-sufficiency—that, so to speak, "it *is* the economy, stupid!" after all—aligns with contemporary conceptions of indigenous sovereignty as tied to economic independence from the US government. It also bears out Vine Deloria Jr.'s assertion in *Custer Died for Your Sins* that the only viable path to reducing Indian-settler violence is indigenous retribalization. *Three Cherries!* reaches for the historic archive, then, to establish the historical precedent for critical contemporary indigenous issues. The palimpsestic layering of nineteenth-century political contexts in Tsinhnahjinnie's piece restores historical depth to contemporary indigeneity, which has been flattened into a one-dimensional performance of cultural difference by multicultural misrecognition.

The interplay of different historic planes implicit in Tsinhnahjinnie's and Aguilar's photography has its graphic equivalent in Pamela Shields's work. We see it explicitly embodied in her images' palimpsestic layering of multiple fragments of the historic photo archive, of which *Kainawa* is an excellent, but not the only, example. Shields's crowded palimpsests set out to counteract photography's generic denotative univocality (Sekula "The Body"), its atomizing impulse (Sontag), and North American settler photography's compression of multiple indigenous realities (Rickard "Exposures" 71). Digitally layered fragments of the historic archive transform a photograph from a moment of time sliced away from the historical continuum and frozen in timelessness (Berger) into narratives unfolding in the space of history. The juxtapositions and overlaps of different layers, the spaces suddenly opened up between them, evoke the idea of time passed, of migrations completed, of history having taken place, and, as the exaggerated damage of the archival materials' quality suggests, having exacted its toll. Subverting photography's impulse to atomize and disaggregate, Shields's palimpsests reconnect and contextualize as they bring together representations of a variety of times, locations, and people. By emphasizing the gaps among different visual planes brought together in the frame of one piece, they open up spaces between the layers of photographic fragments, spaces that demand a narrative, thus reconstituting a history decomposed into images back into a narrative of events and processes. They turn Sekula's mute portraits into narratives of complexly intertwined histories, indigenous and settler. As they decompress and reveal the multiple realities of indigenous lives in North America, they make photography voice "the polyphony of the oppressed" (Sekula 64) and offer a countertestimony to the official photo archive of American history.

The central role of archival photographic material in this endeavor depends on the historical photograph's ability to assert photography's indexical relationship to reality, especially in the contemporary age of digital photography and computer manipulation of images. That the historical archive would play this role is surprising because so much early critical and creative work with colonial photography focused on exposing it as mystification serving the specific ideological needs of the colonial state. But fundamental transformations in the critical understanding of the photographic medium precipitated by the advent of new visual technologies make clear the old photograph's new appeal to contemporary indigenous artists.

Digital technology, some though not all historians of photography agree, fundamentally altered the very nature of the medium.[46] In a parallel to mid-nineteenth-century exclamations that painting was dead welcoming the invention and popularization of daguerreotype,[47] many contemporary theorists and historians of photography proclaimed, in turn, photography's irrevocable demise. With the arrival of computer-assisted manipulation of images for the first time in its history, photography has parted ways with its indexical relationship to reality, a relationship that was at the heart of photography as a unique representational medium. Photographic images no longer had to be "stenciled off the real" (Sontag); they could now be generated from the binary code of digitized data banks, which now also included software programs for the photographic real itself.

André Bazin has argued that the invention of photography was one of the most important developments in modern art because "it has freed plastic arts from their obsession with likeness" (240). While photography, and later cinema, went about satisfying viewers' desires for realist representation, Western painting regained its aesthetic autonomy by returning to art's main business—that of creating illusion (240–43). But with the advent of digital technology, photography appears now to have been similarly liberated. It comes closer to art; it returns to painting, from which it departed as a preferable mode of mimetic representation. As such, photography too becomes more explicitly the art of illusion, a way to tell invented stories, to create rather than represent realities. In this context, the historical photo archive functions as a rhetorical evocation of photography's prior indexical relationship to reality and all that this relationship implies: documentary authority and the historical reality of persons, places, and events. Paradoxically, then, digital imaging allows contemporary American Indian photographers to evoke the truth of the indigenous historical experience obscured in settler colonial photography, precisely by incorporating fragments of that photography's historical archive. It allows them to expose these old photographs as ideologically inflected constructions while also relying on them, and their presumed status as traces "stenciled of the real," to represent contemporary indigenous realities as saturated with officially suppressed histories.

Unlike the Foucauldian critique of photography in the work of Sontag, Sekula, Berger, and others, the indigenous account of settler photography has never been a critique of the photographic medium itself. Rather, it has been a critique of the historic uses of photography, of the aesthetic strategies deployed to subtend particular ideological tenets regarding the place of indigenous peoples in American history. American Indian critics and photographers have not attempted to dismiss the medium; on the contrary, they recognize and assert photography's potential as a useful tool in an ideological struggle and emphasize the imperative to reappropriate it for the specific needs of contemporary indigenous nations and communities. In that sense, contemporary indigenous commentary on photography as a representational system has been very much prescriptive; it routinely sets out a political program for photographic art. And contemporary indigenous photographers have obliged. The collective project at stake is not to put into question the proper documentation of the very idea of the real, and by implication, of history or of the present. The project of contemporary indigenous photography is revisionist rather than deconstructive; it bespeaks hope in the ethical possibilities of photographic representation despite, or perhaps precisely because of, contemporary American mainstream culture's ever-growing appetite for visual displays of indigenous cultural difference. Digital palimpsests by artists such as Aguilar, Shields, Tsinhnahjinnie, and many others offer dialectical images, in Walter Benjamin's sense, as a cure for the lack of historical depth in the interpretive frameworks inspired by multicultural misrecognition. Benjamin described dialectical images as "critical constellations" of past and present that in the adept hands of their creators, be they historians or photographers, open cracks in the official accounts of historical continuity, making possible new points of purchase for alternative accounts of tradition and progress. Benjamin's preferred structural mode for such images was montage, which by juxtaposing irreconcilable images, ideas, or contexts refused harmony or continuity and hence disrupted mythical representations of history (Buck-Morss 67). Contemporary American Indian digital fine artists certainly capitalize on all the possibilities offered by montage, but they augment it with palimpsestic representation in a series of sedimented, and now newly upturned, layerings of historical struggles over material presence and its enduring political meanings. If, as Geoffrey Batchen suggested, "we look into the photograph to witness the past and imagine the future" (*Each Wild Idea* 127), then Indian photographs of the settler archive serve as anchors to indigenous historic realities that resist erasure while the contemporary digital photographic art in which they appear extends the promise of better futures.

4
Of Turtles, Snakes, Bones, and Precious Stones

Jimmie Durham's Indices of Indigeneity

> I absolutely do not want to communicate anything to you! . . . I do not want to entertain you in any sense of the word. I would hate it if you all came to understand me. And I'd really hate it if I wrote something like those "sensitive and honest" novels some black writers are doing, so that any white person with a few bucks could spend a quiet evening being entertained by our sorrows, and gaining in power by "a better understanding" of our predicament, our dreams.
>
> Jimmie Durham, "Those Dead Guys for a Hundred Years" (1987)

It takes a blatant paradox—a lengthy explanation of one's lack of desire to explain—to articulate the defining predicament of any contemporary indigenous artist, that is, this sense of an insurmountable impasse in confrontation with the specific set of rhetorical constraints I've been calling multicultural misrecognition. And yet for Durham, a multimedia artist of Cherokee ancestry, an impasse becomes a fruitful opportunity to transform the contemporary scene of indigenous representation. In the fragment above, he aims his critique at faith in the redemptive power of knowledge to overcome intolerance, a belief fundamental to the contemporary politics of recognition. In particular, he singles out the undisputed value of insider experience, a presumption that turns all minority artists into native informants in the service of the settler public's multiculturalist reformation via educational entertainment. His impatient refusal to participate in the project of achieving tolerance through "better understanding" begs several crucial questions about the possibilities of indigenous self-representation under multiculturalism. How does one formulate a convincing critique of the very conditions of indigenous speech in North America and in a multiculturalist art market that puts a premium on self-authorized representations of minority subjects' suffering and complaint? By what means do indigenous artists enter the cultural commons on their terms when such commons are, as Durham puts it elsewhere, "America's own show," in which they are enlisted as bit-players rewarded for being authentic in precisely the ways set out clearly in the multiculturalist program (*A Certain Lack of Coherence* 224–25)?[1] How does one refuse to occupy the positions of native informant, on the one hand, and authentic entertainer, on the other, while continuing to participate in the public cultural dialogue? What can an indigenous subject say, and how can he or she say it, without being immediately interpolated by the multiculturalist valorization of exclusively cultural difference?

Jimmie Durham's work—as an artist, art critic, and political activist—has always been focused on the issue of effective indigenous speech in North America. Whether they occur as political declarations on behalf of indigenous peoples at the United Nations, in his capacity as director of the International Indian Treaty Council in the 1970s, or as critical assessments of, and artistic challenges to, the multiculturalist art scene in New York City in the 1980s, or through continued creative and curating efforts undertaken abroad, Durham's interventions foreground the specifically North American rhetorical ground and the predicament of representation it poses for indigenous peoples. The artist's acute conviction of the impossibility of indigenous speech in North America, on the one hand, and his uncompromising belief in interventionist minority discourse as "always *possibly* effective," on the other (*CLC* 228), thoroughly determine the defining formal strategies of Durham's writing and visual art. Durham brings these seemingly mutually exclusive stances together through the concept of insubordinate indigenous art, which like the speaker in the essay I quote above refuses to deliver on the multiculturalist mandates of better understanding through access to experiential insider knowledge. The insubordination of Durham's art plays out through two related rhetorical strategies. The first strategy, a kind of preliminary preparation of the rhetorical ground, is a parodic reinscription of settler discourses of Indianness, a move that turns his art into an ethnography of settler desire for authentic indigeneity. Viewers of Durham's plastic art and readers of his poetry and essays routinely find their attention redirected from the piece as a wellspring of insider information about Indians and their authentic culture to their own desire for just such information. Via direct narrative address, symbolic and literal mirroring, and other modes of imposed self-reflexivity, they are invited—or forced—to ponder the sources of their interest, along with the interpretive approaches they bring to indigenous art and literature in efforts to reach "a better understanding" of indigenous experience. The second strategy, the one that cinches the transformation of the rhetorical ground that Durham pursues, is a deployment of a recalcitrant indigenous sign, offered in the form of an index, a sign that simultaneously eludes settler decoding and asserts indigenous materiality. In semiotics, the index is one of three kinds of signs, the other two being the symbol and the icon, all distinguished from each other by their relationships to the objects they signify. While symbols generate meaning through interpretive convention and icons do so through shared quality or likeness with the referent, indices are signs that point to an object by virtue of having a factual or "real" relation to it, or in some instances by being identical with the object; this relation is "real" because it is irrespective of any interpretive conventions or processes. Found objects such as stones, driftwood, turtle shells, animal skulls, bones, and skin serve in Durham's art as recalcitrant signs, recovered from their native ground and deployed as challenges to settlers' decoding and circulation of Indianness and as reminders of ongoing indigenous presence on the continent. They are Durham's best hope for the "always *possibly* effective" Indian discourse, his escape from the trap of multicultural misrecognition.

In this chapter, I trace the development of Durham's strategy of indexical representation as a response to the interpretive constraints of multicultural misrecognition. I begin by reviewing Durham's critical writings to outline his theory of the conditions of indigenous speech under multiculturalism. Then, I show how this theory is illustrated in Durham's works that showcase his parodic reinscription of settler discourses of Indianness. In a separate section focusing in detail on *Red Turtle*, one of his most challenging and interesting installations, I explain how and to what effects Durham deploys found objects as indices of indigeneity. I follow with an analysis of how Durham's historicism, which stems from indexical representation, differs from the historicism implied in the palimpsestic representation in digital fine art, discussed in the previous chapter. Given museum and art gallery exhibition conventions, which as I describe in chapter 1 reduce indigenous material culture and art to solely ethnographic or aesthetic dimensions, I conclude my discussion of Jimmie Durham's negotiations of multicultural misrecognition by considering the potential risks of an object-focused art and by highlighting Durham's inventive ways of bypassing such risks.

Speaking Indian

In numerous essays published in the 1970s and 1980s, Durham argued at length that specific rhetorical conditions in North America confront indigenous people—activists, politicians, and artists alike—with the risk of engaging in mere *playing Indian* with their settler counterparts. This is so because of the compounded effect of the imposed colonial language, the settler audience's presumed conceptions of culture and tradition, and the impact of multiculturalism's commodification of indigenous authenticity. In a 1974 essay on "American Indian Culture: Traditionalism and Spiritualism in a Revolutionary Struggle,"[2] for example, Durham explains that the imposition of European concepts through the translation of indigenous social and political terms into English is at the root of this representational predicament. If we consider pairs of words such as *tribe* versus *nation*, *band* versus *state*, *medicine man* versus *doctor*, *brave* versus *soldier*, and *war chief* versus *general*,[3] it becomes clear, argues Durham, that English romanticizing vocabulary "is designed to prove that [Indians] were inferior" to Europeans in all aspects of their political and social organization (*CLC* 5). The problem, however, does not end with this rhetorically accomplished demotion of America's indigenous nations to a lower civilizational level. The English language is a trap, because "words in English that we have been taught mean certain concepts in our own language, do in fact mean those concepts for us. But when we speak to outsiders it often sounds as though we are all mystics or romantics, or naïve, or primitive, or 'tribal.' That phenomenon reinforces the racial stereotype that non-Indians have about Indians" (*CLC* 6). Because of its romanticizing bias, which imprisons indigenous peoples in European fantasies of American premodernity, the English language adopted by them turns its speakers into inadvertent collaborators in the reproduction of these fantasies. At the moment of articulation, language betrays the indigenous subject by testifying to his or her otherness and to whatever version of indigeneity dominates the settler public sphere at that particular historical junction. This dynamic applies in equal measure to textual and visual expression. As this book explores, American Indian writers and artists confront generic aesthetic conventions and forms historically developed to account, from the European perspective, for their very existence: a vast encyclopedia of settler images of Indians compiled over time by the settler society in order to orient its members in the topography of the Americas. In using settler linguistic and visual codes to make their idioms recognizable to colonizers, indigenous politicians, activists, performers, and artists are trapped by the presumed ways in which these codes signify. Thus, whenever they speak as and on behalf of indigenous peoples, they potentially contribute to a predetermined understanding of their meaning, one that differs sharply from their own conception of the things communicated. And since ethnic art is typically taken to be representative of its presumed constituency in a way that settler art is not, it thus contributes to a skewed understanding of indigenous peoples in general. For Durham, this lack of control over one's means of expression constitutes the true meaning of indigenous illiteracy: it turns American Indians into ESL speakers, even in the absence of their own mother tongues (*CLC* 7).

The narrow interpretive acumen of the settler public compounds the limitations resulting from indigenous peoples' linguistic orphanhood. The North American public sphere has been thoroughly saturated with a historically developed master narrative of Indian-settler relations. Any indigenous interventions into this narrative are hobbled not only by the nationalist imperatives of American history, US or Canadian, but also by dominant conceptions of culture and tradition and particular versions used to understand "Indianness." It's worth remembering here that the modern conceptions of culture, developed in North America in the work of Franz Boas, sprang from his effort to account for specifically indigenous difference. And while Boas's ethnographic approach offered an alternative to earlier American ethnographers' racist evolutionary models of human difference—especially in its shift from the concept of a universalized Culture to particular cultures and from diachronic to synchronic accounts of social phenomena—it had the long-term effect of transforming indigenous political nations into ethnographic cultures and freezing them in an ahistorical vacuum, where presumed authentic essence is manifested in material culture and daily social rituals.[4] What Durham describes as "the nefarious tendency to consider manifestations of material culture as traditions" (*CLC* 108) has persisted, resulting in the broader equation of Indianness with material culture, or in other words, in its perception as artifact. In his critical essays, Durham juxtaposes this ethnographic culture-oriented understanding of Indianness characteristic of multicultural misrecognition with a thoroughly politicized conception of indigeneity as nationhood, calling for attention to "our political system, not our well-made arrowheads" (*CLC* 8). He insists that we understand traditionalism as adaptation to changing historical conditions. He equates it with the "people's vision (political system)" and links it to indigenous efforts at decolonization: "our 'traditionals' are the people who are struggling to conserve our cultural ways and values, as well as being leaders in our struggle against colonialists" (*CLC* 9). Durham's emphasis on the political understanding of indigeneity reverberates with many other instances of strategic shifts from culturalist to political conceptions of indigeneity discussed in other chapters of this book.

As I argue in the introduction, this effort to politicize American Indian identity, undertaken with renewed energy in the 1970s in the initiatives of AIM and the broader Red Power movement and continued through legal battles over treaty rights in the US courts from the 1980s to the present, has been significantly hobbled by the ascendance of multiculturalism and the politics of recognition in North America. The irony of this outcome is not to be missed, given that the most enduring legacy of the new social movements of the 1960s and 1970s is the current consensus regarding the importance of group rights and the conception of cultural difference as a social good. Durham was one of the earliest—and remains one of the most insightful—critics of the ways in which the multiculturalist art market of the 1980s transformed the politically inspired and politically oriented art of minority groups into the performance of cultural difference benefiting North American states intent on solidifying their newly asserted multicultural credentials. Durham's attack on multiculturalism has been relentless and scathing. The very same year that Charles Taylor published his eloquent call for a politics of recognition, Durham observed astutely in "Legal Aliens," an essayistic rejoinder to the Colombian Quintencenary celebrations sweeping the continent, that "self-empowerment and multiculturalism become an absurdity under colonialism" (*CLC* 225). The newest tool in the Euro-American hegemonic arsenal, multiculturalism is an "arrangement of 'separate but equal' under the administration of colonial power"; it effects "enclosure in a colonial context which pretends the opposite" (*CLC* 225). And he further predicted that "as America becomes more comfortable in redeploying its Indian myths, the more invisible [Indians] become as people. This is true even if—or, more likely, *especially* if—Indian artists are allowed to participate" (*CLC* 437). And even though, Durham declares, "one wants, of course, to develop ideas for effective strategies for intervention in the American narrative. . . . To accept any idea of ourselves as the subject matter of our art is potentially a trap" (*CLC* 435–7). It is a trap because of the particular dynamics of the multiculturalist exchange of recognition between the indigenous author and the settler reader or viewer, an exchange taking place across Indian-authored representations. To illustrate this dynamic, Durham cast many of his early art reviews and critical essays in the rhetorical form of a direct address to the mainstream consumer of indigenous art. These essays are simultaneously critical and performative in an ironic enactment of subordination and resistance to multiculturalist imperatives, one inseparable from the other. Here's one example from a 1988 essay, "The Ground Has Been Covered," in which Durham undertakes to elucidate what he calls the insurmountable problem of audience for indigenous artists. The essay begins with a presumably Cherokee version of American early history, startling the readers only to apparently reassure them:

> In the early days we bent over backwards to accommodate whites. Ultimately, however, our efforts proved dista yohi, because tlunh yunh, ani yosgi unadduli squatsi ola yadi! Da n'tunh sga, na?
>
> Don't worry—I am a good Indian. I am from the West, love nature, and have a special intimate connection with the environment. (And if you want me to, I'm perfectly willing to say it's a connection white people will never understand.) I can speak with my animal cousins, and believe it or not, I'm appropriately spiritual. (Even smoke the pipe). (*CLC* 137)

The essay concludes thus:

> Let's see, what else? I hope I have been authentic enough to have been worth your time, and yet educated enough that you feel conversation with me has been intelligent. I have been careful not to reveal too much: understanding is a consumer product in your society; you can buy some for the price of a magazine. Like the TV ad says, "*Time* puts it all in your hands." Once you've bought some understanding, it's only natural for you to turn it around and make a profit from it—psychological, economic, or both. Then you'd get even fatter, more powerful. And where would I be? (*CLC* 142)

The essay's opening is tricky because what appears to be an indictment of America's colonial policies and a clear denunciation of indigenous collaboration, authenticated but then rendered unintelligible (at least to settler readers) by the speaker's presumed slide into his native tongue and graphic expressions of agitation if not anger, by the second paragraph turns out to have been an act, a benign joke played on an audience that often cannot decide whether it expects hostile or friendly Indians, whether it desires to be threatened or reassured, or both. Durham presumes both and begins in the mood of cooperation: "Don't worry, I am a good Indian," "I have been careful." This mood of cooperation, however, very quickly turns sour and begins to resemble a performance of indigenous red minstrelsy, an Indian in redface solicitously attending to his audience's expectations: "If you want me to, I'm perfectly willing . . . ," "Let's see, what else?" "I hope . . ." With this shift, the speaker effectively undermines the premise of authenticity that he establishes in the opening paragraph's angry indictment and the second paragraph's reassurance of the validity of the reigning Indian stereotypes. Ultimately insubordinate, the speaker concludes with a diagnosis of the inescapable commodification of indigenous expression on the American publishing market, in a Foucauldian equation of knowledge with power.[5] The unconstrained direct access of minority subjects to the national imaginary through literature, arts, and benign forms of political activism has been, arguably, the greatest achievement of multiculturalism. For Durham, however, such self-representation is anything but unconstrained; it traps the writer or artist in a dynamic that exacerbates the very condition of subjection it was designed to ameliorate.

Self-Portrait (1987) (fig. 4.1) offers a helpful visual counterpart to Durham's critical essays on the predicament of indigenous expression in America because it illustrates in vivid color this ensnarement, the replica of the artist's own body figured as the very trap of Indian art. (All chapter 4 figures appear in Mulvey and Snauwaert.) A life-size sculpture of canvas, wood, paint, feather, shell, animal fur, human hair, turquoise, and metal, *Self-Portrait* offers the entire Indian body, with the face and genitalia in three-dimensional and ornamented detail and the rest as an outline fashioned out of canvas and hung from the gallery wall, the kind reminiscent of the chalky figures marking the sites of deadly accidents or crime scenes. To augment the effect of transparency, the figure is nude and liberally inscribed with explanatory captions; a roughly cut opening in his upper chest, canvas skin flapping to the side, promises access to the psychic interior demanded by publishers and art dealers but reveals instead ragged emptiness where a heart would be. A naked Indian with a paint-splashed face and a ripped-out heart cannot fail but evoke some of the oldest stereotypes of Indian savagery, and yet he declares in an earnest tone in a caption inscribed across his upper chest: "Hello! I'm Jimmie Durham. I want to explain a few Basic Things About Myself. In 1986 I was 46 years old. As an artist I am confused by many things, but basically my health is good and I am willing and able to do a variety of Jobs. I am Actively seeking Employment." Other autobiographical declarations include "I am basically light hearted," "I have 12 hobbies!," "11 house plants!," "I have a crooked back," "People like my Poems," and "My skin is not really this dark, but I am sure that many Indians have coppery skin." This autodiegetic account is further supplemented by third-person reporting, rhetorically ranging from the discourse of medicine and social work—"Mr. Durham has stated that he believes he has an addiction to Alcohol, Nicotine, Caffiene [sic], and does not sleep well," "His Abdominal Muscle Protrudes Aprox. 3–12 inches," and "Appendix Scar"—to the ethnographic modes of specimen description—"Hands are small, sensitive"—and type generalization—"Indian Penises are unusually large and colorful." Durham's attempt at self-portraiture yields a flat surface of flayed skin, the flapping Redskin straight out of Durham's 1987 poem, "One of Those Indians."[6]

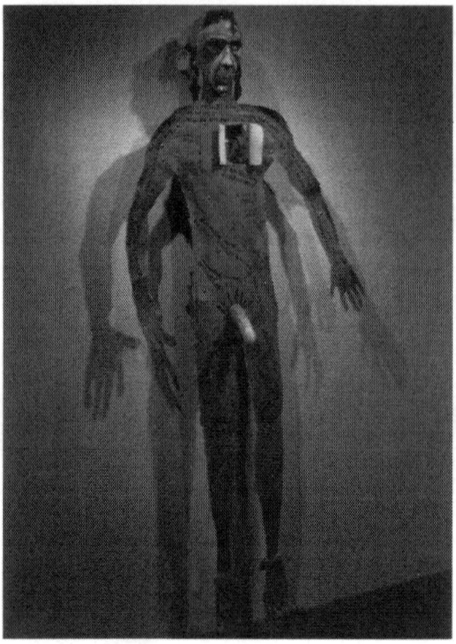

Fig. 4.1. *Self-Portrait*, Jimmie Durham, 1987.

It serves as a catalogue of formal discourses, such as autobiographical declaration, ethnography, social and medical pathology, unemployment benefit application, erotic titillation, and accusations of communist sympathizing,[7] all ways through which Indians typically enter mainstream acknowledgment. Even when the Indian artist is the speaker himself, he is only spoken by the established institutional discourses of the settler society. He cannot (stoically or not) return the viewer's gaze, either; although the Indian in *Self-Portrait* resolutely faces the audience, his eyes are missing: one leaves a gouged socket and the other is replaced by a globe of dull turquoise, yet another stereotyped Indian artifact. Durham's refusal of communication extends to the subaltern's returned gaze, which postcolonial theory has invested with productive potential. Durham's Indian refuses transparency, but he is also devoid of agency.

Critics have linked the tension between such gestures of exposure and withholding to specifically indigenous forms of self-representation, arguing that they function to reassert indigenous agency in the circumscribed colonial contexts of indigenous speech. For example, Doris Sommer has suggested that the recurring assertion of intentional secrecy in *I, Rigoberta Menchú* (1983), a *testimonio* by the Guatemalan Quiche political activist and a winner of the Nobel Peace Prize, served to put distance between Menchú and Elisabeth Burgos-Debray, the French ethnographer who recorded and transcribed Menchú's narrative. Menchú's insistently repeated rhetorical gesture helped her regain control within the overdetermined framework of the resulting text.[8] Mary Lawlor has described a similar technique of displayed withholding at work in tribal museums in North America, which often feature empty display cases with captions explaining that missing materials have been deemed out of limits for public viewing. The point of such displays, she argues, is less the actual protection of restricted objects than the assertion of tribal control over the circulation of its material culture. Whereas Sommer's and Lawlor's arguments imply that the outcome of these withholdings is effective, the blinded mask of the Indian artist's face (a death mask?) along with his body, which has been reduced to a racially signifying surface, exhaustively captioned and displayed for settler cultural self-mirroring, suggest that any attempt at indigenous self-representation in the continuing colonial context of North America is doomed to failure.

Like the body of the Indian artist in *Self-Portrait,* Durham's art often functions as a satirical catalogue of settler foundational discourses, narratives of national self-definition that have prominently figured representations of indigeneity. For example, a 1987 installation titled *She Rose from Her Warm Bed* (fig. 4.2), included in the exhibition *We, the People*, juxtaposes two versions of female heroism, one drawn from cowboy lore and the other from Indian captivity narratives. The piece consists of several Indian "maidens": one life-size figure composed of a dress hanging on a closet hanger, adorned by a beaded necklace and topped by a sculpture of a woman's head, and two rows of smaller stick dolls with female heads, vaguely reminiscent at once of folk spoon dolls and of shrunken heads, displayed on the gallery walls like trophies. This display is captioned by two textual fragments; the one in the top left corner comes from Woody Guthrie's song "The Ranger's Command" and extols the bravery of an Annie Oakley-like cowboy's lover: "She rose from her warm bed / with a gun in each hand / she said come all you cowboys / and fight for your land." The other, in the bottom right corner, reverses the standard eighteenth-century narrative of captivity among the Indians by commemorating those white women who, unlike Mary Rowlandson, found life among American Indians preferable to settler society: "Cynthia Parker was / rescued from the Comanches / on five different occasions. / She kept going back to them. / When her family locked / her up for her own good / she starved herself to death."[9] Durham's more recent solo exhibitions, *Building the Nation* (London's Matt's Gallery, 2006) and *The West* (Compton Verneys, 2005), take up another American foundational discursive cluster: Manifest Destiny, the settling of the frontier, and the literary and cinematographic western. Other examples of Durham's reinscriptions of the nation's foundational narratives include installations featuring Pocahontas and La Malinche (in *Pocahontas and Attakullakulla in London,*

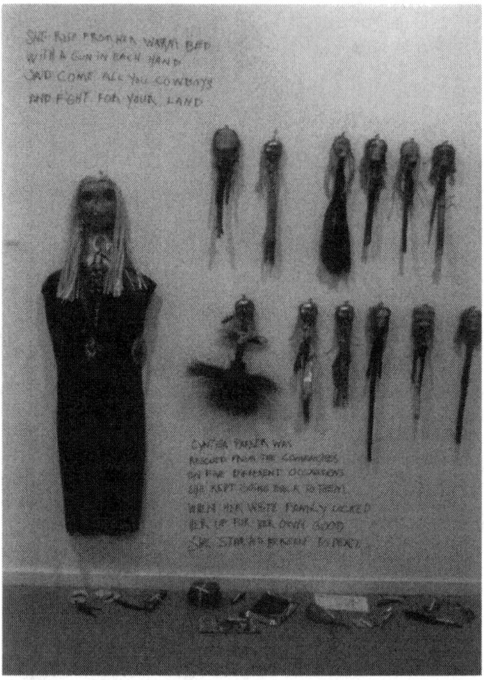

Fig. 4.2. *She Rose from Her Warm Bed*, Jimmie Durham, 1987. Installation: *We, the People,* Art Space, New York.

1988 Matt's Gallery, and *Original Re-Runs*, 1994 ICA, London), which depict these founding mothers of the Americas as conquerors' and settlers' fantasies of passionate collaboration with indigenous women, constructed in an effort to rewrite the conquest itself as a family romance.

Durham does not spare the institutions of the museum and the art market, either. His 1991 exhibition titled *On Loan from the Museum of the American Indian* satirically targets the Western exhibitionary complex and its varied discourses of indigeneity in particular. For example, *Types of Arrows*—displaying three examples of arrows, labeled "tiny," "wavy," and "fat and short"—parodies the systematizing imperatives of Western science and ethnography. A contemporary color photograph of Durham's parents captioned *The Indian's Parents (frontal view)* evokes the long tradition of portraiture of indigenous peoples, in painting and photography, which treated its subjects as ethnographic specimens or as typological evidence of retardation or pathology in evolutionary narratives. *Current Trends in Indian Land Ownership*, consisting of a series of maps documenting indigenous land loss between 1492 and 1992 in North America, in turn, euphemistically rewrites the history of indigenous expropriation and displacement as a narrative of economic ebbs and flows. And lastly, *Pocahontas' Underwear*, featuring red lace bikini panties adorned with feathers and beads, sets up, as Laura Mulvey has argued, resonances between different kinds of fetishistic display, the museum ethnographic and the erotic, pointing out the conjunction of museology and pornography and all the while leaving "Pocahontas" an empty, ironic sign (Mulvey and Snauwaert 38). In an earlier series of fake artifacts—including *Bedia's Muffler* (1985) and *Bedia's Stirring Wheel* (1985), both featuring car parts dressed up with paint, feathers, and beads and appended with explanatory captions—Durham spoofs ethnographic discourse and exhibition practices, especially their need to provide essentializing explanations and the misrepresentation they perform in doing so.[10] In addition, while substantiating the indigenous understanding of tradition as dynamic change, including appropriation of European settler material culture in everyday life, both pieces imagine a process of thorough, albeit symbolic, reindigenization of American realities in the future.

Contemporary art, and especially its late twentieth-century postmodernist and multiculturalist orientations, comes under critique in Durham's work for the ways in which it deploys emblems of indigeneity to testify to its own enlightened multiculturalist stance. For example, in *Not Lothar Baumgarten's Cherokee* (1990), Durham takes aim at a prominent German conceptual artist while facetiously cribbing from Magritte himself. Much of Lothar Baumgarten's work has involved reinscription of indigenous names or forms of writing onto contemporary European and American surfaces in gestures that commemorate while appropriating. Some of his better-known pieces include a 1984 Venice Biennale installation consisting of a marble floor engraved with the names of indigenous peoples from the Amazon and the 1993 exhibition at the Guggenheim Museum in which he imprinted the inner curves of the museum's rotunda with the names of the North American indigenous nations. Durham's piece explicitly references Baumgarten's installation for the Carnegie Museum of Art in 1988, which featured letters from the Cherokee alphabet hand-painted on the exhibition hall ceiling. Unlike Baumgarten's monumental and carefully crafted syllabary, Durham's piece is steeped in a minimalist and provisional aesthetic. Rather than reproducing Cherokee writing in a gesture that smacks of playing Indian, Durham builds a collage including a fragment of an old Cherokee manuscript appended by a nonsensical transcription into the Roman alphabet. His piece works at several levels: satirically, it plays with the possibility of viewers reading the transcription as authentic; analytically, it uncovers the complex dynamic of such prolegomena to translation; and aesthetically, it emphasizes the labor and materials involved in attempts at reading across linguistic and aesthetic barriers. Instead of being a ritual symbolic commemoration of American indigeneity reduced to a form of writing, a gesture that authenticates American claims to multiculturalism, Durham's work zeros in on the inevitability of impasse in encounters between different systems of signification. This impasse, brought on by an indigenous sign that refuses decoding, here in the form of Cherokee syllabary, recurs as the potentially productive moment of transformation in many of Durham's artworks. In the following section, I explore its effects in more detail, via an analysis of *Red Turtle*, to argue ultimately that it constitutes the very core of Durham's approach to negotiating multicultural misrecognition.

The Index and Insubordinate Indigenous Art

Red Turtle (fig. 4.3), a 1991 part-sculpture-part-installation, embodies this approach particularly well by confronting the spectator with a question: What can any Indian speech act mean, given the layered and contradictory contexts of its enunciation? From a distance, *Red Turtle* appears as a large black X on the white page of the gallery wall; it announces itself, all at once, as a mark of the unknown or as the inscrutable other; as an equation requiring solution or as "the Indian problem"; and, perhaps most insistently, as the first Indian writing recognizable to the Europeans, the X mark on a treaty. Durham appends this foundational Indian signature, the very signature elicited to authorize European settlements in North America, with a couple of crucial amendments, which come into view as one approaches the piece. The first, a somewhat ragged slip of paper tacked to the X's lower limbs, offers an exasperated admission hand-printed in black ink: "We have tried to train them; to teach them to speak properly, to write and to fill out forms. We have no way of knowing whether they truly percieve [*sic*] and comprehend or whether they simply imitate our actions." This note, which Laura Mulvey has described as the frustrated cri de coeur of a colonial educator (51), rehearses the problem of mimicry inherent to colonial contexts by reiterating the fundamental binary structure of colonial arrangements, the "us and them" model of social relations. It reinforces the image of the colonial other as a cipher, and yet it also undermines the colonizer's conviction about his epistemological superiority. Such self-doubt hints at the possibility of indigenous speech that remains puzzling to the colonizer while giving voice to the new forms of indigenous experience arising out of the confrontation with and adjustment to the settler presence, a possibility celebrated in Homi Bhabha's conception of colonial mimicry as inherently creative and potentially liberatory. This self-doubt undermines not only the legitimacy of the colonial project of acculturating the subal-

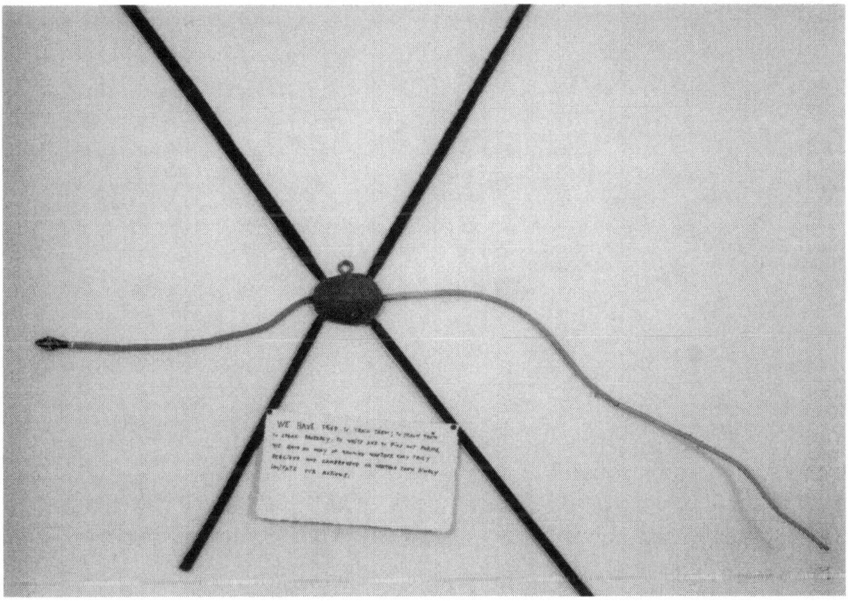

Fig. 4.3. *Red Turtle*, Jimmie Durham, 1991.

tern but also, especially in the context of North America, the legitimacy of European and later American title to North American land.[11] The problem with Indian speech and writing, Durham suggests, is not that it is unrecognizable to the colonizers; rather, the problem consists in the fact that the meaning behind the speech and writing is multiple and contradictory and that it raises a suspicion of insubordination. An Indian sign is always an X in need of decoding and in danger of being misunderstood. It is a sign that generates a compulsion to read and reread and yet escapes the colonizer's presumed mastery of the code. Thus Indian speech is potentially insubordinate and, given that the United States is founded on the idea of Indian cooperation attested to by the Indian X, however manufactured, this insubordination has far-reaching consequences.

The second amendment comes in the form of a composite figure placed at the crux of the X, offering another form of indigenous writing, an alternative to the X that mimics European literacy. It deeds the colonizer's interpretive predicament to the contemporary viewer. This addition is constructed of a turtle shell and two slim tree branches, one with a finely sculpted and ornamented snake head substituting for the turtle's missing head and the other, long and undulating, for its missing tail. It appropriates the limbs of the X for the turtle's legs. Painted vivid red, blue, yellow, black, and white, the turtle-snake figure engages the X in a representational duel of sorts, a contestation of visual inscriptions: the turtle-snake's colorful playfulness against the X's sharp black inexorability; the one's fluid movement against the other's categorical fixedness; the organic forms and natural surfaces of the branches and the shell palimpsestically reaching from underneath the layers of paint, seemingly hurriedly brushed on by the artist, against the X's pointed angular shapes machined out of wood and amplified by the uniform application of the black paint. From this vantage point, *Red Turtle* becomes intelligible as a contest of two forms of writing, two inscriptions on the landscape: the Indian X mimicking Western textuality, a signature that literally changed the American landscape as the fences of settler husbandry and agriculture replaced indigenous forms of land management,[12] versus the indigenous trace in and of the land, the turtle-snake marking its continuous progress across the continent.

But these seemingly clichéd oppositions—Western alphabet versus indigenous pictographs, textuality versus visuality, culture versus nature, and so on—are complicated by their intersections within a changing field of signification, the virgin land or the blank page of America. The series of apparent symmetries of form and color—manufactured versus natural lines, straight versus oblique angles, black and white versus saturated colors—does not clarify matters. The X stands not only for Western literacy and textuality but also for indigenous mimicry of it, just as Durham's installation mimics the Western art object and the exhibitionary order that gives it meaning. Indian writing both reproduces and exceeds Western literacy. At both levels of signification, the spectator viewing the Indian sign is confronted with its potential import and its enigma, its conformity and its insubordination. The colonial educator ponders the meaning of the Indian X while potentially doubting the efficacy of the colonial civilizational project; the contemporary viewer ponders the meaning of the Indian X while questioning the legality of the transaction that the X authorized and the meaning of *Red Turtle*, a contemporary, albeit equally slippery, example of Indian speech. At first, the X figuring as the turtle's splayed legs points to Western textual literacy and the treaties, including the land cessions they extracted, as the twinned causes of the indigenous incapacitation, the reasons behind the turtle's arrested movement across the land. This is a reading familiar to the settler public educated on earlier narratives of Manifest Destiny and civilizational progress and also, more recently, on "sensitive and honest" novels about Indian suffering celebrated as multicultural literature *par excellance*. And yet the particular contest the piece stages between the X and the turtle-snake takes on different meanings depending on the spectator's proximity to the piece, reminding the viewer that meaning depends on the angle of vision. From far away, we notice above all the X's signature on the gallery wall's white page—or map—and presume its power of erasure as the piece's focus. From this vantage point, *Red Turtle* indicts the Americanization of the continent as a process predicated on indigenous expropriation, displacement, and genocide. Far from offering insubordinate speech, such indictments, as Durham argues in his 1992 essay "Legal Aliens," are part and parcel of expected contemporary Indian speech; the Indian indictment and accompanying complaint thereby add poignancy to the historic emergence and continuing mandates of an America always in the process of self-transformation. But close up, we notice the caption that throws into doubt the X's abilities to signify and authorize in predictable and stable ways. In addition, the turtle-snake's placement on top of the X, rather than underneath it, along with the suggestion of its ongoing movement, further complicates, if not altogether reverses, the relations of power implied in the piece's initial cast of visual oppositions. On close approach, *Red Turtle* asserts the persistence of indigeneity as an escaping target, or, as many contemporary American Indian writers would have it, it evokes survivance, that specifically indigenous ability to survive and resist past and present colonialism. Unlike a butterfly immobilized by the collector's pin, or an ethnographic object captured in the museum display case, or an artwork tacked on the gallery wall, Durham's turtle-snake slithers away in a perhaps doomed but nevertheless persistent attempt to avoid fixture in the state's legal frames and the public's representational ones.

This particular reading of the turtle-snake is made possible by Durham's use of an actual turtle shell as an index. *Red Turtle* accrues meaning through a play of its two dueling signs—the X and the turtle shell—and their symbolic, iconic, and indexical valences. The X functions both as an icon of an Indian signature on the treaties authorizing the handover of land to colonial settlers and as a symbol of the erasure of indigenous tenure in the land, given that the treaties cleared the way for European settlement, transforming landscape husbanded by the indigenous nations into a wilderness of virgin land. The actual, as opposed to manufactured, turtle shell at the heart of the piece is deployed as an index of the indigenous ground, Turtle Island, and thus of indigenous tenure on the continent; it invokes the persistence of indigeneity against the many iconic and symbolic representations that work to efface it from material reality, all the while celebrating its abstract versions. But the ironies of the piece multiply further: since it is fashioned out of machined wood, the X is also a kind of ironic index of settler picket fences, which transformed indigenous land into a commodity and thus ushered European modernity into indigenous lives. Through the prism of indexical signification, *Red Turtle* foregrounds the residual materiality of indigeneity persisting in the American ground against an equally material settler presence that has irrevocably transformed this very ground. Lastly, if Scott Lyons is right, in its function as an inked mark made on the final page of a treaty, the X also serves as an icon and symbol of the Indian "assent to the new," the indigenous gambit at participating in that modernity in one way or another. In his 2010 book *X-Marks: Native Signatures of Assent*, Lyons reinterprets the Indian treaty signature as "a sign of consent in a context of coercion," one that "signifies power and lack of power, agency and lack of agency" (1, 2–3), precisely the condition embodied in Durham's red turtle splayed over settler fences, a figure captured and escaping simultaneously, one contained by and attempting to exceed the settler legal, political, and cultural interpretive frameworks. The crucial point of the piece, though, inheres in the shift from the X as an icon of indigenous mimicry of settler modernity back to the turtle shell as an index of a residual indigeneity that exceeds settler interpretive codes. Because they signify independently of interpretation, in Durham's art indices of indigeneity in the form of found objects and raw materials such as turtle shells, animal bones, stones, and driftwood, all recovered from the American ground, supply the recalcitrant indigenous signs. The indexical sign becomes for Durham a remedy for the indigenous lack of control over linguistic and visual means of expression.

Durham imbues the index with a critical agency that targets settler multicultural reading conventions and intimates indigenous speech in excess of settler interpretive mastery. In *Not Joseph Beuys' Coyote* (fig. 4.4), for example, Durham returns to the notorious *I Like America and America Likes Me* performed by German artist Joseph Beuys at the René Block Gallery on East Broadway in 1974. Considered pivotal in opening the North American art world to the German avant-garde, Beuys's performance involved the artist, equipped with a felt blanket, a shepherd's staff, leather gloves, and a flashlight, spending eight hours over three days with a wild coyote in a room stripped bare of furnishings but supplied daily with multiple copies of the *Wall Street Journal*, all adding up to a neat juxtaposition of "nature" and "culture," a juxtaposition that, one cannot fail but note, was hardly put into question by the performance. In yet another example of European Indian playing, Beuys fashioned himself as a shaman engaged in a process of healing what he saw as the fundamental American trauma but described rather elliptically using a cliché of "the Red Man" (qtd. in Sandler 92). Through a series of fabricated ritual gestures, Beuys attempted "a reckoning with the coyote" (qtd. in Sandler 92) in order to lift, or exorcise, this specifically American trauma while, of course, being photographed and filmed in the process. Ac-

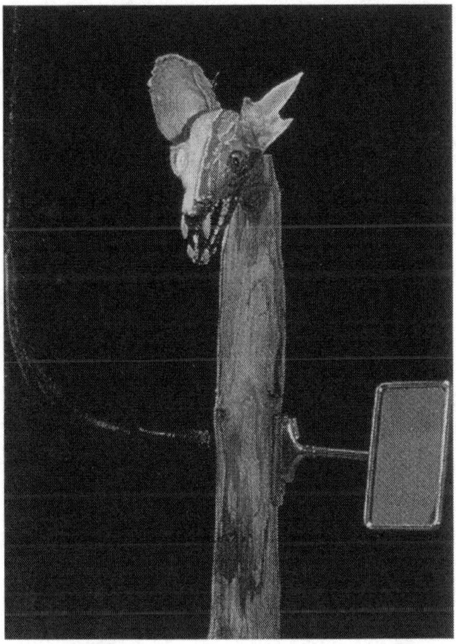

Fig. 4.4. *Not Joseph Beuys' Coyote*, Jimmie Durham, 1990.

cording to accounts of the event, the coyote, although hostile and even aggressive at first, had by the end of the performance become friendly toward the artist and even allowed him to touch it. While commentators on Beuys's work have noted the irony of the performance's title, no one has commented on the irony of the reckoning itself, which required the confinement of the coyote, thereby unwittingly extending the history of specifically American kinds of exploitation of indigeneity oriented at the definition or recuperation of a Western self.

Durham's 1990 sculpture zeros in on the ironies and paradoxes manifest in Beuys's performance but missing from critical assessments of it. In place of a live animal, Durham places at the center of his work a Frankenstein-like coyote, a composite figure featuring a wooden log stripped of bark and topped with an ornamented coyote skull recycled from Durham's previous work. The coyote extends its front legs—one fashioned from a black animal horn, the other from a car's rearview mirror—toward the viewer, trapping her in a moment of forced self-examination of her fascination with the exhibited object. A far cry from Beuys's emblem of uncontaminated American wildness, Durham's coyote collapses any distinction between nature and culture. Beuys's performance implied that the Western man could still come into the presence of the wild, even if he had to cage it, and that, therefore, a return to premodern time was still an option; viewed from the vantage point of the twenty-first century, the attempt appears quaintly, though unapologetically, naïve in a New Age kind of way. With Durham, the viewer is entirely within the realm of representation, yet not allowed simply to appreciate the piece, the presumed authentic Indian artwork, as a beautifully executed artifice. As she leans in to observe the crafted details of the real coyote skull, what confronts her is an image of her own curious leaning-in reflected in the mirror. In Durham's signature gesture, the coyote returns the viewer's look upon herself and the installation becomes an ethnography not of indigenous culture but of settler subjects. Rather than a window into Indian spiritual life, a gateway offering passage away from modernity, Durham's coyote is a mirror, flashing back at spectators their need for Indian authenticity. The fact that this settler ethnography is forcefully imposed on the spectator by the presence of the mirror, that she is tricked by a coyote, is crucial here. On the one hand, Durham's strategy confirms one of the best-known stereotypes regarding indigenous lore: coyotes are superb tricksters. At the same time, however, this strategy evokes the structural limitations attending the supposedly free Indian expression in contemporary multicultural America. If the spectator's image of herself, captured in the mirror the coyote flashes at her, is necessarily a record of her reaction to the Indian other, so, by extension, Indian self-representations, whether in speech, writing, visual arts, or political action, are also determined to a large degree by indigenous peoples' forced coexistence with settler society. In this complicated context, authenticity is not a useful category of analysis or understanding. Beuys's *I Like America and America Likes Me* managed—in the middle of the 1970s, in the immediate aftermath of the occupation of Alcatraz Island and the Siege of Wounded Knee—to evacuate indigeneity of its political meanings by reducing indigenous America to a wild coyote, an iconic stereotype of indigenous spirituality in popular imagination but one that eerily evokes the demographic disasters that nearly emptied the hemisphere of its indigenous inhabitants following the arrival of Europeans. In response to this elision of indigenous peoples and their political aspirations, Durham's *Not Joseph Beuys' Coyote* reaches for the real coyote skull to commemorate the damage and, via the skull's indexical authority, to animate the coyote with contemporary critical agency.

The profound effects of Durham's turn to indexical representation become clear if we recall George Catlin's understanding of the governing mandates of his art. A precursor to late nineteenth- and the early twentieth-century proponents of the vanishing-race discourse, Catlin wrote in 1841, in volume I of his *Letters and Notes on the Manners, Customs and Conditions of the North American Indians*, that he had long "contemplated the noble races of red men. . . . their rights invaded, their morals corrupted, their lands wrested from them, their customs changed, therefore lost to the world. . . . At last sunk into the earth, and the ploughshare turning the sod over their graves" only to decide to come "to their rescue—not of their lives or of their race (for they are 'doomed' and must perish), but to the rescue of their looks and their modes" so that "yet phoenix-like, they may rise from the 'stain on a painter's palette,' and live again upon canvas, and stand forth for centuries to come, the living monuments of a noble race" (16). Catlin's art rescues the idea of the Indian, who is otherwise obviously and unavoidably vanishing. In doing so, it exculpates settler society for the Indians' inadvertent and lamentable, but historically necessary, demise. Catlin's Indian paintings allow settler society to have its Indian cake and eat it, too, so to speak. They do not feature Indian bones upturned by the settler plows; rather, Catlin's response to the real sight of such bones is to offer icons and symbols of a glorious Indian past. His paintings transform historic Indians into noble warriors and celebrate them as such.[13] To reinforce the idea that such nobility is a thing of the past, they occasionally lament (or lampoon?) his assimilated Indian contemporaries.[14] In Durham's art, Indian bones do show up, insistently: they return as real bones and skulls transformed by the artist into indexical signs. They are never displaced by their symbolic or iconic equivalents, as is the case in Catlin's paintings. Like Marcel Duchamp's ready-made art did early in the twentieth century, Durham's found-object pieces certainly challenge the concept of artistic creativity understood as originality, as he capitalizes on his predecessor's idea of art as an act of changing an existing object or shifting its context (for example, from that of daily utility to that of artistic exhibition, as was the case with Duchamp's notorious 1917 *Fountain*). More importantly, however, Durham's art puts into question not only the originality of the art object but also, as Laura Mulvey has observed, the very issue of origin itself and thus, by extension, the conception of America as the New World (52). Durham's bones, skulls, stones, and driftwood bring the indigenous precontact past into the American present, exposing the very idea of a *new beginning* as the most cherished redundancy of the American classic ideology. Like the archival photographs in the contemporary digital fine art of Pamela Shields, which I discuss in chapter 3, Durham's found objects anchor his artworks in the historical past and in the indigenous ground in which they have been buried and from which they emerge.

Excavating Buried Political Histories

As Durham's indices block the specifically settler kinds of meanings that work to bolster American nationalist myths, they smuggle in meanings intelligible to viewers open to indigenous perspectives; in Durham's art they become portals for indigenous political histories. For example, *Red Turtle* recalls the tradition of treaty negotiation in its use of the X, but the piece's political references do not end there. The turtle's transformation into a snake also inserts politics into the picture by evoking specific histories of political resistance to settler colonialism. It calls up the Crazy Snake movement, an early twentieth-century Muskogee resistance against forced allotment in Oklahoma, named after its leader Chitto Harjo.[15] After Harjo's death, the movement's adherents constituted the Four Mothers Nation, a broader intertribal political organization advocating against the allotment of tribal lands, most recently described in LeAnne Howe's novel *Miko Kings*. The Crazy Snake movement collapsed in 1926 after a quarter century of political resistance against the loss of tribal lands, but it is often credited with inspiring pan-Indian political mobilization throughout the twentieth century. In the context of the Crazy Snake movement, Durham's *Red Turtle* figures the history of America as an ongoing political contest over land, one between European and American attempts at usurpation and indigenous efforts to hold on to ancestral territories. Durham's turtle-snake, which slithers off the gallery wall right over the X mark of the treaty and the picket of the settler fence, reclaims indigenous land as it escapes settler captive frameworks.

Untitled (fig. 4.5), a 1992 sculpture, illustrates Durham's strategy of embedding thick historical layers into his art as well, but with an added twist. It offers a historical genealogy of contemporary militant activism and provides links between past and present political struggles and their counterparts in the sphere of cultural production. Like *Red Turtle* and many of Durham's works combining text and sculpture, *Untitled* consists of two objects, a large tree branch and an attached handwritten note from the artist that highlight the symbol-index tension and the opposition of textuality and materiality as different forms of signification. The branch is roughly the size and shape of a human arm and has been painted vivid red, its knots and other natural characteristics accrued through both growth and decay remaining visible through the glossy paint. In the lower left corner, the artist has embedded a glass eye where a branch used to sprout to the left, an eye turned to confront the spectator. To the right of the red arm is an "Open Letter to the Public to Whom It May Concern" written in ink, in cursive on a single lined sheet of paper, the kind you would rip out of a school notebook or a legal-size writing pad. It reads:

> I intended to tie this piece to a hammer and a sickle and call it "Red Herring", which means a non-sequitur. But I could not find a sickle in New York City and anyway it does not look very much like a herring. (Gabriel, a herring is a kind of fish).

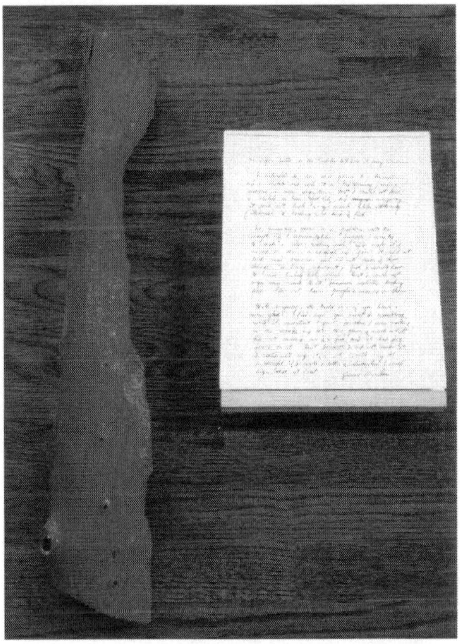

Fig. 4.5. *Untitled*, Jimmie Durham, 1992.

> No, anyway, there is a problem with the concept of representation. Suppose I wanted to make a real-looking fish: if I make it of wood or stone or canvas and paint it could not look real because fish are not made of those things. To truly represent a fish I would have to use living fish flesh. But I could not sign my name to it because realistic-looking fish do not have people's names on them.
>
> Well, anyway, the truth is, if you have a nice glass fish-eye you must do *something* with it, mustn't you? So then I was walking in the woods and saw this piece of wood, which did not remind me of a fish, and it had dog feces on it. But because I did not make it I could not sign it, so who would buy it? I thought if I wrote a letter of introduction I could sign that, at least.
>
> Jimmie Durham

Durham's appended letter singles out the issue of representation, and the universally abstract and arbitrary relationship between the sign and the signified, along with the question of authorship, as the focus of the piece. And yet, this thematic focus on the sculptor's relationship to his materials appears to be the red herring of the piece, intentionally failing to distract from the artwork's multiple referencing of diverse political histories. Most immediately, the tree branch resembling a raised human arm serves as an icon of

AIM and Red Power activism, the red clenched fist their ubiquitous symbol. The color red, aside from its most obvious association with American Indians, one reappropriated by the activists themselves, evokes the accusations of communist sympathizing leveled at AIM, and at Durham himself, by the federal government. But the piece also, when considered as an index, could be described as a "red stick," thus excavating yet another precursor to the twentieth-century indigenous militant activism in the military resistance of a faction of Muscogee Nation, the Red Sticks, to US settler encroachment on tribal lands in the early nineteenth century. The conflict between the Red Sticks and the White Sticks, who opposed military resistance and sought accommodations with American settlers, led to a civil war within the Muscogee Nation, a conflict that ultimately became intertwined with the War of 1812.[16] For a viewer conversant with the recent history of American Indian federal law, the question of authorship takes on specifically political meanings given that *Untitled* was completed and exhibited soon after the signing into law of the American Indian Arts and Crafts Act (AIACA) in 1990. Designed as a "truth-in-advertising" law to protect American Indian artists whose work competed on the market with fake Indian artifacts, the law had unintended consequences. Since it required artists to have a Certificate Degree of Indian Blood (CDIB) card in order to sell their work as American Indian art, it effectively declassified as Indian those artists who had never secured tribal enrollment, refused to do so, or could not secure it due to blood quantum restrictions on tribal membership.[17] In the political context of the AIACA law, the pressing problem of representation at the heart of *Untitled* is not so much the question of the artist's relationship to his materials but rather his certifiable relationship to tribal citizenship and to the colonial governments, state and federal, that recognize it.

The metaphors of excavating buried indigenous histories recur throughout Durham's body of work and culminate in *The Banks of the Ohio* (fig. 4.6), included in the 1992 exhibition *Will/Power,* at the Wexner Center for the Arts in Columbus, Ohio, organized in response to the official celebrations of the Columbus Quincentenary. This installation brings together diverse contexts and materials to prompt reflection on historical amnesia as fundamental to nation-building and to indict historical obscurantism as the quintessential American mode of self-creation. The artwork consists of PVC pipe sections of ever-increasing size emerging out of a gallery wall and winding through a series of corridors, ultimately rising up into the air. A snakehead, fashioned out of mud and horned with tree branches, comes out of the end opening of the PVC duct, the animal appearing simultaneously as trapped and emerging free, an ancient snake rising up from the modern-day sewer.

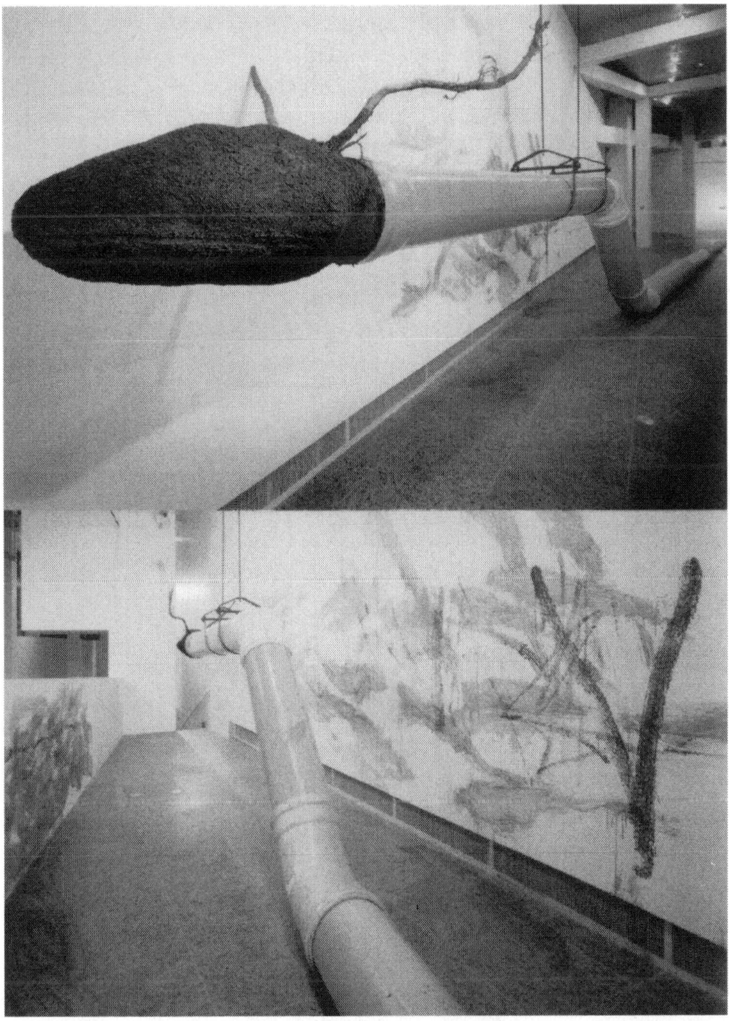

Fig. 4.6. *The Banks of the Ohio* (details), Jimmie Durham, 1992. Installation: *Will/Power,* Wexner Center for the Arts, Columbus, Ohio

The walls of the gallery halls are patterned with brown paint, which, depending on the perspective, evokes sloppily mopped up dirt (in close-up), tracks of rubber tires or of a snake slithering along (in middle view), or, as Laura Mulvey suggests, "elegant vegetal forms, like growth of river plants" (in long view) (72). By virtue of this imagery as well as the installation's location in Columbus, Ohio, *The Banks of the Ohio* evokes the Serpent Mound, a 1,330-foot-long and 3-foot-high prehistoric mound located in Peebles,

Adams County, Ohio. Thought to have been built about 1070 by the Fort Ancient culture, people descended from the Hopewell culture and sometimes referred to as Mound Builders, the Serpent Mound has been designated a National Historic Landmark and is today maintained by the Ohio Historical Society both as a historical site and as a tourist attraction. For Laura Mulvey, the Serpent Mound and other ancient effigy earthworks "stand as a testimonial to the way that the amnesia, imported by settler communities, was imposed, blanket-like, on the past of the country and its landscape" (74). And yet such ancient mounds, especially those transformed into sites of explicitly national history, are testimonials to both amnesia and memorialization. If indeed, as the French historian Ernst Renan first pointed out in 1882, nation-building requires conscientious acts of forgetting of the "deeds of violence which took place at the origin of all political formations" (11), then the Serpent Mound reminds us again that the Union was made "by means of brutality" (11). It serves as evidence of manufactured forgetting on behalf of the new nation and, simultaneously, as a conduit for remembering the price the nation exacts in its very acts of creation.

At the same time, in its memorialization as a National Historic Landmark, itself a process of complementary forgetting and remembering, the Serpent Mound, and the evidence of social and cultural development in North America prior to European arrival and settlement that it represents, is repurposed for the US nationalist narrative. As Martha Sandweiss has explained, beginning in the late nineteenth century, archeologists deployed to the Southwest and other sites of ancient ruins and earthworks worked to appropriate these sites for US nationalist genealogy.[18] As a result, these sites became unavailable to contemporary indigenous peoples for the same purposes. This repurposing severed the link between the historical indigenous peoples and their contemporary counterparts, who were at the time subject to a relentless project of economic, social, and cultural assimilation. In these acts of nationalist memorialization, the Serpent Mound and other ancient earthworks were and continue to be both exposed and buried again, made visible for some ideological functions while obscured for others. In this broader context, *The Banks of the Ohio* makes sense as a play with the ever-present possibility of another emergence,[19] or excavation, this time by the hand of the artist rather than an archeologist or a national park curator. The title of the piece, taken from a popular nineteenth-century murder ballad, which was further popularized by a host of twentieth-century performers, reinforces this dynamic of burying and exposure while also evoking the idea of the American continent's original sin. The ballad's basic conceit remains the same across its many versions.[20] In the voice of the suitor, the ballad dramatizes a refused marriage proposal and the ensuing killing and disposal of the murdered woman's body in the Ohio River. Given the long discursive tradition of casting the settlement of America in the idiom of seduction,[21] the ballad's lyrics can be understood as depicting frustration at the land not giving in to the masculinized settler's control, resisting settlement and its attendant narrative of the family romance and marital union. The body of the woman dumped in the river threatens to resurface and expose the brutal cost of the domestication of the continent. If she emerges from the sewer of the river as an ancient serpent, hers is the buried and exposed body of indigenous America returning to trouble settler consciousness and potentially threaten settler claims to full legal ownership of the land. Considered as an index, the mud serpent of Durham's installation recovers the severed link between contemporary and historical indigenous peoples of the Ohio Valley and the continuity of indigenous tenure in the land. In the midst of the Columbus Quincentenary, *The Banks of the Ohio* turns the glorious story of the nation's Manifest Destiny familiar from artworks such as John Gast's 1872 *American Progress* into a sordid tale of unrequited passion and vengeful murder, on the one hand, and into the reemergence of never-vanished, always-residual indigeneity, on the other.

Durham's kind of historicism—his attention to the American ground as a palimpsest, its multiple layers ever contending for surface visibility—draws its persuasive power from the artist's reliance on indexical representation, or, to put it differently, from the very mud of the Ohio River, from the actual turtle shell at the center of *Red Turtle*, from the real coyote skull in *Not Joseph Beuys' Coyote*. And thus it operates with different emphases than the historicism of contemporary digital art practitioners such as Shields, Auguilar, and Tsinhnahjinnie, who rely on palimpsesting photographic representation. While Durham's works, in all media, employ symbolic and iconic signs, it is his emphasis on the index that makes his art distinctive and particularly politically relevant for contemporary indigenous nations. Once inserted into the artwork, animal skulls and bones, turtle shells, snake skins, stones, driftwood, and Durham's other found objects demand that viewers rethink the concept of representation in ways that do away with some of its fundamental organizing assumptions, perhaps even abandon them altogether. They invite us to think about Durham's artworks in a way similar to Walter Benjamin's thinking about photography and his claim that the people depicted in old photographs possess such a powerful aura of presence that they continue to be real and will "never perish into art" (Trachtenberg 30). Benjamin's formulation betrays his suspicion of art as that discursive medium that mediates historical people and events out of contemporary existence (a dynamic we see at work in, for example, Catlin's paintings), a sentiment shared by many American Indians with regard to their representations in settler popular media. This suspicion is certainly part of the reason why contemporary American Indian photographers/artists turn to the historical photographic archive and rely on the indexical aspect of its images, and the documentary authority the photographic index implies, to evoke the realness of indigenous experience in the age of digital media and the forsaken original. But as contemporary scholar of early photography Geoffrey Batchen points out, photography, too, is a medium caught up in its own haunting: an image, however repurposed, ultimately surpassing its own referent. To escape this particular representational dilemma, in whatever medium, Durham turns to a whole other kind of index, not the analog photograph but the object itself, and stages this object's refusal to perish into art via the potential of its indexical signification. Unlike those settler photographs of Indians, which appropriate a settler representational medium for the mandates of contemporary indigenous art, Durham's indices offer themselves as recalcitrant indigenous signs that can but do not have to circulate via settler technologies of meaning. In photography, the index as a concept refers to the specific nature of the photographic process; that is, to the fact that the image is a record of a particular play of light and shadow created by the object photographed. Thus, it testifies to the object's factual realness at the moment of the photographic event. But, the photographic event is itself a process of mediation, of transforming real, three-dimensional objects, people, or landscapes into their two-dimensional equivalents, which are then available to circulate as photographic icons. Durham's use of found objects as indices bypasses that moment of mediated transformation. Certainly, the artist routinely changes these objects by painting or embedding them with stones or gems. Certainly, even unchanged, they could be taken up and deployed for a variety of means. But the very materiality of the object does not disappear through these transformations, it is never superseded by its equivalent; the object never cedes the space to an image. The turtle shell at the center of *Red Turtle* remains the same turtle shell it has been for years, decades, or centuries. The coyote's skull is fundamentally the same bone now, however changed by exposure to the elements, as it was when it was animated by an animal's body. In this sense, though it might undergo transformations, the index is not mediated out of its fundamental materiality. It simply *is*; it persists. Like his photographer counterparts, Durham capitalizes on the advantages of palimpsestic representation to recover indigenous historical experience. Many of his pieces deploy motifs of memorialization and reemergence from historically imposed obscurity. But his specific use of found objects as indices of indigeneity adds an important dimension of signification via their independence of interpretive codes and their materiality, which points to a stubborn residual materiality of indigenous presence in the Americas. If archival settler photos of American Indians serve in contemporary digital fine art to illustrate the extent of the disruption of indigenous life under colonialism, Durham's indices of indigeneity recompose the shattered tradition into a continuous, incontrovertible material presence.

This insistence on materiality made possible by indexical representation turns Durham's artworks into alternatives to the pervasive American discourse of Indian spectrality, from the historic precedent of the vanishing Indian to a variety of Indian ghosts populating contemporary American culture. In *The National Uncanny*, Renée Bergland has argued that the rhetoric of Indian ghostliness has become "a triumphalist American aesthetic that repeatedly transforms horror into glory, national dishonor into national pride" (22), all the while obscuring the reality of Indian survival (3). And she points out that when American Indian writers themselves turn to that trope, they gain in rhetorical power and authority, but at the price of foregoing Indian political presence in the contemporary context (3). I would add to Bergland's assessment that ghosts and haunting have become such popular American tropes because they substitute ethical reckoning for political engagement with indigeneity. Ghosts inspire the colonizers' desire to settle with their own conscience by offering belated representational respect to historic Indian people and places through landmark naming, dedications, and commemorations. They do not press the need to consider contemporary indigenous peoples; to the contrary, they obscure their existence all over again. In this context, Durham's bones, skulls, stones, turtle shells, and other indices of indigeneity circulating through his artworks become primary tools in the project of dissipating Indian ghostliness so that an engagement with contemporary, living indigenous peoples can take place instead.

La Malinche (original 1988–91, included in a 1993 *Original Re-Runs* installation at ICA in London; fig. 4.7) and the 1988 *Pocahontas and the Little Carpenter in London* installation at Matt's Gallery in London (fig. 4.8) offer two particularly poignant illustrations of the use of indexical representation to trouble the discourse of Indian spectrality. Both works feature composite figures of these indigenous women, their bodies constructed of cotton, snakeskin, turquoise, feathers, beads, driftwood, and wood machined into lumber. The figures share the same head, sculpted out of wood and adorned with turquoise, snakeskin, and paint, La Malinche's head recycled to become Pocahontas's or vice versa. Durham's renditions of these historical figures and symbolic mothers of two different American nations highlight simultaneously their syncretic nature and the stubborn material persistence of indigeneity on the American continent. In Durham's pieces, Pocahontas and La Malinche clearly are settler phantasms of the indigenous woman's sexual and ideological openness to European penetration. *La Malinche's* figure, barely clothed in white canvas and a golden brassiere hanging loosely from her wooden shoulders, appears to parade her tattered historical reputation as both the ur-mother and *la chingada*, the whore of Mexico.[22] Pocahontas's body in *Pocahontas and the Little Carpenter in London,* in turn, is reduced to her head, a sculpted image evoking the numerous paintings of the supposed Powhatan's daughter, John Smith's lover, John Rolfe's wife, and the first mother of Virginia's settler aristocracy. A wooden chair partially covered by a large swath of dark fabric, drapery-like sliding down to the floor and pooling there like blood, stands in for her body, a kind of placeholder for the many identities imputed to her by her contemporaries and later historians alike. But what arrest the viewer's attention in these pieces are the indices in the form of the stone eye fixed on the spectator, the cheek fashioned out of snake skin, the lace-clad gnarled driftwood hands folded in La Malinche's lap and her feet resting on the gallery floor, one petrified nearly beyond recognition. If Pocahontas and La Malinche are to be the emblems of America, then the European conception of American land as a virginal seductress is replaced in Durham's works with America as a graveyard rendering up arrowheads, pottery, and most importantly bones, all indexically testifying not only to the prior indigenous occupation of the land but also to the stubborn persistence of indigenous life, changed but enduring, throughout the long colonial period. Pocahontas's and La Malinche's eyes emerging out of the rubble of history and of their own bodies are trained on the contemporary viewer and demand the acknowledgment of indigenous presence and agency. Durham's indices return material presence to Indian ghosts, insisting on crowding out the immaterial ways of representing indigeneity. At the same time, the artist's aesthetic of provisionality, one that combines bones and stones with objects of settler modernity, such as machined lumber, paint, and PVC piping, makes clear that "the Indian" continues to be a composite figure, a juncture of historical reality and the myriad discourses invented to account for it.

And yet, because it puts such a premium on the object itself, indexical representation as practiced by Durham has its dangers, especially given the long tradition and the legacy of the reductionist perception of indigenous culture as material culture in ethnography (recall Durham's plea to ethnographers to pay attention to Indians' governance systems rather than to their

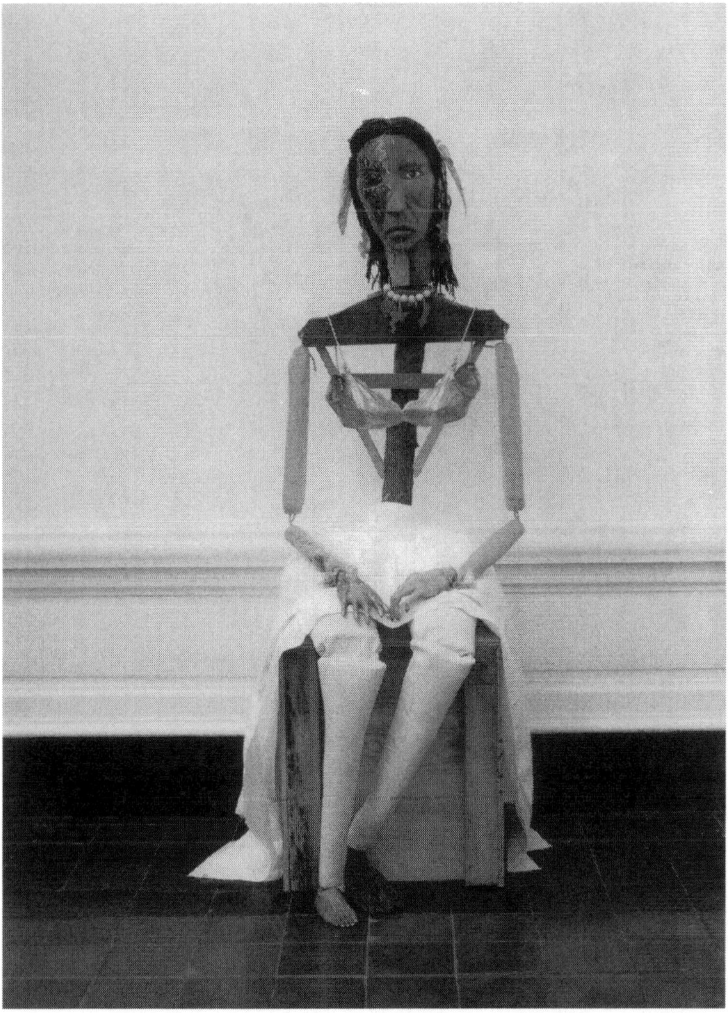

Fig. 4.7. *La Malinche*, Jimmie Durham, 1988–91.

well-made arrowheads) and of the aestheticization of indigenous material culture as art in gallery exhibition. Art focused so centrally around an object may fall prey to existing institutional ways of framing it; Durham's early beautifully crafted pieces, such as the bone and skull sculptures ranging from *Badger* (1971) and *Armadillo* (1976) to several untitled works collected in the 1982 *Manhattan Festival of the Dead* installation, quickly found their way onto the coffee tables and into the display cases of those enthralled by the sheer beauty of authentic American Indian art. Faced with this com-

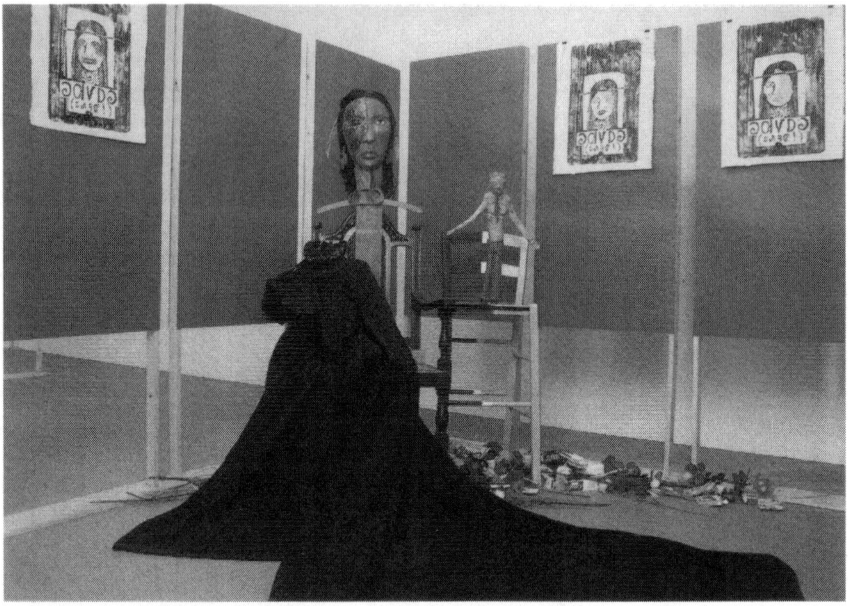

Fig. 4.8. *Pocahontas and the Little Carpenter in London*, Jimmie Durham, 1988. Installation: Matt's Gallery, London.

mercial success, Durham worried that his art at the time contributed to the stereotypical perception of an indigenous aesthetic, and ultimately to the commodification of indigenous suffering on the multiculturalist art market.

Durham's response to this dilemma comes in several forms. In his fake artifacts, the artist turns to the minimalist, provisional collage aesthetic to forestall the perception of his pieces as ethnographic evidence. The messy, half-finished quality of his later composite works, along with their insistent dialogism, denies spectators the experience of Indian art as a beautiful object for detached aesthetic contemplation or as a wellspring of Indian cultural authenticity. While not wanting to communicate anything to the viewer as an *Indian* or as an *Indian artist*, Durham nevertheless continues to create individual pieces and complex installations that function as invitations to engagement that he extends to viewers, who in the process of often inadvertently pursuing Indian authenticity find themselves compelled to examine their own selves ethnographically. These strategies of provisional composition and dialogic engagement foisted upon spectators supply creative responses to earlier settler conceptions of Indian aesthetics, which stressed supposedly inherently authentic traditional Indian patterns and motifs along with the flat, two-dimensional perspective. By contrast, Durham's pieces expand into space, transforming galleries into places that have to be negotiated like obstacle courses, where visitors are prompted to do often uncomfortable interpretive work that involves moving their own bodies through space, submitting to transformation in response to strategically chosen and placed objects. His situational art showcases objects that have had prior lives outside of the artist's studio, found objects that circulate endlessly, this process of recycling emphasizing their inherent *and* changing meanings. While indexing indigeneity, Durham's stones and bones, turtle shells and snakeskin, pieces of driftwood and turquoise function not as emblems of essential authenticity but rather as repositories of historical meaning; their very qualities of incompleteness and damage mark them as chronicles of historic transformations.

Indexical referencing combines in Durham's artistic practice with the parodic reproductions of settler symbols of indigeneity in order to recuperate indigenous representation from the symbolic to the indexical as a testimony to the incontrovertible indigenous continuity on the continent. Actual bones, shells, driftwood, and stone, rather than their replicas created in the artist's studio, tie indigeneity back to the ground from which they come. Durham's art, thus, is best understood not as clever musings on the artist's relationship to his materials in the postmodern metacritical vein but rather as a politically relevant statement about indigenous tenure on the continent. Durham's art reaches beyond an intervention that simply dismisses settler discourses of indigeneity by redirecting the audience's gaze from the exoticized indigenous object to the desiring audience—spectator and reader alike—and its interpretive practices. Via its reliance on indices of indigeneity, which function as insubordinate or recalcitrant signs, it supplies a form of indigenous discourse that is "always *possibly* effective" in counteracting multicultural misrecognition by proposing new narratives of indigenous political histories and contemporary realities.

5
Fictions of the Gruesome Authentic in LeAnne Howe's *Shell Shaker*

LeAnne Howe's novel *Shell Shaker* (2001) opens with an idyllic image of an ancient Choctaw village, where food is plentiful and life is "like a party," "a series of games and dances." We learn that "every day, the men sang with a drum in the square grounds while the women tended their children and drank from gourds filled with sweet peach juice" and that the villagers dancing together at night were beautiful: "Their skin was smooth, and their teeth were white and straight" (1).[1] A few pages later, however, this paradisiacal vision of abundance, leisure, health, beauty, and harmony is replaced by a scene of ritual execution in which a woman's head is smashed with a wooden club. Far from avoiding the brutality of the killing, Howe narrates the event as attentively and vividly as possible, in the voice of the executed woman herself: "I feel an icy hot explosion in my head. Deafening. Blood gurgles from my mouth. My hands spring to my head involuntarily, blood is seeping out of my head and flecks of bone are strewn through my hair. My arms jerk wildly, like a wounded bird trying to fly away, as the old man hits me again. . . . I feel my body twitch, perhaps someone turns me over. I can no longer see, my head is unraveling" (16). Howe makes sure we are repulsed by the scene's gruesomeness, emphasizing the anatomical detail of a body in extreme trauma: the flecks of bone, the seeping, gurgling blood, and the twitching flesh all do their rhetorical work well here, particularly in contrast to the idyllic scenes from the village square grounds, scenes that focused on the perfection and beauty of similar bodies. Aware that we might pass over the scene too quickly, inured as we are to the spectacles of bodies undergoing violent harm that pervade contemporary popular culture, Howe stops us in our readerly tracks. We do not merely witness the execution; third-person narration would serve that purpose perfectly well. Instead we suffer through it vicariously as we mouth the dying woman's words and for a moment inhabit her consciousness.

The first-person narrative increases not only the visceral quality of the scene but also our regret at the woman's violent death. In the course of the first chapter, we are invited to admire this woman, who has been narrating the story from the beginning. Her opening instruction to us—"*Ano ma Chahta sia hoke oke*. Call me Shakbatina, a Shell Shaker" (1)—may momentarily disorient those readers who do not speak Choctaw. Like the elder woman storyteller who declares in the voiceover during the initial shots of Isuma's *Atanarjuat* that she can tell her story only to those who already understand it,[2] Shakbatina first alienates her readers by asserting her linguistic difference.[3] Immediately after that, however, unlike Isuma's film, which subjects non-Inuktitut speaking viewers to a prolonged period of disorientation, Shakbatina, and Howe, put us at ease by offering some easily recognized Americana: they extend a metaphorical helping hand by evoking the famous opening line of Herman Melville's *Moby Dick*. And yet, clearly drawn distinctions once again follow after this acknowledgment of cultural commonality. Unlike Ishmael, whose assertions of individuality generously pepper the opening of *Moby Dick*, Shakbatina dwells in collective history. She emphasizes her precise placement in a network of social relations: as a Shell Shaker she is "an *Inholahta* woman, born into the tradition of our grandmother, the first Shell Shaker of our people" (1). As she explains that Shell Shakers "are the peacemakers for the Choctaws," Shakbatina's individuality folds into the collectivity of her clan. Instead of Melville's suicidal individualist, who substitutes a ship deck "for pistol and ball" (1), Howe offers a narrator with a high degree of awareness of her embeddedness in history and a specific, politically inflected, kinship genealogy.[4]

We—and I have been using this collective pronoun advisedly to emphasize the readerly experience presumed in the novel and to draw you, my reader, into its interpretive complexities—have trusted Shakbatina as our native informant; she has introduced us to the world of preconquest North America and reported on its violent unraveling following the arrival of Europeans. She has been a persuasive chronicler and a lyrical storyteller. We are invited to regret her death and see it as unnecessarily brutal: by 1738, when the execution scene takes place, the Choctaw had already acquired guns, which would assure a cleaner and more expedient death. We likely see it as unjust: Shakbatina committed no crime; in fact, she attempts to save a daughter falsely accused of murder and to temporarily forestall a war between two tribes. Recalling the scenes of human sacrifice readily available in

European discourse on the New World from the first encounters on, we may zero in on the wooden club, the gurgling blood, the flecks of bone. Transfixed by this gruesome and therefore seemingly accurate description of the ritual—an example of a rhetorical strategy I will call the *gruesome authentic*—we may have also conveniently forgotten that the scene takes place in the mid-eighteenth century, amid intertribal conflicts precipitated by engagement with the French and the English. So we tend to see Shakbatina's unjust death as an anachronistic remnant of a primitive ritual, a fitting reminder of the savage ways of precontact America.[5] In other words, we may resort, or fall victim, to what Roy Harvey Pearce calls *savagism* and defines as a discursive "solution to a major human problem" (xviii) in the Americas: the European encounter with indigenous difference.[6] And this is, precisely, where Howe wants us: teetering on the borderline between sympathy inculcated by contemporary multiculturalism and revulsion inherited from earlier discursive formations, uncertain whether we are able to extend recognition and respect to the historic Choctaws in the face of their apparently repugnant alterity.[7]

Like all contemporary American Indian artists, Howe has inherited the predicament of multicultural misrecognition, a contemporary rhetorical circumstance shaped by a long history of Europeans playing Indian, which articulated American identities as radically different from their Old World counterparts, and by the legacy of salvage ethnography, which welded Indian authenticity to its precontact versions.[8] In tandem, these performative and discursive traditions led to the equation of indigeneity with a necessarily doomed form of (first racial, later cultural) difference ever irrevocably in retreat before encroaching European modernity. As a result, any representations of indigenous difference must navigate between the proverbial Scylla and Charybdis of appropriation and exoticization, between what Chadwick Allen called *saming* and *unsaming* arguments structuring most of the past and contemporary approaches to the study and representation of indigenous societies. As Allen explains, "saming arguments approach American Indian topics as though they are similar to 'other' national, multicultural, ethnic or postcolonial topics and, thus, as though they are amenable to the same critical methods. Unsaming arguments, in marked contrast, approach American Indian topics as though they are in some significant way distinctive—perhaps even radically distinctive—from other national, multicultural, ethnic, and postcolonial topics, thus, that they require distinctive methodologies, critical interventions or theories" ("Indigeneity Inside and Outside the Metropolitan Conversation" 110). Allen's model extends readily from the realm of scholarly methodology to that of literary, and more broadly cultural, representation. If mainstream historians or literary critics are reluctant to articulate any kind of difference when describing precontact societies out of fear of appearing to exoticize indigenous peoples and thus confine them to the past, American Indian writers also confront this dilemma. Thus we encounter accounts of precontact societies that make them look just like contemporary democratic capitalist societies: dynamic, open, and culturally pragmatic—always already multicultural—engaging in continental trade in material and intellectual goods in some kind of precursor to the North American Free Trade Agreement.[9] We can see Howe deploying that very option through the depictions of historic Choctaws in the novel's opening chapters as a dynamic society open to multiple networks of economic and political alliances. But whenever, either in artistic representation or academic argument, we translate indigenous difference into the parallel forms of the social present or consign it to the past as irremediably savage, we forfeit the chance to apprehend it as a viable contemporary alternative to settler forms of sociality. In other words, we exclude it from the intellectual public commons as anything but an auxiliary to the articulations of the Western, the modern, the contemporary.

This limited representational horizon has shrunk further under the rhetorical strictures of postcolonial criticism and then multiculturalism because, as Robert Young explains, "since Sartre, Fanon and Memmi, postcolonial criticism has constructed the antithetical groups, the colonizer and the colonized, self and Other, with the second only knowable through a necessarily false representation, a Manichean division that threatens to reproduce the static, essentialist categories it seeks to undo. In the same way, the doctrine of multiculturalism encourages different groups to reify their individual and different identities at their most different" (5). The latter of Young's indictments in particular comes as a surprise. After all, as I described in the introduction, multiculturalism first emerged as a panacea to a long history of representational erasure or misprision of difference. It promised a kind of representational liberation to all of America's putative historical and contemporary others, one depending precisely on a far-ranging appreciation of difference as crucially constitutive of the American past and present. To be sure, the minority artists and writers have taken full advantage of the hard-won opportunities that multiculturalism presented, first as a fighting creed and later as a state-sponsored cultural program. Arguments on behalf of a politics of recognition, the ideological heart of North American multiculturalism, gave rise to the concept of cultural citizenship and led to a vastly increased cultural, and occasionally political, representation of minority subjects in North American democracies.

Still, early on it became clear that the conception of difference informing the politics of recognition presented the dangers of reification and essentialism—a transformation of history into identity, understood as a set of a priori understandings about who we are,[10] and ironically a contemporary version of the ahistoricism typically imputed to indigenous thought. Since articulation of cultural—rather than political, social, or economic—difference is the only way to emerge as subjects within a national imaginary governed by multicultural misrecognition, Howe, along with other contemporary indigenous artists, confronts a specific dilemma: How does one represent historic and contemporary indigenous difference in a rhetorical situation in which emphasizing difference and minimizing it are equally bad solutions? How can one depict the concrete historical specificity of indigenous societies, past and present, in a way that does not imply their fundamental similarity to mainstream cultural formations or, by contrast, foreground their unredeemable difference, an alterity that excludes them from the realm of modernity? In other words, how is it possible to avoid the presentism of saming approaches to the representation of indigeneity without feeding the multiculturalist appetite for performances of merely cultural difference, performances that ultimately sustain the self-assertion of contemporary liberal states and obscure indigenous nations' demands for political sovereignty?

As I argued in preceding chapters, this predicament of multicultural misrecognition has elicited innovative strategies of resistance from indigenous artists in Canada and the United States. A great deal of contemporary indigenous artistic and critical energy focuses on decolonizing the mind by seizing creative control over representations of indigeneity in literature, film, plastic art, and criticism. As Linda Tuhiwai Smith, an aboriginal scholar from Australia, declares, "indigenous peoples want to tell our own stories, write our own versions, in our own ways, for our own purposes" (28). Many of these stories, in whatever genre, chronicle tribally specific political and intellectual traditions in an effort to preempt multicultural interest in indigenous cultures with an insistence on indigenous nations' historic claims to nationhood and sovereignty. The community galleries curated by tribal curator teams at the National Museum of the American Indian, which I discuss in detail in chapter 1, provide the best example of this particular approach. Other stories offer trenchant analyses of the changing rhetorical ground on which indigenous peoples, be they artists or political activists or both, articulate their accounts of historic and contemporary realities. Howe adds to this latter effort in her attempt to radically transform this rhetorical ground by retraining those contemporary readers who are willing to examine and potentially suspend their multiculturalist reading practice. In this sense, her work supplies the literary equivalent of Jimmie Durham's efforts to turn indigenous art into an ethnography of settler culture's desire for Indian difference and a statement about indigenous claims to political histories and contemporary realities. Howe's approach differs from Durham's in that rather than exposing settler desire for indigenous difference, she capitalizes on it by engaging the reader in a series of rhetorical moves that invariably lead to ever more confounding interpretive impasses, leaving the reader entangled in her own critical acumen. As I describe below, some of her rhetorical moves, such as a palimpsestic layering of different historical planes or the deployment of indigenous languages, recall those of the artists discussed in previous chapters. Her unique contribution consists in her exploitation of both the long tradition of savagism in settler thinking about indigeneity and our contemporary desire, inspired by multiculturalism, to leave such conceptual frameworks behind. The gruesome authentic, first deployed in the opening chapter's execution scene, serves to heighten the precarious interpretive stance the settler public tends to assume in its encounters with contemporary representations of indigeneity.

To explain how Howe's gruesome authentic functions to disrupt the mechanisms of multicultural misrecognition—that is, how it guards against multiculturalist appropriation of Choctaw historic political distinctiveness as a mere cultural difference—we need to backtrack to the novel's beginning. The opening chapter of *Shell Shaker*, significantly, goes to great lengths to counteract misperceptions regarding the purported savagery of the early Choctaw, even as it invites them in its unflinching description of Shakbatina's death. Howe insists that the execution is the final act of a long process sanctioned by tradition (hence the wooden club rather than the gun). It is a process of intricate and persistent negotiation between the two nations engaged in a dispute, one involving highly ritualized strategies of persuasion and sustained patience to secure unanimous consent: Shakbatina "must keep talking until all the *Inholahta* people agree to support [her] decision" (5). Shakbatina herself initiates and insists upon the act, seeing her sacrifice as a way of bringing (at least temporary) peace to the two warring tribes. There is nothing impulsive, spurious, or forcefully imposed about the event (unless, of course, we acknowledge that culture itself is nothing but an imposition). In fact, the entire process that precedes Shakbatina's chosen death is fundamentally no different from democratic social and legal mechanisms firmly in place today.

To prepare us for this particular insight about the execution—its political reconciliatory function—Howe has already offered, early in the chapter, a different scene of brutality, one perpetrated by the Spanish invading Choctaw lands in the sixteenth century under the command of Hernando de Soto: "The whole town was burned. Unspeakable acts were then committed by *Hispano Osano*. They fell into a barbaric blood lust and cut off the heads and hands of the stickball players, and the Mabilians. Later, the *Hispanos* displayed them wherever they went as souvenirs of their courage" (3).[11] In this account Howe reverses the settler culture's favorite equation, which aligns savagery with the indigenous inhabitants of the Americas and civilization with the arriving Europeans. However, lest we become facile with such reversals, Howe is careful not to draw the lines of distinction too categorically. Just a couple of pages after the scene of the Spanish collective rage, *Shell Shaker* offers another account of beheading. In this scene, a younger Shakbatina watches a Choctaw warrior perform a ceremony following his victory over an enemy: "Ilapintabi, Kills It Himself, jammed the head of his victim onto a post, then thrust his sharp blade into the soft flesh of the neck, fastening it to the wood. Then he painted his own face red. Tied hawk feathers in his hair. Danced and sang in a defiant gravel voice" (6–7). The differences between the two scenes at first appear obvious: in place of a crazed bloodthirsty horde sowing indiscriminate, gratuitous death and destruction, we witness a solitary warrior who, through his enemy's dead body, confronts the enemy's spirit. Shakbatina's account of Ilapintabi's ceremony makes clear that it is a reenactment of the kind of violence visited on the Choctaw warriors by the English. She watches because, as she says, "even though I was young, I had known warriors who'd been dragged off by marauding bands of *Inkilish okla*. I wanted to see what would happen to me if I were captured by our enemy" (6). Her witnessing has the effect she desired: "Ilapintabi's cries washed over me like a soothing rain. . . . After his song I was cleansed of fear" (7). Ilapintabi's ceremony has a double function: it serves to process a violent event (the warrior lapses into a prolonged trance afterward) and it models courage for others while purifying them of fear. However, both scenes are governed by the same fundamental logic—the emphatically ideological function of public displays of violence—and by the same reliance on the aesthetic of gruesomeness to evoke a visceral response in readers. By pointing out similarities as well as differences between these separate scenes of violence—de Soto's raid, Ilapintabi's ceremony, and Shakbatina's execution—Howe asks us to consider the context in which violence unfolds. In the raid scene, brutality is spurious rather than considered, useless rather than constructive, deployed and experienced en masse rather than singly and deliberately. It is portrayed as a temporary lapse, literally a fall from civilization into unrestrained rage, into barbarism.

By contrast, far from being an emblem of savagery, Shakbatina's execution is part and parcel of a highly organized society. If the gruesomeness of the execution allows readers to indulge in interpretive strategies governed by the logic of Allen's unsaming approaches to the understanding of indigenous societies, the sociopolitical background Howe provides to contextualize the same execution invites the opposite reaction: the appropriation of the saming approach and a resulting recognition of the historic Choctaw as a highly organized, deliberative, and democratic society. Howe invites her readers to dwell on the choice between these two interpretive approaches. And with each subsequent rhetorical move she multiples such impasses and raises the stakes of our choice.

As if all of this ethnographic and historical context were not enough to ease the blow of the execution scene, Howe concludes the chapter with a brief lesson in Choctaw spiritual belief. Shakbatina speaks in the wake of her death from a different temporal and spatial realm, where she can observe relatives left behind but where she is freed from the limitations of materiality: "I feel myself growing younger in this place. . . . An unknown language floats around me. Each word is an Old Code that I must decipher. Suddenly there are streaks of white and the delicious scent of tobacco fills the air as the spirit of an animal appears. Big Mother Porcupine walks into view and takes me by the hand. I open my mouth to speak but my thoughts escape into the wind" (16). Shakbatina's death is her release into freedom—though one fraught with ongoing responsibilities not only to decipher the language and to speak but also to grieve over her people—and it creates the conditions for the novel's fundamental structural conceit, one calculated to translate the Choctaw cosmology into a formally specifiable aesthetic form. After her death in 1738, Shakbatina is free to travel across time; she can reappear, over two centuries later in 1991, in the Choctaw tribal government offices in Old Durant, Oklahoma, to pull the trigger of the gun that kills the nation's chief, Redford McAlester. She can also return to narrate this event in the novel's final chapter, invalidating all the conclusions readers might have reached about the McAlester's murder.

To represent this specific cosmology, Howe designed *Shell Shaker* to unfold through two separate plotlines situated in two geographically and historically separate spaces and times: mid-eighteenth-century Mississippi and several contemporary locations: Old Durant, Oklahoma; New Orleans, Louisiana; New York City; and London. Each historical plane is inhabited by a separate set of protagonists. However, early on in the novel, it becomes clear that the contemporary Choctaws are either reincarnations-with-a-difference of their historic predecessors or living out the same historical processes, the same political entanglements, that their ancestors did, with the additional charge of bringing satisfactory conclusions where their predecessors failed to do so. In *Shell Shaker*, people move through time and space—from the eighteenth century to the twentieth and back—but they always inhabit bodies that are historically and geographically specific; no Connecticut Yankee in King Arthur's Court here. In their insistence on historicity, which counteracts the common perception that traditional indigenous societies operate outside of time, that they are ahistorical, Howe's multiple time frames recall Pamela Shields's digital palimpsests. However, while Shields turns to the photographic archive to reinsert indigenous histories into flat images of Indian cultural difference, Howe is intent on bending Western narrative conventions to fit Choctaw cosmology. We are familiar with the readily available antitheses of the mythical, astronomic, or cyclical understanding of time characteristic of premodern cultures and the modern understanding of time as linear, as unfolding in history. From its first paragraph, *Shell Shaker* stakes a claim to both modes of locating events in time. Before the narrative begins, Howe specifies: "Yanàbi Town. Eastern District of the Choctaws. September 22, 1738. Autumnal Equinox" (1). Here and on numerous occasions throughout the novel, she anchors events in both astronomic time and the Gregorian calendar brought to the Americas by Europeans. She thus suggests that indigenous consciousness is not oblivious to historicity but operates in time differently: according to Western conceptions of the historical and across them, within their strictures and through them, but not outside of them at all.

Some of these apparently impossible travels across time can be explained as dream sequences, as when the twentieth-century protagonists lose consciousness in 1992 and find themselves in the bodies of their eighteenth-century ancestors and living their lives. Others, such as Shakbatina's presence at the chief's killing or her husband's appearance in the form of a panther in his daughter's hotel room, cannot be explained within the rationalist logic of the European West. Rather, they serve to substantiate the idea of bodies moving in Choctaw space, the space that is time then and now, a logic that Howe's novel emphatically embraces in its conclusion.[12] In this context, Shakbatina's closing description of the chief's execution as the moment when "past and present collide" (222) does not merely reveal the identities of the killers; it asserts a specific Choctaw cosmology, especially its conception of time, place, and subjectivity. *Shell Shaker*'s particular narrative structure becomes a formal figuration of a system of belief and a crucial component of Howe's ultimate novelistic goal and challenge: to represent a contemporary traditional tribal society as an extension of historic

Choctaws, and their surviving system of belief as a foundation for a viable political, and not just merely cultural, alternative to the contemporary liberal settler state.

To prompt our careful consideration of these two different forms of philosophical belief and political organization organizing the Choctaw Nation, on the one hand, and the settler society, on the other, Howe resorts to a familiar generic convention: a murder and detection plot featuring a contest between two different conceptions of justice, the retributive justice governing the settler society's judicial and penal systems and the traditional Choctaw ethics of restoration. Legal, scholarly, and popular disputes over tribal justice and jurisdiction have taken place in the United States since the inception of the state. They reached a weighty culmination late in the nineteenth century when the famous Crow Dog trial allowed the federal government to curtail tribal jurisdiction and impose settler judicial systems on tribal societies through the Seven Major Crimes Act.[13] To this day, justice systems in indigenous national territories are thoroughly syncretic, combining administrative forms of local tribal and federal legal oversight and often offering conflicting consequences for crimes.[14] From its opening pages, Howe's *Shell Shaker* asserts the viability of the indigenous notion of justice as a restoration of balance. This understanding of justice has been passed down among Choctaws through generations of women, the shell shakers of the novel's title, whose primary social function as peacemakers is to "make things even" (2). Lest, tempted by etymological confluence, we too easily equate tribalism and retribution, it merits pointing out that the notion of justice characteristic of many of the America's indigenous societies differs significantly from Western identificatory retributive justice. "Making things even" does not mean seeking retribution for specific trespasses by meting out punishment to identified perpetrators, but rather restoring the original balance in the material and spiritual universe typically presumed by indigenous cosmologies.[15]

Howe contrasts these two conceptions of justice, along with the legal practices they inform, in two parallel but intricately interlocking plot lines. She tells the story of the assassination of the eighteenth-century Choctaw warrior and leader Red Shoes, and of the killing of the contemporary Choctaw Nation of Oklahoma's chief, Redford McAlester. Both murder plots are embedded in detailed accounts of the political and economic conditions of their times. Howe's mid-eighteenth-century Mississippi is rife with conflicts between the French and the English, who solicit allegiances from the numerous Indian nations inhabiting the region—the Choctaw, the Chickasaw, and the Alabama Conchaty central among them—thereby irrevocably changing intertribal relations throughout the region. It is a world pervaded by often random, unmitigated, and always graphically rendered violence, a world in which indigenous peoples struggle to maintain their traditional societies and their sense of ethics while also changing in response to the European presence on the continent. The Choctaw in the 1990s are no less caught up in the exchanges with American settler society than were their historical predecessors. Debates over the proper forms of tribal governance, over the effects of gambling operations, and over economic development on tribal lands more broadly all provide a subtext to the plot's central dramatic development: McAlester's murder.

Like the classics of the genre, Howe's novel uses the enigma of the crime to cognitively map out historical and contemporary realities in their political, economic, and social totality. But unlike the genre's typical big reveal at the end, *Shell Shaker* relies on two contradictory conclusions to bring the detection plot to its culmination. The novel first offers an extended court scene during which the main suspect in McAlester's murder is exonerated. Based on testimony by an elder who is the tribal government's telephone switchboard operator and on the material evidence she provides in the form of taped conversations, the chief's killer is identified and the circumstances of the chief's death described in detail sufficient to satisfy the demand for a rational cause-and-effect explanation of the mystery. The arrest warrant for the killer is promptly issued and Auda Billy, McAlester's lover and assistant, who was found unconscious at the murder scene, smoking gun by her hand, walks free. As far as the court is concerned, the investigation is concluded and the expectation of justice met.

And yet the novel does not end there. The final chapter, titled "The Shell Shaker," offers another explanation of McAlester's murder, one that explicitly contradicts the court's conclusions and implicates Auda all over again. We learn that Auda did, indeed, point the gun at McAlester that fateful afternoon, but she was aided by the spirit of her ancestor, named Shakbatina, who helped squeeze the trigger. We learn all of this from Shakbatina herself as she speaks in a first-person directly to us in the novel's conclusion:

> Now I must tell you what really happened. Since I had acquired the knowledge of splitting myself in two, I must be the one to tell the story of *Itilauichi*, who came back to Choctaw Country when day and night were in perfect balance, and Indians had all the luck.
>
> My story is an enormous undertaking. Hundreds of years in the making until past and present collide into a single moment. Auda did hold the gun in her hands, gently, as if it were inlaid with jewels. It

> was then that I slipped my hands in front of her hands, and together we struck the pose. The day was hers, all hers, but it was my day, too.
>
> *Nuklibishakachi*, my breath is warm with passion; we Choctaws are *hatak okla hut okchaya bilia hoh illi bilia.* Life everlasting.
>
> *Hekano,* I am finished talking. (222)

By claiming that she collaborated with Auda in killing McAlester, Shakbatina exposes the court-sanctioned version of events as a ruse devised by the defense team in order to circumvent one kind of justice and make another kind possible. Unlike the court decision, which left Auda not guilty but disempowered, Shakbatina's confession both implicates and exculpates Auda, without depriving her of agency. By killing McAlester, Auda acts as a responsible clan mother, one more in a long tradition of Billy peacemakers, most notably including Anoleta and Haya, who assassinated a corrupt Choctaw leader, Red Shoes, in 1747. She removes a compromised tribal chief from power, a task traditionally undertaken by clan mothers in matrilineal indigenous societies. What's harder to accept is that Shakbatina, too, pulled the trigger. Shakbatina's account makes sense within traditional Choctaw cosmology, but just as the Choctaw language passages in the text are not accessible to most readers, neither is that system of belief. Shakbatina's explanation is viable only if readers share Choctaw cosmology. If they do not, if they instead subscribe to Western rationalism to make sense of the world, then it is no explanation at all. In fact, it can come across as a joke, a taunt directed at readers: *I will tell you what happened. See if you can believe it. Shell Shaker* tells us exactly "what really happened." It is this *really*, though, that becomes the problem, the unsolved enigma of Howe's novel. Thus Howe presents us with yet another interpretive impasse: How do we, and can we, determine what *really* happened, in the presence of multiple and contradictory explanations?

Instead of an ongoing enigma regarding the identity of the murderer, as is the case, for example, in Sherman Alexie's 1996 novel, *Indian Killer*, in *Shell Shaker* we have an abundance of interpretive options, each presenting a different solution to the murder plot.[16] If we choose Shakbatina's version, then we acknowledge that the sequence of events accepted by the court is false. If we stick to the court version, then we explicitly dismiss Shakbatina's account. There is a third possibility, too: we grant that Auda committed the murder but believe that she did it herself, without any unearthly intervention. In other words, we maintain our allegiance to Western rationalism. Or, as another option still, we decide that all the accounts are true. In this last instance, we suspend our disbelief and, like all good contemporary American multiculturalists feel compelled to do, recognize the existence of different belief systems. Both Western rationalism and Choctaw cosmology are valid; they can cohabit the multiculturalist universe. The novel, however, does not take this relativist position at all. It aligns itself with Shakbatina by giving her the last word. After she is "finished talking," no one else gets to speak. Yet importantly, if the novel sides easily with traditional Choctaws, Howe makes it difficult for the majority of readers to follow. *Shell Shaker*'s conclusion precipitates a specific interpretive problem: how to solve detection plots when radically different, if not contradictory, systems of belief are available. Each solution to the central detection plot requires allegiance to a separate system of belief. Selecting one excludes the other. This dilemma exemplifies a specific impasse of contemporary multicultural exchanges of recognition: the difficult question of how to negotiate the different cosmologies coming into contact in such exchanges.

Howe's novel takes up several times the issue of translation between radically different cosmologies that have come face-to-face in America. The wider American public is typically familiar with the problem from only one perspective. We have been taught about the long tradition of Europeans coming to terms with America's distinctive societies—all those travelers, missionaries, and anthropologists describing the indigenous societies they encounter in the New World, transcribing and translating their languages, interpreting their customs and beliefs. A tentative list of such endeavors could begin with the letters of Christopher Columbus, the chronicles of Bartolomé de las Casas, narratives by Garcilaso de la Vega and Álvar Núñez Cabeza de Vaca, John Smith's reports to King George and Roger Williams's linguistic work, George Catlin's paintings, and Edward Curtis's photographs, and continue all the way to twentieth-century anthropologists fanning out across American continents in an attempt to comprehend and represent for the rest of us the essence of the indigenes. *Shell Shaker* depicts some of these endeavors, often ironically, in the episodes concerning Jean Baptiste le Moyne Sieur de Bienville and the Jesuit father Renoir's history-writing. The latter, in particular, exposes European history-writing as a process motivated by attempts to resolve the conflict between the desire for the indigenous life (Renoir abandons the church and embarks on a life with a Choctaw woman, Nashoba, whom he loves) and the culturally ingrained imperative to offer a supposedly objective, but in reality politically motivated, record of historic events, one that will justify the European colonizing project in the Americas.

But more importantly, *Shell Shaker* gives us the opportunity to reverse this ethnographic dynamic in which Europeans are the observers and the indigenous the observed. Throughout the novel, Howe depicts the eighteenth-century Choctaw as they make sense of the European traders, settlers, and missionaries who intrude upon their world. For instance, we overhear two warriors condemning the English for trading with the Attakapa, a local tribe known to practice cannibalism, because they believe that trading has an ethical dimension beyond its pure economic utility. In another striking example, a young Choctaw woman, Anoleta, disputes eternity with a Jesuit priest. In a reversal of early European discourse on American cannibalism,[17] her rendition of the Eucharist ceremony reveals a thoroughly cannibalistic imagination at the heart of the Christian Mass, all the while opposing to it the Choctaw conception of life everlasting. In an example I mention above, we watch a group of traditionally minded contemporary Choctaw successfully subvert the workings of the BIA tribal court to substitute traditional Choctaw justice for the Western logic of retribution. As she depicts Choctaw historic and contemporary figures interpreting the world changing around them and actively engaging European modernity, Howe participates in what scholars have called the project of cultural decolonization.[18] At stake in this project is an attempt to represent Choctaw history and the present from an emphatically Choctaw point of view—in other words, to have Shakbatina speak and be understood by listeners/readers, both indigenous and settler, beyond the traditional Choctaws.

These extended ethnographic lessons in Choctaw cosmology and social and legal systems appeal to our multicultural acumen, allowing us to translate Choctaw otherness into familiar terms. However, the brutality of Shakbatina's execution interferes with this sympathetic identification with ancient Choctaw sociality. It is here that readers encounter the most demanding impasse of the novel. Howe's gruesome authentic, first deployed here, leaves us uncomfortably suspended between a facile recourse to the idea of savagism and the equally easy multiculturalist truism about the need to recognize and respect cultural difference—and searching for alternatives to these interpretive options. The execution scene thus functions as a preview of a specific narrative strategy that is repeated in the novel and that culminates most forcefully in the lengthy depiction of the Choctaw bone-picking ceremony, which Howe places at the center of the novel.[19] The passage describing the ceremony deserves to be quoted at length because it exemplifies how Howe combines disparate representational registers to evoke contradictory (and often visceral) responses from her readers, a strategy that is central to her larger effort to render Choctaw specificity without succumbing to the multiculturalist appetite for performance of cultural difference. Through a third-person narration, we witness a scene involving the most tenacious of settler society's taboos: necrophilia and the dismemberment of dead bodies. Koi Chitto, Shakbatina's husband, is compelled to perform a bone-picking ceremony earlier than is customary because of impending military conflict; Shakbatina's body has been laid out for only three, rather than the requisite six, months on a scaffold, exposed to weather and animals. Koi Chitto has been preparing himself for this ceremony for three days by fasting and inducing trance-like states:

> The drums grow louder.
>
> They seem in rhythm with Koi Chitto's heartbeat, and he drops the basket. At last, the roar of the forest, the constant drumming, and he begins to chant to the crowd gathered below the scaffold.
>
> "I am the Bone Picker, dancer of death, transformer of life, the one who brings sex, the one who brings rebirth. You must have death to have life. The people live by killing, by stripping the flesh from the animal corpse. The people live by dying. That which dies is reborn."
>
> A shrill moan comes from the belly of Koi Chitto. He dances faster, and rolls his eyes back in his head. He is again in the center of *na tohbi*. . . . He sees his wife dancing towards him, and he shouts. "Shakbatina is coming. She is here!"
>
> She looks like she did so many years ago. Her skin is vibrant brown and she is half-naked. Her calf-length hair glistens in the moonlight. She comes very close, puts her hands on his penis. He puts his hands around her hands and together they stroke him, until he ejaculates on her body and screams, "Flesh of my flesh, I will be with you always. Flesh of my flesh, I will return with you always. Until nothingness becomes everything. I am the Bone Picker, dancer of death, transformer of life, the one who brings sex, the one who brings rebirth."
>
> Shakbatina's spirit dances around the platform and Koi Chitto can hear her talking to him. "Dance with me, my husband, this is the dance of life and rebirth. This is my body. Pull away my remaining flesh. I charge you to get inside me. Release me now, so I may watch over our people. Dance the dance that releases me."
>
> She smiles and entreats him to touch her corpse and tear the remaining flesh from her bones. "*Hatak holitopa*, beloved man, release me and dance the dance of life and death. *Che pisa lauchi*. I will see you."
>
> Hearing her promise of return, Koi Chitto gathers his courage and tears Shakbatina's skull and spinal column from the rest of her bones. He holds them in both his hands high above his head and salutes the four directions. He believes when he finishes this spirit dance, and

> Shakbatina's bones are painted and placed in a box, he will not see her again for a long time. Until then he lets her fading scent engulf him. He closes his eyes. They are together, dancing the dance, both knowing that this is the ecstasy of life and rebirth. (106–7)

Like Shakbatina's execution, this scene follows an extended tour through a mid-eighteenth-century American landscape strewn with burning villages and charred bodies left in the wake of the encroaching English. As before, Howe inserts lengthy ethnographic passages explaining the meanings of the ritual about to unfold: "Koi Chitto believes, as all Choctaws believe, that the spirit is related to the body as perfume is to the rose" (105) or "They also pierced her stomach and bladder in order for the bloating gases to escape to the wind. This was to announce to the animal world that a woman of the people was coming" (105). This time, she also aestheticizes and eroticizes the ceremony: Shakbatina's "small jawbone and teeth lie surrendering to the sun, like gleaming pearls . . . [her] smell was erotic" (105) and borrows generously from the language of Catholic liturgy: "Flesh of my flesh. . . . This is my body" (107).

As in the case of Shakbatina's execution scene, what captures our attention are the details that historically settler society has rarely failed to associate with Indian savagery: the deafening rhythm of the drums, the trancelike state of the people performing the ceremony, Koi Chitto's fingernails, which have been cultivated into claws since his wife's death, and ultimately his act of masturbating and ejaculating on his wife's partly decayed body, just before he proceeds to tear her head from her spinal column and pick the remaining flesh from her bones—all related to us in unflinchingly meticulous detail. Howe abandons reliance on the ethnographic and the rational and engineers, instead, readers' visceral response to what has been designated by settler culture as repugnant. To amplify this effect, she also abandons the first-person narrative in this instance. Unlike in the scene of Shakbatina's execution, which rhetorically invited our identification with the woman about to die, here Howe reverts to third-person narration: we observe Koi Chitto from the outside. This narrative mode facilitates our disidentification from Koi Chitto and makes it easier to resort to savagism to account for what we are witnessing, even as we hear his invocations to Shakbatina and attempt to sympathize with his particular predicament.

This insistence on the repugnant as an emblem of savage authenticity and as a sustained attempt to evoke revulsion is surprising and appears to undermine all the autoethnographic efforts of Howe's writing. *Shell Shaker* is clearly invested in representing contemporary indigeneity. Howe's late twentieth-century Choctaw are modern people, often living outside of their nation, thoroughly embedded in settler culture and society: they are actresses, historians, newspaper editors, stockbrokers, and lawyers. They argue about contemporary Indianness. They worry, for instance, whether Indians who learn to play the piano cease to be tribal, and they dispute the ideological effects of Indian collaboration in the commodification of Indian culture. *Shell Shaker* is a reflection on contemporary indigeneity, one strung between the notions of tribalism, authenticity, and modernity.

Howe is aware of the long and persistent tradition that Pearce names savagism. When a BBC reporter investigating McAlester's killing asks one of her Choctaw interviewees whether it would be "fair to say that [the] savage-style assassination was an ancient Choctaw ritual" (54), Howe cautions us that her lapses into stereotypical Indian imagery are not accidental. As the reporter collapses Pearce's paradigm—"savage-style assassination"—with the multiculturalist interpretive cop-out—"ancient Choctaw ritual"—she reiterates the interpretive problem regarding representation of the indigenous. Howe's reaching for the repugnant is a creative response to what Elizabeth Povinelli identifies as the core dilemma that the politics of recognition poses for the indigenous: "how to present a form of difference that is maximally other than dominant society and minimally abrasive to dominant values" (68). In Australia, Povinelli's case study, aboriginal societies seeking restitution of their land title confront a particularly vicious circle, what Povinelli calls the cunning of recognition. They are required to establish their distinctiveness and historical continuity through adherence to rituals often considered repugnant and prohibited by Australian law.

In the United States, at least for the indigenous nations that signed historic treaties with the US government and therefore are not compelled to seek federal recognition, the issue of claiming entitlements pertaining to their status as "domestic dependent nations" is simpler. All the courts demand before extending such entitlements is a tribal enrollment card testifying to a genealogical connection to members of historical nations. There's no requirement of proven continuity of traditional belief and practice.[20] And perhaps for that reason, the repugnant—that is, the ancient practices now prohibited by law or found reprehensible by a public sense of ethics—furnishes an opportunity for Howe to mount a critique of the very conditions pervading the late twentieth- and early twenty-first-century multicultural democracies under which indigenous artists undertake self-representation. The gruesome authentic deployed at several strategic junctions throughout *Shell Shaker* becomes a strategy that allows Howe to escape the integrative thrust of multicultural misrecognition and to stake a claim to an identity that would be recognizable as other than that required by the settler community's political discourse. To put it another way, Howe is after an otherness *different* from that demanded by multiculturalism, after a difference other than cultural difference.

Inviting both identification with and revulsion from indigenous ritual practices, Howe elicits Chadwick Allen's saming and unsaming interpretive approaches simultaneously. She constantly alternates between disparate representational registers, so to speak. In the ethnographic narration of customs that interrupt the twentieth-century mystery novel plotline, her detailed renditions of bone-picking ceremonies or ritual executions represent these potentially repugnant rituals in terms intelligible to Euro-American readers. In the description of the bone-picking ceremony we hear the scientific language of rationalism in the body preparation scene, the religious language of liturgy, the philosophical language of the sacred and sublime, the ethnographic language of social difference, and the aestheticizing language of beauty and eroticism. Howe offers plenty of opportunities to assimilate what's taking place, even to appreciate deeply the terrifying—and sublime—beauty of the ritual. At the same time, however, she thwarts such assimilation, giving unrelenting play to the gruesomeness, potential horror even, of the traditional Choctaw practices she describes. She forces her readers to visualize crushed skulls, half-decayed bodies coming apart in other people's hands, and necrophilic sex. The novel takes time to explain ancient Choctaw rituals and yet, paradoxically, readily exploiting the reader's voyeuristic inclinations, withholds full comprehension from its readers as they recoil at what they are witnessing. The gruesome authentic works to block our strategies of sympathy by cultural analogy, even as Howe reminds us that these strategies are available to us. We teeter on the precarious line between what we continue to perceive as savage and civilized, despite the now decades-long education in multiculturalist tolerance and the appreciation of difference.

In a reversal of the multiculturalist truism linking knowledge and tolerance, Howe's depictions leave a strong residue of revulsion to elicit respect without full comprehension. One of the central premises of the multiculturalist experiment in North America—including the official recognition of racial and cultural difference, revamped school curricula and publishing programs, updated museums and other sites of national and regional commemoration—is a belief that lack of knowledge about the racial, and later, cultural others of settler America was at the root of prejudice and the resulting inequality. What multiculturalism stresses, then, is a program of tolerance through education. Patchen Markell calls this model *cognitive recognition* and explains that "unlike toleration, which can be grudging, and is consistent with utter ignorance of the people to whom it is extended, recognition involves respecting people precisely in virtue of, not despite, who they are; and so proper relations of recognition must be founded on accurate mutual knowledge among the people and groups involved" (40). In a multicultural democracy, reading minority literature, viewing minority art, and attending minority cultural festivals is good citizenship; "eating the other" (22), to recall bell hooks's formulation of this social dynamic, is part and parcel of the larger integrative national project. One way to disable the appropriating mechanisms of multiculturalism, then, would be to forestall cognitive recognition by withholding information. Literary and cultural scholars have argued that the cultivation of secrecy—a strategy deployed by a variety of minority artists[21]—works to refuse the mainstream audience's efforts to master cultural otherness through knowledge, a mastery we expect to obtain from ethnic literature and art. In *Shell Shaker* we see a different strategy. Howe disrupts the mechanisms of cognitive recognition not by withholding information but by flooding us with it. Like Shakbatina with her final promise to tell us what *really* happened, Howe seems to tease the reader, saying: *I will tell you everything you might want to know, with meticulous detail and expert ethnographic gloss, and still you will not understand.*

Because the semblance of knowledge is dangerous given that it has historically sustained discourses of indigenous savagery and the inequality those discourses justify and perpetuate, Howe insists on refusing to grant mainstream readers a sense of understanding and potential identification. Her strategy forestalls multicultural misrecognition by resorting to representations of the repugnant as a way to preempt identification through difference, contemporary multiculturalism's main tool of national integration. Her gruesome authentic serves to sustain and deepen a kind of impassable epistemological gap that Howe produces throughout the novel, from its opening juxtaposition of historical and astronomic time as well as Standard English and transliterated Choctaw, all the way to Shakbatina's concluding explanation of the circumstances of Red McAlester's murder, her telling us that this is "what really happened" (222). This gap emerges because of our inability, or reluctance, to suspend disbelief, a reluctance subtended by Western rationalist logic—still the intellectual genealogy of the majority of contemporary American readers—which makes it difficult for us to "really" believe Shakbatina's story. The novel's final sentences highlight this difficulty in graphic ways: as Shakbatina's words transition from English into transliterated Choctaw, this epistemological gap becomes visual, and we remember that Choctaw language is the ultimate imagined horizon and the frame that holds the novel together in ways that will not be fully intelligible to the majority of its readers.

But Howe also knows that in the late twentieth century, North American readers have at their disposal interpretive strategies that can mitigate such an epistemological inadequacy too vividly felt in encounters with radically different systems of belief. Token cognitive recognition, swift translation into our own terms, and the ensuing toleration of cultural difference, which has been officially sanctioned not only as an undeniable social good but also as a necessary corollary to nationalist projects in contemporary multicultural democracies, are always available as interpretive options. Howe's representations of the repugnant make these approaches to indigenous difference difficult or facile. Her reliance on the gruesome authentic heightens the interpretive dilemma posed by the multiple solutions to the novel's detection plot. It makes us pause in our multiculturalist reading practice, which is characterized by an easy recourse to multicultural misrecognition and its reliance on culture as the fundamental category of understanding, to consider its ramifications. By making that pause possible, by disrupting the literary exchange of multicultural misrecognition, Howe's rhetorical strategies impede the easy consolidation of a "transcendental national monoculturalism" (Povinelli 29)—an integrative logic according to which we are all the same because we are all different—operating behind the smokescreen of multiculturalism's celebration of difference. Within this logic, difference is tokenized to such an extent that its performances are fully interchangeable—it does not matter whether we read a novel by a Native American or African American writer, for example, as long as we are reading multiculturally, that is, extending recognition to our putative others and, as critics have charged, in the process reasserting our sovereign agency as liberal subjects engaged in the process of national reformation. Howe wants us to know and understand enough to recognize the distinctiveness of the historical and contemporary Choctaw, enough to see their spiritual universe and social organization as viable, even preferable, alternatives to settler society. But she wants us to understand just short of enough to comfortably cross the boundary into Choctaw epistemological territory, just short of enough to appropriate and to celebrate and then go on to knowingly dismiss.

In effect, Howe's novel offers an acutely perceptive diagnosis of contemporary multiculturalist reading practices and the representational predicament those practices pose for indigenous artists. It provides a literary counterpart to the efforts of contemporary indigenous visual artists, whose work, as I argue in the preceding chapters, showcases the paradoxes of the

North American exchanges of recognition taking place privately and publicly between settler and indigenous subjects and societies. *Shell Shaker* is also, and perhaps more urgently, a plea for alternative strategies of apprehending difference in contemporary North America, whether we attempt it through reading literature, watching cinema, or visiting museums and art galleries. Howe's novel extends an invitation to consider replacing the politics of recognition that underlie our current multiculturalist interpretive strategies with what Patchen Markell calls the politics of acknowledgment. Markell, through a meticulous critique of recognition from Hegel all the way to contemporary multiculturalism, argues for a concept of recognition devoid of the dynamics of appropriation and mastery. Inspired by Hannah Arendt's famous declaration that "if it is good to be recognized, it is better to be welcomed, precisely because this is something we can neither earn nor deserve" (qtd. in Markell, 180), Markell defines the politics of acknowledgment as a process of coming to terms with one's ontological condition of finitude and vulnerability in interaction with others, on the one hand, and, on the other, of recognizing the relations of privilege and subordination structuring such encounters.

Howe's novel invites two kinds of acknowledgment, then. In refusing to grant readers interpretive mastery of the indigenous text—in a literary counterpart to Jimmie Durham's insubordinate indigenous art—it facilitates a Markellian acknowledgment of one's ontological condition of finitude and of the resulting limits on one's ability to know and understand the other. By redefining the interpretive ground of contemporary reading practices, *Shell Shaker* clears space for the potential welcoming of the (indigenous) other despite freshly experienced limits of understanding, a welcoming that, unlike cognitive recognition, is not predicated on exacting the prize of transparency in exchange for acknowledgment. And yet further, in keeping with Howe's project of representing contemporary Choctaw tribalism, the novel prompts an acknowledgment of contemporary indigenous nations, and contemporary versions of indigenous traditionalism in particular, as viable forms of governance and sociality, forms that already successfully constitute political, rather than merely cultural, reality in North America. In this latter sense, Howe's writing offers an instructive imaginative corollary to efforts to recover and revitalize indigenous political traditions that lie at the heart of contemporary American Indian intellectual work.

Conclusion

Unsettling Misrecognition

> We are from the past, but we echo and reverberate in the present. What a responsibility! It is necessary that, with great urgency, we all speak well, and listen well. We, you and I, must remember everything. We must especially remember those things we never knew. Obviously that process cannot begin with longer lists of facts. It needs newer, and much more complex, kinds of metaphors. Perhaps we must trust confusion more, for a while, and be deeply suspicious of simple stories, simple acts.
>
> Jimmie Durham, *A Certain Lack of Coherence*, 1988

As I wrote this book, I was struck by a paradox. Although the artists I explore work within a cultural context that puts a premium on insider knowledge supplied by minority cultural production, they often choose to stonewall rather than to cooperate. They do capitalize on the multiculturalist demand for performances of cultural difference simply by creating and selling their art, but their artworks appear intent on thwarting understanding and engineering confusion instead of providing knowledge. They stump rather than elucidate. They refuse to deliver on the expectations of multiculturalist enlightenment that the settler public brings to their appreciation.

I have pointed out such gestures of refusal throughout the preceding chapters. Recall the opening voice-over in *Atanarjuat (The Fast Runner)* and its warning that the story about to unfold will be intelligible only to those who already understand it—that is, to the Inuit who heard its lesson in ethics as children rather than to the broader Southern or international public. Or Jimmie Durham's persistent refusal to provide "better understanding through entertainment," a promise delivered via a variety of deflecting tactics, be they Xs refusing solution, mirrors reflecting the spectator's gaze, hearts missing from dissected ribcages in his sculptures, or the red herrings of his critical writing and poetry. There are LeAnne Howe's multiple and mutually exclusive solutions to murder plots and her protagonists who deliver explanations that readers unfamiliar with traditional Choctaw cosmology are not equipped to comprehend; Pamela Shields's and Hulleah Tsihnahjinnie's photographic palimpsests that bring back historical figures obscured by settler nationalist narratives but then refuse to identify them; and the exhibitions at the National Museum of the American Indian that amass objects of material culture but withhold the expected ethnographic gloss. Such refusals are not just peripheral rhetorical gestures that make things more edgy or interesting; neither are they idiosyncrasies that the public should, in a classic gesture of multicultural misrecognition, chalk up to Indians' quirky cultural authenticity. Rather, these refusals are the first and most visible manifestations of a recurring strategy that consists in repeated stagings of interpretive impasses: instead of achieving a clear understanding of indigenous cultural difference, we, somewhat like the colonial educator pondering the Indian X in Jimmie Durham's *Red Turtle,* often end up disabled by our critical acumen. Such impasses aim for nothing less than a transformation of the rhetorical ground of indigenous cultural production; the goal is a disruption of the multicultural misrecognition that so pervasively defines current settler engagement with indigenous art, a disruption that clears discursive space to make room for indigeneity's political meanings.

Historically, it makes perfect sense that the interpretive or conceptual impasse has become such a recurrent and powerful mode of creative expression in contemporary indigenous art in North America. Today's indigenous peoples experience a disjunction between, on the one hand, their knowledge of their unique legal status and that status's acknowledgment in current political discourse and legal practice, and, on the other, popular discourse's insistence on understanding indigeneity as merely cultural identity. Negotiating this conundrum is the daily challenge of contemporary indigenous lives. The culturalization of social identities resulting from the late twentieth-century mainstreaming of multiculturalism has solidified this predicament.

Because the fighting words of the early debates over multiculturalism, such as identity politics, culture wars, political correctness, and so on, have disappeared from our everyday vocabulary, we might not realize how defining this culturalist model of social relations continues to be. As scholars and critics we rarely debate the politics of recognition because we take for granted the founding assumption of multiculturalism about the value of cultural difference to national cohesion in contemporary democracies. The results of a quick search on various iterations of the word "multicultural" in the mainstream daily press show that the concept has thoroughly permeated settler thinking about the nature of social relations in North America. It not only survived post–9/11 backlash, in which the value of diversity was challenged on the basis of worries that ethnic and religious enclaves might harbor domestic terrorists, but also has been redeployed as testimony to a reconceived North American exceptionalism, a means of distinguishing Canada and the United States from fundamentalist Islamic states. This has been largely good news for a variety of minority groups making up North American polities as the conception of cultural citizenship extends a sense of belonging to previously marginalized populations, though critics continue to point out that multiculturalism fetishizes culture and obscures socio-economic inequality. In the case of indigenous peoples, this emphasis on culture perpetuates a fundamental misrecognition of their history and their contemporary realities.

As I describe in the introduction, a successful refocusing on the political conceptions of indigeneity in diplomacy and law has been accomplished thanks to decades of indigenous activism in the second half of the twentieth century. It has also met with measured success in academe, where newly created American Indian and indigenous studies programs have highlighted colonialism as the proper framework for the study of indigeneity via nationalist and transnationalist methodologies. All of this critical work, however, has had minimal impact on the popular settler understanding of indigeneity. It seems that the more established multiculturalism becomes as a model for social relations, the *less* likely the settler public is to embrace the idea of indigenous nations as distinct political entities. And yet, as indigenous political, legal, and academic activism bears fruit in the return of the political conception of indigeneity to these disciplines, the persistence of the culturalist conceptions in popular discourse is increasingly difficult to ignore. Occasionally, the issue comes to broader public attention when indigenous nations or their individual citizens act on the presumption of their unique legal status—always, it seems, to the general public's surprise. Typical press coverage of such instances illustrates the dilemma I'm describing. To consider one of the most recent examples, we might remember the Iroquois Nationals lacrosse team's passport controversy in 2010. The Iroquois Nationals, for the first time ever, were refused entry to England for the 2010 Lacrosse World Cup in Manchester because their Haudenosaunee passports had not been digitized; that is, they were not in compliance with the new requirement resulting from increased international travel security strictures following 9/11. When offered US passports by the federal government, the team declined, explaining that they were representing the Iroquois Nations and not the United States, which had its own national team at the competition in Manchester. No matter the amount of remedial education in political history provided by *Indian Country Today* and other indigenous news outlets to contextualize the team's decision, it was met with incredulity on the part of the general public along the familiar lines of *Indians should just get over it.*[1] These and similar examples suggest that interventions in the form of direct, explicit assertions of the political conception of indigeneity do change things in crucial but limited ways. While they readjust legal, diplomatic, and occasionally educational practices, they have not transformed how the general settler public thinks about American Indians. The ideological allure of multicultural misrecognition can, after all, be difficult to resist: witness the tribal community galleries at the National Museum of the American Indian in Washington, DC, discussed in chapter 1, whose outright assertion of treaty rights and indigenous sovereignty is so easily muffled under the broader discourse of First Americans at a Native Place evoked in the museum's building and grounds. Such examples beg the question of why the political conception of indigeneity, now easily available elsewhere, has not permeated settler popular culture and remains unrecognized by settler society.

Throughout this book, I have been making the case that studying contemporary indigenous art offers critical insight into the workings of multicultural misrecognition as well as into potentially effective ways of resisting its incorporative pull. Because of the considerable cultural capital that minority art and literature wield in the contemporary art and publishing markets, they provide indigenous artists, writers, filmmakers, and curators with an unprecedented opportunity to articulate their worldviews on their terms while reaching ever-larger segments of the settler public. This opportunity brings its own risks of cooptation, but as I have described in the preceding chapters, some indigenous artists have demonstrated an acute understanding of the treacherous rhetorical ground they tread as they ply their varied arts. They realize that, prompted by multiculturalist imperatives of good citizenship and national reformation, the settler public brings to their artworks conceptions of indigeneity that urgently need unsettling. Designed to obscure the historical and ongoing colonialism, multiculturalism offers a particularly inhospitable ground for narratives that seek to revise this colonial history or to reinsert its ongoing legacies into accounts of the present. As long as multiculturalism dictates our vocabulary regarding social relations, multicultural misrecognition will shape public perceptions of indigeneity. Thus multiculturalism simultaneously offers opportunity in the form of a greater demand for indigenous cultural production and poses a seemingly insurmountable obstacle to the dissemination of the political meanings of indigeneity in its presumption that all social identities are reducible to culture. The sites and texts of indigenous cultural production I have explored capitalize on this contradiction in order both to expose it and to experiment with potential routes of escape from its grasp.

Contemporary indigenous artists insistently turn to the potential for transformative encounter that art offers by engineering conceptual impasses for their viewers and readers. Having rejected customary exhibition conventions, the National Museum of the American Indian frustrates visitors, who find themselves at a loss without familiar interpretive guidelines and are invited to wonder anew how one might think about indigenous lives, past and present, in the absence of the ethnographic framework. Isuma's filmmakers both invite spectators to identify with the Inuit and reestablish distance and boundaries, giving the interpretive edge to Inuit insiders. LeAnne Howe offers her readers all the interpretive tools available to translate ancient Choctaw sociality into familiar terms, and yet she forestalls such translation via gruesome depictions of ancient rituals. Visual artists who resort to palimpsestic representation disrupt the public's recognition of the vanished Indians by resurrecting suppressed histories, but the many photographic layers of these histories often confound, leaving spectators with even more questions. Each of Jimmie Durham's artworks appears intent on bringing us to our interpretive knees, luring us with recognizable icons of Indianness only to turn them into insubordinate indices of indigeneity. All of these artists invite the public to experience confusion, to acknowledge unexpected difficulty, to linger in a space of a conceptual paradox. Ironically, such recognition of our lack of interpretive mastery is harder to dismiss than a reasoned argument offered in a legal brief, for example, because it evokes no counterarguments, just a sense of limits, an experience particularly useful in encountering difference. Contemporary indigenous art asks that we master ourselves rather than our perceived cultural others; that we fully apprehend our desire to experience cultural otherness, a desire that may serve to disguise a fear of all other kinds of difference, particularly those kinds of difference that might require rethinking our fundamental modes of living (how we vote, what we consume, where we live), rather than merely our aesthetic practices (what we read or view, what exhibitions we frequent).

Ultimately, however, these humbling impasses serve to clear discursive space for a potential return of the political meanings of indigeneity within popular discourse, as this discourse is adjusted through ongoing exchanges of recognition transacted across contemporary indigenous art in museums, in movie theaters, in art galleries, in classrooms, and in private reading. The main strategy might be an emphasis on the dialectic of recognition, as in the National Museum of the American Indian, where the staged tension between the conception of indigeneity as culture and the conception of indigeneity as nationhood opens up space for critiques of colonialism paradoxically within the very framework designed to conceal it. Or it could be a deft deployment of the gruesome authentic in literary fiction to block the multicultural translation of difference into equivalence so that contemporary indigenous traditionalism is perceived as a viable alternative to settler forms of sociality. The political implications of rootedness in the form of claims to national territory may also arrive via indexical signs that simultaneously frustrate decoding and imply residual and re-emergent indigeneity. These conceptual impasses serve as reminders of the political foundations of contemporary indigenous nations and acknowledge that while indigenous sovereignty is inherent and prior to contact, its contemporary versions are necessarily enacted in the context of the politics of recognition—that is, in adaptation and resistance to the interpretive and political imperatives of multiculturalism. The impasses of contemporary indigenous art clear paths for interpretive options beyond those conceptually tethered to culture. We must learn to read such impasses not as cognitive cul-de-sacs but as opportunities for indigenous discursive freedom beyond multicultural misrecognition.

Notes

Introduction

1. While the initial responses have been removed from No Doubt's Facebook page along with the video, "An Open Letter to No Doubt, Supersonic Public Relations and Interscope Records in Response to No Doubt's Video, 'Looking Hot,'" written by Angela Riley, the director of the UCLA American Indian Studies Center, made public on November 5, 2012, effectively summarizes the main charges. The letter is available on various blogs, for example, the National Indigenous Women's Resource Center at <http://www.niwrc.org/?attachment_id=1837> (accessed April 10, 2013) and Turtle Talk, the blog of Michigan State University Law School's Indigenous Law and Policy Center at http://turtletalk.wordpress.com/2012/11/05/ucla-indian-studies-director-angela-riley-open-letter-to-no-doubt/ (accessed April 10, 2013).

2. For an argument on the ideological functions of settler Indian play, see Deloria, *Playing Indian*.

3. In its entirety, No Doubt's statement of apology reads as follows:

> As a multi-racial band our foundation is built upon both diversity and consideration for other cultures. Our intention with our new video was never to offend, hurt or trivialize Native American people, their culture or their history. Although we consulted with Native American friends and Native American studies experts at the University of California, we realize now that we have offended people. This is of great concern to us and we are removing the video immediately. The music that inspired us when we started the band, and the community of friends, family, and fans that surrounds us was built upon respect, unity and inclusiveness. We sincerely apologize to the Native American community and anyone else offended by this video. Being hurtful to anyone is simply not who we are. (<http://www.nodoubt.com>, accessed November 3, 2012)

4. The anthropologist Renato Rosaldo coined the term "cultural citizenship," which he defines as "a deliberate oxymoron, a pair of words that do not fit comfortably together. Cultural citizenship refers to the right to be different and to belong in a participatory democratic sense. It claims that, in a democracy, social justice calls for equity among all citizens, even when such differences as race, religion, class, gender, or sexual orientation potentially could be used to make certain people less equal or inferior to others. The notion of belonging means full membership in a group and the ability to influence one's destiny by having a significant voice in basic decisions" (402).

5. The Indian Arts and Crafts Act, passed by the US Congress in 1990, requires all artists marketing their work as Indian to document their enrollment/citizenship in a federally recognized Indian tribe.

6. I borrow the concept of the ethnoracial pentagon from David Hollinger's 1995 *Postethnic America*, where he uses it to describe the five ethnoracial categories, such as "Euro-American, Asian American, African American, Hispanic, and Native American" (23), that organize the US population census, and with it, American thinking on group difference in the age of multiculturalism.

7. In chapter 2, where I discuss the Inuit Isuma Productions and its first feature film, I fill in the Canadian context in more detail.

8. In "The Politics of Recognition," Taylor argues that "our identity is partly shaped by recognition or its absence, often by the misrecognition of others, and so a person or a group of people suffer real damage, real distortion, if the people or society around them mirror back to them a confining or demeaning or contemptible picture of themselves" (25).

9. Glazer was a critic of multiculturalism and saw its emergence as the price US society paid for its inability to integrate African Americans.

10. Some historians argue that the treaties were simply a convenient expedient for the European courts and later American governments and were never intended as acknowledgments of the indigenous nations' sovereignty on the continent. However, apart from the intentions of the signatories, in legal terms the historic treaties serve as evidence of a diplomatic practice that presumes indigenous nations to be political entities in control of their territories and social organization.

11. For a reading of the sculpture's rhetorical effects, see chapter 1.

12. For a detailed account of these diplomatic maneuvers, see Hoxie, *This Indian Country*.

13. For a comprehensive account of this process, see Cheyfitz. On Indian Federal Law, see Wilkins and Lomawaima's *Uneven Ground*.

14. Some American Indians opposed US citizenship as an abrogation of indigenous sovereignty, while others advocated for it, seeing it as a path to civic and political participation that would lead to ensuring tribal rights.

15. Here, for example, is Catlin writing in 1841 in volume I of his *Letters and Notes*:

> I have, for many years past, contemplated the noble races of red men who are now spread over these trackless forests and boundless prairies, melting away

> at the approach of civilization. Their rights invaded, their morals corrupted, their lands wrested from them, their customs changed, therefore lost to the world; and they at last sunk into the earth, and the ploughshare turning the sod over their graves, and I have flowed to their rescue—not of their lives or of their race (for they are "doomed" and must perish), but to the rescue of their looks and their modes, at which the acquisitive world may hurl their poison and every besom of destruction, and trample them down and crush them to death; yet phoenix-like, they may rise from "the stain on a painter's palette," and live again upon canvas, and stand forth for centuries to come, the living monuments of a noble race. (16)

16. John Wesley Powell, the founding director of the American Institute of Ethnology in 1878, argued thus for the creation of the office: "The field of research is speedily narrowing because of the rapid change in the Indian population now in progress; all habits, customs and opinions are fading away; even languages are disappearing; and in a few years it will be impossible to study our North American Indians in their primitive conditions, except from recorded history" (qtd. in Elliott 10). To gather support for his project "Vanishing Tribes of North America," Franz Boas argued that "future generations will owe a debt of gratitude to him who enables us to preserve this knowledge, which, without an effort on the part of our own generation, will be lost forever" (qtd. in Elliott 10).

17. Contemporary critics have argued over the ideological ramifications of Curtis's work; however, the extensive financial support he received in the initial stages of his project testifies to the wide appeal of his pitch for salvage ethnography. Alluding vaguely, in an introduction to the 1906 edition of *The North American Indian*, to the "great changes in practically every aspect of the Indian's life that have taken place, especially within recent years," and reminding the public that "the passing of every old man or woman means the passing of some tradition, some knowledge of sacred rites possessed by no other," Curtis urged that "the information that is [still] to be gathered, for the benefit of future generations, respecting the mode of life of one of the great races of mankind, must be collected at once or the opportunity will be lost for all time" (21).

18. Flaherty's supposed documentary opens with a title card informing the viewers that the film's protagonist, Nanook, has since died of starvation during an apparently unsuccessful hunt while simultaneously asserting that *Nanook*, the film, has toured the globe to enthusiastic reviews gaining a global visibility the humble Eskimo hunter could not even dream about. The film concludes with a shot that effectively melds the two Nanooks, an extreme close-up of the sleeping hunter's head. *Silent Enemy*, in turn, is framed by a prologue, in which Yellow Robe attired in Plains Indian dress extends thanks to the settler society, for through their "magic" his people, the Ojibwe, will live on into posterity. The prologue juxtaposes precontact Ojibwe life, depicted in an ethnographic and romance mode in the film, with the solitary Indian figure against a black background, here abstracted as an Indian performing on the stage. In this way, the film unwittingly depicts the evolution of the most enduring of the settler culture's Indian stereotypes, that of an Indian as a

living monument to Plains Indian culture, an abstracted image made available for the settler national mythmaking, one returning so insistently and recognizably in No Doubt's "Looking Hot" music video.

19. On how historic Indians intentionally used settler conventions of Indian representation to gain access to broader publics, see Deloria, *Indians in Unexpected Places*, and Goodyear, *Red Cloud*.

20. Over a couple of decades, Dixon orchestrated several media events—from slide lectures and theatrical productions of the *Song of Hiawatha* in the Wanamaker store in Philadelphia, to the Last Council, a staged meeting and departure of the last of old chiefs, to the groundbreaking for the Indian Memorial in New York Harbor and several expeditions for citizenship to the Western Indian nations and scheduled educational visits to American public schools, especially those educating the children of immigrants. See Trachtenberg, *Shades of Hiawatha*, for a detailed history of the Wanamaker-Dixon educational ventures.

21. During the same period, despite the predominance of culturalist conceptions of indigeneity in public discourse, some among indigenous nations insisted on the language of the treaties and on the indigenous sovereignty these treaties implied. For example, the Haudenosaunee Confederacy issued a separate declaration of War on Germany to point out that Haudenosaunee were fighting on the US side as allies rather than as US citizens.

22. Ironically, the termination policy's effect of Indian migration to cities resulted in a development of politicized pan-Indian communities, which spurred the American Indian Movement.

23. For a detailed account of the changing political priorities of the NCAI, see Hoxie's *This Indian Country*.

24. The fish-ins in the Northwest in the 1960s and in the Great Lakes in 1972–73, along with the Mohawk blockade of the international bridge between Canada and the United States in 1968, for example, publicized treaty-guaranteed rights to fishing and hunting and to free passage across the US-Canadian border. In 1972 the Trail of Broken Treaties concluded in Washington with the delivery of a twenty-point document demanding reversal of the 1871 decision and re-establishment of treaty-making with Indian nations. In a most memorable example of the time, AIM leaders, with Oglala traditional leaders' support, acted on the assumption of their tribal sovereignty by announcing the creation of the Oglala Nation, declaring its independence from the United States and establishing its historic boundaries after the 1868 Treaty of Fort Laramie, action that resulted in the confrontation with the federal government known as the Siege of Wounded Knee in 1973.

25. Hoxie points out in *This Indian Country* that by the very divisive presidential elections of 2008 and 2012, perhaps the only issue that was not a bone of contention and an opportunity for candidates to differentiate themselves from their opponents was the official commitment to indigenous sovereignty.

26. Some of these legal victories included compensation to Penobscot and Passamaquody over land lost in contravention of the 1790 Indian Trade and Intercourse Act, the ruling asserting Indian political sovereignty in the *Santa Clara v. Martinez*

case over tribal membership, and rulings in various cases over water rights in the Southwest.

27. However, as many scholars of Indian law have pointed out, as long as the paternalism of the federal government first developed in the Marshall Cherokee cases persists as precedent and the doctrine of plenary power asserted in *Lone Wolf v. Hitchcock* remains in place, this sovereignty continues to be circumscribed by the ongoing colonial nature of indigenous-US relations. With the colonial framework firmly in place, the legal victories of the 1970s and 1980s, along with the series of acts pertaining to Indian education, health, religious freedom, gaming, and repatriation of human remains and cultural patrimony written into law during these decades, led indigenous nations in the direction of self-administration rather than self-governance.

Chapter 1

1. Anecdotal reports describing the opening ceremonies are often appended to writing on the NMAI; see Lonetree, "Critical Engagements with the NMAI," for representative accounts of the day's celebratory tenor. For a view that insightfully and forthrightly accounts for the celebratory experience despite the author's serious misgivings about her participation, see Kauanui.

2. Such international lobbying resulted, for example, in the signing of the Declaration on the Rights of Indigenous Peoples by members of the United Nations on September 24, 2007. The United States, Canada, Australia, and New Zealand declined to sign the declaration. Since 2007, however, all four countries have officially supported the Declaration: Australia in April 2009, New Zealand in April 2010, Canada in November 2010, and the United States in December 2010.

3. Public Law 101–185, the document establishing the NMAI at the Smithsonian Institution, specifies in paragraph 80q-3, section (e), regarding the initial appointments to the NMAI Board of Trustees, that "at least 7 out of 23 members appointed shall be Indians," and in section (f), regarding subsequent appointments, that "(a) 7 members, 4 of whom shall be Indians, shall be appointed for a term of one year," and "(b) 8 members, 4 of whom shall be Indians, shall be appointed for a term of 2 years" (Public Law 101–185, 111–2).

4. *The Museum Guide* states that "roughly one-fourth of the staff of the National Museum of the American Indian is Native" (12).

5. For other examples, see the special issues of *Public Historian* (28.2) and *American Indian Quarterly* (29: 3–4) and (30:3–4).

6. For a representative example, see Lonetree, "Continuing Dialogues." A notable exception is "Performing 'Indian' in the National Museum of the American Indian," a 1999 essay by Hilden and Huhndorf on the opening exhibitions of the NMAI's Gustav Heye Center in New York City. In a rare critique of the rhetoric of Indian authenticity guaranteed by Indian control deployed in the NMAI's public relations materials, Hilden and Huhndorf argue that "regardless of the ethnic origins of curators or boards of directors, most ethnographic museums remain

memorials to wealth and privilege, educating the public to accept the relations of power extant in given societies." While the new museums have potential to "clarify national histories, revealing aspects obfuscated in more celebratory narratives . . . if they painstakingly avoid . . . the simple construction of an alternative, but still equally triumphal, master narrative of the nation's past," the Heye Center obviously fails at that task, and this failure begins with the museum's building, the old Custom House, which the authors see as an architectural apotheosis of American imperialism. It culminates in what the authors find "most shocking—living exhibitions in the persons of the tour guides (called 'cultural interpreters') and of those Native people hired to sit in a 'talking Circle' . . . ready to answer tourists' questions and . . . to embody authenticity . . . for Museum visitors" (162–65). Hilden and Huhndorf readily acknowledge the good intentions of the museum curators and believe that "tribal people could assume control of the destinies of objects" (167) from Heye's collection. But they also meticulously chronicle the derailment of these intentions in actual exhibitionary practice, pointing out, among other instances, that the Native interpreters in the Heye Center end up speaking in the voice of "the objective, scholarly viewer of 'their' objects from 'their' culture" and that the exhibits exemplify "a move from the tribal world—the world that grants this voice its authority to speak here—to the Western scholarly one (whose language validates cultural judgment)" (169). The Native voices in the NMAI Heye Center model Western viewing practices. The museum thus, despite its professed Indian control, testifies to the "internalization of colonial dreams of savage others" and an "assumption that Westernness is the norm" (166). For a critique of the NMAI as a pioneer in curatorial practice, see Jacknis.

7. For a summary of press coverage of the opening and early scholarly response to it, see Lonetree, "Continuing Dialogues." For a critique of the press coverage, see Reinhardt.

8. For early scholarly writing on the NMAI in Washington, D.C., see the special issues of *Public Historian* (28.2) and *American Indian Quarterly* (29: 3–4) and (30: 3–4). On the latter criticism, see especially Lonetree, "Continued Dialogues," "Missed Opportunities," and "Critical Engagements with the NMAI," as well as Carpio, DeLugan, and Atalay in these special issues. For a critique of the inaugural exhibits, including their community-curated galleries, see Lujan.

9. I borrow the concepts of the script and the stage and the idea of their inextricable intertwining from George Yúdice, a cultural studies scholar who offers a comprehensive account of American cultural politics in the late twentieth century. In his 2003 book, *Expediency of Culture*, Yúdice argues that any revisionist stance vis-à-vis existing political, social, or cultural conditions and discourses needs to be considered as inextricably intertwined in the "performative force" of these conditions and discourses. For Yúdice, "the problem is not so much the [revisionist] script but the stage (force field) on which they are enacted. If what one is seeking is unadulterated agency, the complexity of the stage will not yield that kind of dénouement" (74). Thus the NMAI's effort at revisionist museological practices needs to be considered in the context of multicultural misrecognition, which defines the rhetorical stage of the contemporary moment.

10. The issue of the origin, age, and size of indigenous populations has been the subject of an ongoing debate. Most recent scholarly arguments have been moving the origin earlier in history and the demographic numbers upward. For a brief summary of recent research, see Mann.

11. I am borrowing the concept of the "vitrine" from Donald Preziosi. A vitrine, a display case for curiosities and goods, familiar from museums, fairs, and shops, serves for Preziosi as a symbol for what he understands to be "the most thoroughgoing and imperialist gesture imaginable": "the collection and containment of all the things and peoples of the world" and their representation from the vantage point of Europe, or the West ("The Art of Art History" 519). In that context, the National Mall becomes the showcase for the United States' newly minted credentials as a multicultural democracy by way of its collection and display of American—and the world's—cultural difference.

12. On the function of the NMAI as a forum for South America's indigenous peoples seeking recognition, see DeLugan.

13. For comprehensive histories of the rise of the museum as a public institution, see Duncan, Bennett, and Greenhill. On the impact of the museum on indigenous nations, see Phillips, "Disrupting Past Paradigms."

14. On the system of objects in the West, see Baudrillard; on the culture of spectacle, see Debord.

15. Mary Lawlor offers an account of the center's ideological functions, especially in tension with the Foxwoods Casino. The critical rift between mainstream and indigenous intellectuals over the question of the nation is visible in academia as well: while many disciplines in the late twentieth century moved away from the nation as an analytical model in favor of postcolonial, transnational, or global approaches, many thinkers within Native American studies turn to the concept of the nation to assert a sovereignist perspective. While investment in national models is sharply criticized everywhere else, it appears to be the main promise of contemporary Native American studies. For nationalist critical approaches, see Cook-Lynn, Weaver, Womack, and Warrior, *American Indian Literary Nationalism*, and Justice. For a critique of the nationalist model in indigenous studies, see Huhndorf, *Mapping the Americas*.

16. Foucauldian critics, for example, note that the museum delivers the community as subject to the surveillance and discipline of the state (see Yúdice, for instance). Marxist critics in turn might point out that the communities articulated and served by the museum function in tandem with capitalism, ultimately upholding its hierarchies (see Žižek and Joseph).

17. At the same time, political scientists such as Anthony Hall and James Tully have argued for the historic treaty as a most appropriate model for federalism in North America.

18. *The Spirit of a Native Place* provides a detailed account of the complex history of architectural direction and curatorial management at the museum.

19. The Jay Treaty, otherwise known as the Treaty of London of 1794, was concluded between the United States and the British Crown to regulate political and economic relations between these two states following the Revolutionary War. Article III of the treaty guaranteed Indians living in the United States and Canada

free passage across the US-Canadian border. This right of free passage was reiterated in the US Immigration and Nationality Act of 1952 (section 289), with an addition specifying that it would pertain only to Indians with 50 percent "Indian blood."

20. The establishment of Nunavut territory included extinguishing the Inuit native title in exchange for rights to a smaller territory and monetary compensation.

21. For a critique of the Heye Center's dioramas and other exhibition practices, see Hilden and Huhndorf.

22. See Phillips, *Trading Identities*, on the category of the authentic in Native art history.

23. See Clifford, "Histories of the Tribal and the Modern" on the ethnographic logic of metonymy.

24. See Hilden and Huhndorf for a discussion of the Heye Center's exhibit, including Ghost Shirts.

25. On Heye, see Clara Sue Kidwell's "Every Last Dishcloth: The Prodigious Collecting of George Gustav Heye" in Krech and Hail.

26. See Hilden and Huhndorf for Chris Eyre's comments on stolen collections and American appropriations of Native history.

27. Yet another reading is possible here, however. The blurring of colonial agency speeds up the time of the European history on the continent, pointing toward a different time frame. Its likening to natural disasters suggests that this time frame extends far into the past and also into the future, a horizon on which the colonial tenure of European states in the Americas might be only a brief interval. This concept of the indigenous "long outwaiting" is present in the classics of American Indian literature. N. Scott Momaday's *The House Made of Dawn* and Leslie Marmon Silko's *Almanac of the Dead* are two of the best-known examples.

28. For analyses of the processes of federal recognition, see Clifford and Povinelli.

29. These have not always been the dominant myths. On English perceptions of Northeast Indians as similar to Europeans in many respects, see Kupperman, Shoemaker, and Paula Gunn Allen.

30. I owe this detail to Joy Harjo, in conversation.

31. See, for example, Hilden and Huhndorf.

32. In their essay on the Gustav Heye Center's inaugural exhibitions, Hilden and Huhndorf quote the following comment from the visitor's book: "We have not seen the exhibits yet, but we're thrilled that the Museum brought us to see this magnificent building—like the Sistine Chapel!" (166).

33. For the Omaha Tribal Interpretive Center and Museum, for example, see the architect's project images at <http://www.jackalopearts.org> and <http://www.omaha-nsn.gov> (accessed June 11, 2014).

34. See Ostrowitz for the account of the design process.

35. In an effort to transmit as much of that information as possible, the building and the guide feed into the stereotype that everything about indigenous architecture, dress, and personal adornment bears deeper spiritual meaning. The stereotype itself has already become a subject of jokes by indigenous filmmakers. For example,

in a conversation with the audience after the 2006 NYC Film Festival screening of his second film, Zacharias Kunuk responded to a question about the religious significance of facial tattoos among Inuit women by stating matter-of-factly that the tattoos were "just make-up." In his 2003 film, *The Edge of America*, Chris Eyre has Wes Studi respond to a similar question from another protagonist about a particular geological formation by saying with a laugh, "Oh no, it's just a big rock!"

Chapter 2

1. On the emergence of contemporary American Indian cinema, see Singer. For an account of Indian filmmakers and actors in early American cinema, see Deloria, *Indians in Unexpected Places*. See Hearne, *Smoke Signals* and *Native Recognition*, for the significance of Chris Eyre's debut feature to indigenous cinema.

2. All quotations in this paragraph are from *Reel Injun*'s soundtrack.

3. All quotations in this paragraph are from the Isuma Productions Inc. website, <http://www.isuma.tv>.

4. On the local distribution and meanings of Isuma's film, see Huhndorf, *Mapping the Americas*, chapter 2.

5. Inuktitut is the mother tongue of Canada's Eastern Arctic Inuit.

6. "Southern" is typically used by the Inuit to refer to Canadian or more broadly American peoples living south of the Canadian Eastern Arctic. But it also can be taken to refer to a specific, though broad, cultural formation we call, in other contexts, "The West" or "Europe." In this chapter, I use the term "Southern" or "the South" whenever I paraphrase Inuit commentators; in all other cases, for the sake of a coherent practice throughout the book, I use the term "settler" to refer to the same concept.

7. Jessica L. Horton's 2012 essay, "Alone on the Snow, Alone on the Beach: 'A Global Sense of Place'" in *Atanarjuat* and *Fountain*," is an interesting exception in the ongoing debate on Isuma's feature film, as it explores the many and intricate ways in which the film inscribes global contexts in its depictions of ancient Igloolik.

8. The two temporal realms of crucial consequence to my argument in this chapter are the premodern and the contemporary, the former referring to the precontact time of the tale recounted in the film's diegesis and the latter to the present historical moment, the moment of the film's production captured in the outtakes and the moment of the film's subsequent reception. In this context, specific to North America, by "modernity" I mean the time period and the prevailing social formations following the arrival of settlers on the continent. In this sense, *Atanarjuat* edits out American modernity, oscillating instead between the premodern and the contemporary.

9. Examples include Greg Sarris and Daniel Sakheim's TV series *Grand Avenue* (1996), Sherman Alexie's film *The Business of Fancydancing* (2002), Adrian Louis's novel and Chris Eyre's film *Skins* (2002), Eyre's film *Smoke Signals* (1998), Valerie Red-Horse and Jennifer Farmer's film *Naturally Native* (1997), Shelley Niro's film *Honey Moccasins* (1998), Randy Redroad's film *The Doe Boy* (2001), Blackhorse Lowe's film *The 5th World* (2004), Sterlin Harjo's film *Four Sheets to the Wind*

(2007), Georgina Lightning's film *Older than America* (2008), and Andrew Okpeaha MacLean's film *On the Ice* (2011).

10. Here is a representative example of such criticism from the late Louis Owens's *Mixed-blood Messages*: "[Sherman] Alexie's fiction . . . too often simply reinforces all of the stereotypes desired by white readers: his bleakly absurd and aimless Indians are imploding in a passion of self-destructiveness and self-loathing; there is no family or community center toward which his characters, like Momaday's Abel, Welch's unnamed narrator in *Winter in the Blood*, Silko's Tayo, or Thomas King's Will in *Medicine River* might turn to for coherence, and in the process of self-destruction the Indians provide Euroamerican readers with pleasurable moments of dark humor or the titillation of bloodthirsty savagery. Above all, the non-Indian reader of Alexie's work is allowed to come away with a sense . . . that no one is really to blame but the Indians, no matter how loudly the author shouts his anger" (80).

11. Isuma's two subsequent features, *The Journals of Knud Rasmussen* (2006) and *Before Tomorrow* (2009), depict, respectively, the suppression of shamanism by Christianity among the Inuit in the 1920s and the first contact between the Inuit and Southerners in 1840. In the context of these films, the rhetorical choices of *Atanarjuat (The Fast Runner)* are even more poignant than at the time of the film's original release.

12. Curtis routinely traveled with a set of props (e.g., feather bonnets, masks, and costumes) that he would furnish to his subjects without much concern for their tribal accuracy. He also, on some occasions, painstakingly airbrushed any traces of indigenous and settler historical co-presence from his photographs. The best known, and oft-cited, example here is the substitution of a clock by a woven basket in a 1911 photograph, titled *Piegan Lodge Interior*.

13. For example, *Starting Fire with Gunpowder* (1991) by Inuit filmmaker David Posey and British filmmaker William Hansen, produced by the Inuit Broadcasting Corporation, opens with a mise en abyme series of shots of an Inuit woman saying, "This is not me. This is my picture" and again, "And here it's not me. It's my picture," while pointing at a picture of herself on TV. This prologue invokes unmistakably the famous prologue from the 1930 *Silent Enemy*, in which the Lakota actor Chief Yellow Robe thanks the settler viewers for the "magic" of cinema that will ensure the survival of his vanishing people in the representational realm. In *Silent Enemy* and in Posey and Hansen's production, the metafictional gesture opens the film; in *Atanarjuat* it is postponed until the outtakes, in order to preserve the illusion of the precontact world as long as possible and reinforce the ideological functions of this narrative.

14. Other examples of films deploying the same strategy include George Burdeau's *Backbone of the World*, Victor Masayesva Jr.'s *Itam, Hakim Hopiit*, and Alanis Obomsawin's *Kanehsatake: 270 Years of Resistance*; as this list makes clear, the strategy is prevalent in documentary film.

15. As is the case with almost all Canadian productions, Isuma's film was partially funded by the National Film Board (NFB). See Gittings and White on the complicated history of this funding.

16. The critical debates over orality/textuality, and the claim of indigenous illiteracy in particular, continue to animate critical work in American Indian studies. For two of the most recent—and most original—examples, see Teuton, *Deep Waters*, and Rassmussen, *Queequeg's Coffin*.

17. Because the representative government in Canada gives every resident of legal age in a particular province the right to vote, the Inuit population in Nunavut (at 80 percent majority) has the leverage to affect major political decisions in the territory.

18. The fact that when Thomas Edison first presented his kinetoscope to the broader public at the 1893 Chicago World's Fair he screened "Hopi Snake Dance" is one more testimony to the intertwining of early film history with representations of America's indigenous peoples.

19. Only in 1988, when Claude Massot released *Nanook Revisited*, did settler viewers learn that the main actor's name wasn't Nanook but Allakariallak and that many others portrayed in Flaherty's film were actors (including Flaherty's two common-law wives) and not a group of actual relatives (Rony 123).

20. In yet another ironic twist, the medicine is seal oil, now packaged in the Southern pharmacy bottle.

21. For more on that history, see Brody, *The People's Land*.

22. We can think here of Akira Kurosawa's *Dersu Uzala*'s scenes with the camera to see how this particular trope has endured across different national cinemas.

23. R. Quinn Duffy's 1988 *The Road to Nunavut* is the most extreme example of the tenacity of this paternalistic discourse. In the preface, the author announces that "this book is structured on the idea of guardianship, of bringing up children until they are old enough and mature to look after themselves" (xxii). And, indeed, the book proceeds from a discussion of "Reluctant Guardianship" in the introduction to discussions of "Supplying Shelter," "Looking after Health," "Providing an Education," "Providing a Living," and "Relinquishing Authority" in the subsequent chapters.

24. Deborah Miranda on the ASAIL listserv, March 4, 2004.

25. See San Juan, Alfred, Povinelli, and Samson.

26. Moreover, in the report of the 1996 Royal Commission on Aboriginal peoples, historic injustices are admitted only in order to clear the way for a new relationship with the First Nations; the report self-servingly insists that "Aboriginal peoples anticipate and desire a process for continuing the historical work of Confederation. Their goal is not to undo Canadian federation; their goal is to complete it" (qtd. in Samson 328).

27. An official term used in Canada and across North America for the cancellation of the sovereignty over territories or "Aboriginal title" of Native people, "extinguishment" is the end result of a political process used to settle outstanding land conflicts. Formerly extinguishment was achieved through written treaties, but in other cases the same result was achieved through violent displacement, the spread of disease, or by Native peoples fleeing in the wake of advancing Europeans. Today, extinguishment entails the official voiding of what the state recognizes as Aboriginal title to land by agreements between the government and political bodies estab-

lished (often in Canada) to represent Aboriginal people. By extinguishing what are recognized as prior rights, Canada assumes unquestionable legal ownership over Native Lands and in exchange confers subsidiary rights and provides cash compensation to Native peoples who have become parties to this process (Samson 9).

28. As Gittings points out, "with three quarters of their books, 98% of their cinema screen time and 90% of their television programming and recorded music originating from foreign, largely American sources, Canadians feel as if they are being taken over by a global, US-dominated culture to the detriment of their own cultural identity" (104).

29. This dynamic operates in a particularly categorical way in Australia. In the United States and Canada, land claims have to be underwritten by indigenous identity as testified to by federal recognition. There is no legal requirement to demonstrate a continuing adherence to traditional lifeways. However, the logic of cultural distinctiveness and authenticity established with reference to earlier forms of tribal/national organizations operates unimpeded within the public discourse on indigeneity in North America. In addition, unrecognized tribes seeking federal recognition carry the burden of proving historic and cultural continuity.

30. The explicit nation-building project of the NFB, which often led to overt discouragement of *auteur*-oriented films, resulted in frequent departures of filmmakers from the board to establish their own private (and underfunded) companies (Gittings 89).

31. Studio D's "remit was not only to make interventions in a patriarchal cinematic tradition by restoring images of women to a history that had repressed them, but also to train women to produce their own images'" (qtd. in Gittings 91). Due to budget cuts it closed in 1996.

Chapter 3

1. For somewhat different versions of this concept, see Benjamin, Bazin, and Sontag.

2. Blankets are thoroughly complex symbols in indigenous representation. Historically, blankets were among the goods distributed to indigenous nations as part of treaty provisions and thus signified dependence on the federal government. Although the concept is disputed by some historians, smallpox-infected blankets are believed to have been used as a tool in what was, effectively, biological warfare against American Indians. And yet in the late nineteenth and early twentieth centuries the so-called "blanket Indian" became emblematic of a rejection of European clothing and the entire project of assimilation and acculturation; wrapped tightly around the body, the blanket stands for adherence to traditionalism and tribalism. See Deloria, *Indians in Unexpected Places*, on the blanket as a sign of tribal resistance. In Tsinhnahjinnie's image the blanket is old and frayed, and it falls off the man's body rather than protecting him. It is a prisoner's blanket, and is especially visible as such because, unlike in the case of images of Plenty Horses featured in Deloria's book, it is not accompanied by any other sartorial emblems of traditionalism and Indian cultural and national difference.

3. The three cherries most obviously signify casino slot machines, but they also remind us that the cherry has a secured, if ambivalent, place in American national iconography, from Washington's cherry tree all the way to Nabokov's *Lolita's* Humbert-coveted cherry.

4. Stereographs or postcards depicting American Indians, acquired during trips out West, often ended up in family albums side by side with images of Western landscapes, various other tourist attractions, and portraits of family members. On the circulation of these images, see Sandweiss.

5. Kainawa is the original name of the Blood Band of the Blackfoot Confederacy; the word's literal translation is "people of many chiefs." Contemporary Kainawa live in southern Alberta, Canada.

6. Compare to Curtis's *Nanivook Mother and Child*, for example.

7. There are numerous photographs of American Indians driving, riding in, or posing with cars, the most famous among them, no doubt, a 1904 photograph by Walter Ferguson titled *Geronimo at the Wheel*, featuring the famous Apache leader in settler clothing and a top hat driving a Cadillac in the company of three other Indian men wearing traditional dress, including the requisite Plains feather headdress. For other examples of such images and their ideological functions in the early twentieth century, see Philip Deloria's essay "I Want to Ride in Geronimo's Cadillac," in *Indians in Unexpected Places*, 136–82. For a somewhat different representation of Indian mobility, see Kiowa photographer Horace Poolaw's 1950s series of images of Oklahoma Kiowas participating in public parades driving, and perched over, cars while displaying traditional regalia.

8. <http://www.thephotographyinstitute.org/all_abstracts/1995.htmld>. Accessed August 15, 2007.

9. With the exception of essays and photographs by Jolene Rickard and Gail Tremblay, all the collection's pieces discuss old settler photographs of American Indians; examples include studio portraits by Frank Matsura, "before and after" boarding-school photographs, images of Indian sports teams, and a picture of the famed Mescalero Apache leader, Geronimo, at the wheel of a Cadillac.

10. The editor's introduction and James Faris's essay are the only exceptions.

11. Reproductions of Curtis's photographs, in the form of posters, calendars, coffee-table books, and anniversary or special theme editions—the latter two often endorsed by some of the most visible figures among indigenous intellectuals in North America—have been appearing steadily since Curtis's work underwent a kind of renaissance in the 1970s, fueled to a large degree by the American Indian Movement and its appropriation of old photographs for the purposes of mobilization as well as political propaganda.

12. For example, Gidley's *Edward S. Curtis and the North American Indian, Incorporated* in 2000; Sandweiss's *Print the Legend* in 2002; Faris's *Navajo and Photography* in 2003; Goodyear's *Red Cloud* in 2003; Bernadin, Graulich, MacFarlane, and Tonkovich's *Trading Gazes* in 2003; and Williams's *Framing the West* in 2003.

13. Rayna Green's discussion of Frank Matsura's photo of two American Indian girls on a fainting couch is particularly illuminating in this respect. For Green's essay, see Lippard's *Partial Recall*.

14. The pervasiveness of this idea is readily attested to by a 1904 photograph by Curtis, titled, of course, *The Vanishing Race—Navaho* and captioned thus: "The thought that this picture is meant to convey is that the Indians, as a race, already shorn of their tribal strength and stripped of their primitive dress, are passing into a darkness of an unknown future. Feeling that the picture expresses so much of the thought that inspired the entire work [that is, his twenty-volume *North American Indian*], the author chose it as the first of the original series" (Cardozo 123). The ideological intention of the photographic construction is exposed here beyond any doubt.

15. Some of the more egregious examples, surely, especially from our contemporary vantage point, come from Curtis's work. See, for example, his 1903 *Mosa—Mohave* or 1904 *A Son of the Desert—Navajo*, appended by the following Curtis-authored captions: "It would be difficult to conceive of a more thorough aboriginal than this Mohave girl. Her eyes are those of a fawn of a forest, questioning the strange things of civilization upon which it gazes for the first time. The Mohave home is on the banks of the Colorado River, an environment into which they have so fitted themselves that they seem to have always been a vital part of it" and "In the early morning, this boy as if springing from the earth itself, came to the author's desert camp. Indeed, he seemed a part of the very desert. His eyes bespeak all the curiosity, all the wonder of his primitive mind striving to grasp the meaning of the strange things about him" (Cardozo 24 and 95).

16. See Sandweiss (2002) for the details of this argument and a remarkable example: a series of photographs documenting the destruction of the Big Mound—one of the Mississippian burial mounds from AD 1000 to 1400—to make room for the urban expansion of St. Louis, a clear record of the process in which the "Indian past was destroyed to become a literal foundation of American future" (254). On the nationalist appropriation of the Western landscape, see, for example, Spence, *Dispossessing the Wilderness*; Keller and Turek, *American Indians and National Parks*; Burnham, *Indian Country, God's Country*; and Solnit, *Savage Dreams*.

17. For the argument on how specific archeological theories appropriated ancient indigenous ruins to serve nationalist US discourse, see Sandweiss.

18. For a sampling of such commentary, from the first pronouncements on daguerreotype by Poe and Baudelaire, for example, all the way to writing by Bazin and Berger in the 1970s, see Trachtenberg, *Classic Essays on Photography*.

19. In compensating for that insecurity, which Americans must have felt in the vastness of the country, photography colluded with the tourist industry. Sontag writes:

> The predatory side of photography is at the heart of the alliance, evident earlier in the United States than anywhere else, between photography and tourism. After the opening of the West in 1869 by the completion of the transcontinental railroad came the colonization through photography. The case of the American Indians is the most brutal. Discreet, serious amateurs like Vroman had been operating since the end of the Civil War. They were the vanguard of the army of tourists who arrived by the end of the century, eager for

> a "good shot" of Indian life. The tourists invaded the Indians' privacy, photographing holy objects and the sacred dances and places, if necessary paying the Indians to pose and getting them to revise their ceremonies to provide more photogenic material. (64)

20. The idea of a photograph as a commodity is further developed in Allan Sekula's 1981 essay "The Traffic in Photographs."

21. Sontag's classic essays remain perceptive and relevant to thinking about photography, despite the changing nature of the medium (Sontag's work, along with Barthes's *Camera Lucida*, remain today the most quoted references in writings about photography). However, read from the vantage point of the early twenty-first century, and especially of the critical and theoretical work developed under the heading of Native American studies since the early 1970s, Sontag's comments about the historic photography of American Indians strike one as less insightful. Sontag appears at times persuaded by the concept of the vanishing race: "for an approach reminiscent of Sander's, one must look to people who documented a dying or superseded part of America like Adam Clark Vroman, who photographed Indians in Arizona and New Mexico between 1895 and 1904. Vroman's handsome photographs are unexpressive, uncondescending, unsentimental. . . . they are not moving, they are not idiomatic, they do not invite sympathy. They make no propaganda for the Indians. Sander did not know he was photographing a disappearing world. Vroman did. He also knew that there was no saving the world that he was recording" (63). And she accepts unquestioningly the stereotypes about indigenous people's response to photography: "Everybody knows, primitive people fear that the camera will rob them of some part of their being" (158). Like almost all critics of photography invoking the medium's indexical relationship to reality, Sontag refers to Honoré de Balzac's fear of photography as documented by his photographer Nadar: "every body in its natural state was made up of series of ghostly images superimposed on layers to infinity, wrapped in infinitesimal films. . . . Man never having been able to create, that is to make something material from apparition, from something impalpable, or to make from nothing, an object—each Daguerreian operation was therefore going to lay hold of, detach, and use up one of the layers of the body on which it focused" (Trachtenberg 158). This is one of the favorite anecdotes among people writing about early photography. Invariably, though, this noted correlation works to have us wonder at the surprising "primitivism" of the realist novel's greatest practitioner rather than marvel at the modernity of the "primitive" mind. This is surprising considering that Lévi-Strauss's argument about the systematicity of indigenous epistemology in *The Savage Mind* has been around since the 1950s. And it is particularly so with Sontag, who in the conclusion of her book returns to Balzac's metaphor (but not to "primitive societies" supposed thinking about photography's power to strip away being) to explain how photography, this "realistic" genre par excellence, in fact subtracts, if not altogether replaces, reality with the proliferation of its images.

22. Sekula's argument rested on his archival work with the first attempts at constructing a photographic record of France's urban criminals and homeless people.

The issue of what constitutes proper evidence—the transcribed oral account or visual record—was particularly urgent at the time. Sekula sees photography as complicit with the state's imperative to survey and discipline its subjects, criminal or not.

23. See Gunning on Western culture's conjunction of the conceivable with the visible and on photography's role as the "guarantor of a new realm of visual certainty" (420).

24. I offer a detailed discussion of Kunuk's work in chapter 2 of this book.

25. This view of photography as centrally engaged in ideological struggles was further elaborated by John Berger in *Ways of Seeing* and in John Tagg's work collected in *Burden of Representation*.

26. This documenting of types was an explicit imperative of official ethnologists as well as amateur salvage photo-ethnographers such as Edward Curtis.

27. See Huhndorf's *Going Native* on the complexities of late nineteenth- and early twentieth-century antimodernism, which was antimodern and colonial at the same time.

28. See, for example, Jolene Rickard's discussion of the ideological function of the woman and the basket stereograph in *Native Visions*, or peruse many of Curtis's photographs purporting to represent tribal types.

29. Historically, American Indians did not turn to photography until the late twentieth century. Even though, as Rick Hill argues, "Indians and photography did not get along for many years" because "the camera was an intrusion on Indian life" and "served outside interests" (9), and because, as Hulleah Tsinhnahjinnie explains, the popularity of photography coincided with the Indian Wars' policies of relocation and termination, during which American Indians were busy struggling for survival (29–30), there exist photographs of indigenous people and their communities taken by indigenous photographers that date all the way to the first years of the twentieth century. Among the earliest indigenous photographers in North America were Richard Throssell, who (as an agent for a federal institution) photographed his adopted nation, the Crow; Jennie Cobbs, who documented the lives of Cherokee women at the Cherokee Female Seminary at the turn of the twentieth century; Horace Poolaw, who photographed his community, the Kiowa, throughout the 1920s; and Lee Marmon, who produced some of the most strikingly beautiful (and most reminiscent of settler historic photography and Edward Curtis's representational strategies) images of the Pueblo peoples and communities in the post–World War II period.

30. On the Micmacs' use of the ethnographic archive in political activism, see Griffiths.

31. See chapter 2.

32. For such examples, see Anne Makepeace's film *Coming to Light*.

33. The photo might have been taken during the St. Louis World's Fair in 1904.

34. For an argument about the relationship between American Indians and modern technology imagined by the settler society and exemplified in Ferguson's photograph, see Deloria, *Indians in Unexpected Places*.

35. Aguilar here, too, evokes, somewhat eerily, Curtis's archival imperative, though

clearly in the service of autoethnography and the indigenous claims on modernity it implies, rather than in the service of salvage ethnography.

36. Other notable examples of this effort include Lee Marmon's portraits of Laguna elders, such as the silver gelatin prints *Platero (Diné), 1958* or *Juana, 1960*; Larry McNeill's sepia-toned silver gelatin prints of Tlingit tribal leaders (for example, a 1984 *Man of the Bear Clan*); David Neel's photographs of Kwakiutl elders and tribal leaders (1990 *Catherine Adams* or 1990 *Chief Alvin Alfred* and *Agnes Alfred*); Richard Ray Whitman's *Street Chiefs* series; and numerous photographs by Gregg Staats, Shelley Niro, and Jessie Cooday.

37. Some commentators on Curtis's work come to his defense in this regard by pointing to those of his photographs that represent their subjects in settler dress or other accoutrements of Western modernity.

38. For the details of this argument about the function of the background in nineteenth-century French portraiture, see Sekula, "The Body." On how the backgrounds of late nineteenth-century photographs testify to "the growing impotence of the imperialist bourgeoisie in the face of technological progress," see Benjamin.

39. David Wallace Adams explains in *Education for Extinction* that

> Armstrong and Pratt [the men responsible first for educating Indian prisoners in Florida and later for establishing the first Indian boarding schools] came up with an ingenious public relations scheme that both would utilize in the coming years with the utmost effect—the use of photographs to illustrate the conditions of Indians both "before" and "after" their institutionalization. Thus, on the eve of Pratt's departure for Nebraska, Armstrong wrote him: "We wish a variety of photographs of the Indians. Be sure and have them bring their wild barbarous things. This will show whence we started." Armstrong advised Pratt that if he liked, he could have the photographs taken in the West whereupon Hampton would purchase the negative, but one way or another, the students must be photographed in their native state. (47)

40. See Deloria's *Indians in Unexpected Places* for this argument on Indians' complicated position in the post-conquest and post-pacification United States.

41. For the full argument about the ideological functions of the parent-child photographs, see Bernadin et al.

42. Images from all three collections can be viewed at the artist's website, www.hulleah.com (accessed June 12, 2014).

43. American Indians are the only group in the contemporary United States required to present identification to attest to their group identity.

44. See note 15 for a couple of particularly egregious examples.

45. Archival photographs of the fleeing Minnesota settlers cannot help but evoke that other example of massive removal, the Trail of Tears, which took place too early to be documented by photography.

46. On digitization of photography, see Ritchin and Mitchell. See Batchen, "Ectoplasm," for an argument that since photography from the beginning was much more

hospitable to manipulation than its enthusiasts admit, on the one hand, and since the world of representation, as deconstruction has taught us, is always mimetically compromised anyway, on the other, the advent of digital technology is less of a milestone in the history of photography than its critics make it out to be.

47. For examples, see the early essays in Trachtenberg's collection.

Chapter 4

1. The title is abbreviated to *CLC* in subsequent references.

2. The essay was inspired by the Third World expatriate artists' appropriation of Marxism that Durham witnessed in Geneva, Switzerland, and was written to address American Marxist supporters of AIM. Later, according to Durham, it was used by the FBI to compromise AIM as a Marxist organization in an effort to alienate it from tribal constituencies.

3. These are Durham's examples.

4. See chapter 1 for a discussion of the effects of Boasian thought on perceptions of contemporary indigenous peoples.

5. The image of settler society getting fatter on the knowledge and understanding of the other reverberates with bell hooks's argument, in "eating the other," about the fundamentally parasitic nature of contemporary American interest in minority texts and bodies.

6. The 1987 poem "I Am One of Those Indians" reads "I am one of those Indians that fly around / . . . Ancestral graves and my specific gravity were all / Terminated in '54 and I act accordingly. I act / like a flapping Redskin. We are not stars or birds / or ghosts; more like flying peeping toms" (*CLC* 13).

7. The red star painted on the poet's forehead evokes both Durham's commitment to a materialist critique of indigenous conditions under colonialism and the FBI's effort to discredit the leaders of AIM by linking them with Soviet communism.

8. Throughout the testimonio, Menchú mentions the existence of tribal secrets and emphasizes her refusal to reveal them. Sommer reasons that, were the preservation of protected information at issue, it would make sense not to mention the matter at all. Menchú's more active and intentional highlighting of her refusal to provide information (or to have opening sections of her public speeches translated) works to emphasize her agency, including her refusal to provide information, in the exchange.

9. Cynthia Parker is a historical figure; so is Mary Jamieson, who was captured by, and decided to remain with, the Seneca. Their captivity narratives have not become staples of American classic literature. For a testimony to the perception of eighteenth-century captivity narratives and the experiences they depicted, see Susan Faludi's recent myopic book, *The Terror Dream: Myth and Misogyny in an Insecure America*, in which she reaches for the captivity narratives to argue that the experience of domestic terrorism—that is, of Puritans being attacked in their own (!) country by Indian foreigners (!)—was fundamental to the formation of the American sensibility.

10. For example, the caption to *Bedia's Stirring Wheel* reads "from: Site B, quadrant 71 White Planes [*sic*], New York. José Bedia, the famous Cuban explorer/archeologist discovered this stirring wheel, sometimes referred to as the 'Fifth' or 'Big' wheel, during his second excavation of the ruins at White Planes in AD 3290. He believes that the stirring wheel was a symbol of office for the Great White Father, often called, 'The Man behind the Wheel.' Bedia claims that the chief would stand behind the wheel to make pronouncements and stirring speeches." The pieces, of course, also function as celebratory callouts to a fellow artist, José Bedia.

11. The treaties authorized land transfers between the indigenous peoples and the arriving settler governments; in this context, the X's two limbs fashioned of machined wood are also recognizable as the pickets of settler fences.

12. William Cronon's *Changes in the Land* offers a fascinating account of transformations in the physical landscape and ecological systems in North America following the settlement of New England.

13. See, for example, *Máh-to-tóh-pa, Four Bears, Second Chief, in Full Dress* (1832), *Pshán-shaw, Sweet-scented Grass, Twelve-year-old Daughter of Bloody Hand* (1832), *Os-ce-o-lá, the Black Drink, a Warrior of Great Distinction* (1838), or *Stu-mick-o-súcks, Buffalo Bull's Back Fat, Head Chief, Blood Tribe* (1832), available for viewing at the Smithsonian's Catlin Virtual Exhibition website: <americanart.si.edu/exhibitions/online/catlin/highlights.html> (accessed June 12, 2014).

14. See, for example, *Pigeon's Egg Head (The Light) Going to and Returning from Washington* (1837–39), also available at the Smithsonian's Catlin Virtual Exhibition: <americanart.si.edu/exhibitions/online/catlin/catlin_highlights2.cfm?StartRow=22> (accessed June 12, 2014).

15. Like other Five Civilized Nations, the Muscogee, or the Creeks, were exempted from the 1887 Dawes Act. However, pressure stemming from the 1898 Curtis Act, which as an amendment to Dawes eliminated tribal governments and courts to clear resistance to allotment, resulted in the majority of Creeks relinquishing their opposition and beginning to register for allotments in 1899. The Crazy Snake movement was made up of Creek dissidents who opposed the allotment as a violation of earlier treaties.

16. After the surprise capture of Fort Mims in 1813, during which they killed all the fort's inhabitants except for the black slaves, the Red Sticks were defeated in 1814 at Horseshoe Bend by the combined forces of the Tennessee militia under the command of Andrew Jackson and their Lower Creek and Cherokee allies. The terms of surrender transferred twenty million acres of Muscogee land, more than half of their ancestral holdings, to the United States. This newly acquired territory was incorporated into the state of Alabama, which joined the union in 1819.

17. Durham, who has always identified as a Cherokee, never secured tribal enrollment and was barred from exhibiting his art in American Indian art shows after the passage of the AIACA.

18. See chapter 3 for a detailed discussion of this process.

19. Many creation stories in the Southwest feature the motif of emergence from underground.

20. Traditional version: "Come my love let's take a walk / Just a little way away /

While we walk along we'll talk / Talk about our wedding day / Only say that you'll be mine / And in our home we'll happy be / Down beside where the waters flow / Down on the banks of the Ohio / I drew my knife across her throat / And to my breast she gently pressed / Oh please, oh please, don't murder me! For I'm unprepared to die you see / I took her by her lily white hand / I let her down and I made her stand / There I plunged her in to drown / And watched her as she floated down / Returning home 'tween twelve and one / Thinking of the deed I'd done / I murdered the girl I love you see / Because she would not marry me / Next day as I was returning home I met the sheriff standing in the door / He said young man come with me and go / Down to the banks of the Ohio."

21. See Annette Kolodny's *The Lay of the Land* for this argument.

22. See Paz for the most influential, though unsympathetic, interpretation of La Malinche as the mother of Mexico.

Chapter 5

1. I note this detail because historically the issues of hygiene, often emblematized through skin and teeth, served to arrange people on the scale of humanity and civilization in North America.

2. I describe the ideological functions of this rhetorical gesture in chapter 2.

3. Since there are only ten thousand speakers of Choctaw in the United States today, most living in the Choctaw Nation of Oklahoma, the chances that readers of *Shell Shaker* will recognize and understand the opening sentence are indeed slim. The issue of preserving Choctaw as a living language is, in fact, of utmost urgency to the contemporary Choctaw, who have expressed alarm at the low levels of Choctaw fluency among the nation's youngest people. For information on language revitalization efforts, see the nation's official website at <www.choctawnation.com> (accessed June 12, 2014). My reading thus presumes a non-Choctaw-speaking readership, both indigenous and non-native.

4. Through Ishmael, *Moby Dick* maps out an outsider's path to the national collective; in that sense, Melville's novel is an auto-American biography (see Bercovitch). Shakbatina, and *Shell Shaker,* reverse the relationship between the individual and the collective; the latter assures the former.

5. In the mid-eighteenth century, Choctaw lands were subject to the contest between the French and English interests. The Choctaw, along with other indigenous nations in the area, were often recruited by either side against the other. Howe makes this history of changing and contradictory political and military allegiance abundantly clear in her novel, even as she baits her readers to think in terms of supposed precontact savagery through her use of the gruesome authentic.

6. As with any object of representation, readers' responses are ultimately unpredictable and cannot be generalized. In building my argument about the rhetorical and ideological functions of the gruesome authentic in Howe's novel, I extrapolate from the reading experience of my students in the course of teaching the novel over the last ten years at a large private university in the American Northeast and a private liberal arts college in the Southeast. An interesting study, which I am unfortu-

nately not able to undertake, would be to examine readerly responses to the novel among American Indian readers, and especially traditional, tribally based Choctaws.

7. Let me add here by way of clarification that violence in *Shell Shaker* is shocking not so much in itself—we see much worse daily in American movie theaters and in mainstream TV programming—but in contrast to the novel's opening scene of peaceful harmony, and, more importantly, in the context of savagism as defined by Pearce. Mutilated bodies showcased weekly on CSI do not prompt us to conclusions about the savage nature of "Miami-an" society or culture; they merely suggest the extent of pathology of a few individual residents of, or visitors to, the city, simultaneously putting into sharper relief the health of all the others. But the long discursive tradition of twinning representations of indigeneity with representations of brutality has resulted in a kind of knee-jerk interpretative behavior, persuasively chronicled by Pearce. Should we find a blood-soaked eagle feather near any of those CSI victims, as Sherman Alexie imaginatively demonstrated in his 1996 novel, *Indian Killer*, our forensic acumen might be readily overtaken by the fear and thrill of Indian savagery.

8. For a detailed discussion of these historical conditions, see the introduction.

9. Examples of exoticized Indian difference are ample in American popular culture; it overflows with figurations of Chadwick Allen's unsaming arguments. But their opposite might be less obvious to readers brought up on American westerns or New Age fads. So here's a good example of a contemporary saming argument about the indigenous from *The Earth Shall Weep*, the critically acclaimed and widely read history of indigenous America by James Wilson: "Anthropologists point to the many similarities of belief, mythology and ceremony among different peoples as a proof that, far from being becalmed in a kind of changeless, timeless prehistory, Native American societies were open, vital and dynamic, pragmatically accepting cultural practices from each other. This appears to be borne out by the evidence of extensive trade networks, linking areas as far apart as present-day Mexico and Canada, which carried, presumably, not only materials and artifacts but people and ideas back and forth across the continent" (28).

10. I borrow this formulation from Patchen Markell's *Bound by Recognition*.

11. *Osano* is a Choctaw word meaning "horsefly" or "bloodsucker" that Howe recovered from a 1933 recording of a traditional Choctaw song. In Howe's Choctaw universe it constitutes the ultimate insult and is applied equally to the Spanish, English, or those among the Choctaw who prey on or exploit others, their own people included.

12. Howe develops this concept further in her novel *Miko Kings* (2007), where she creates a protagonist, Ezol Day, who formulates the Choctaw theory of language, reality, and time early in the twentieth century and returns to help the present-day narrator understand that she, too, is "a body moving in Choctaw time" (221).

13. The Seven Major Crimes Act was later expanded to the Twelve Major Crimes Act. See Prucha on the changing federal Indian laws and policies.

14. For a recent depiction of the workings of tribal courts, see David Treuer's *Rez Life*, especially chapter 3. Treuer's point is that the tribal courts can, in effect, offer justice that accommodates tribal ethical imperatives of restoration.

15. For accounts of indigenous cosmologies, epistemologies, and notions of justice, see Waters, Deloria and Salisbury, Thornton (1998), Alfred (1999), Martin, and Kidwell et al.

16. In that sense, as Ken McCullough pointed out, *Shell Shaker* is more Greek tragedy than Tony Hillerman whodunit. Provided we share the Choctaw belief system, we know what did and what will happen.

17. On the ideological functions of cannibalism in accounts of early encounters with the indigenous peoples in America, see Samuels.

18. On *Shell Shaker* as a decolonizing narrative, see Hollrah (2004).

19. The material from the chapter, including the bone-picking ceremony, was the first to see print, long before the publication of *Shell Shaker* itself, appearing as "Bone Picker" in *Fiction International* 20 (Fall 1991), and reprinted in *Looking Glass* in 1991, where it was titled "Dance of the Dead: From the Bone Picker."

20. This is not the case for nations that are seeking federal recognition. Their situation bears similarities to that of the Australian Aborigines.

21. See chapter 4 for an expanded discussion of this issue; also see, for example, Sommer on the openly announced secretive nature of Rigoberta Menchú's narratives and on the strategies of refusal of readerly mastery in Toni Morrison's fiction, Mary Lawlor on the displayed withholding of objects deemed inappropriate for public viewing in tribal museums, and Rob Appleford on Jimmie Durham's *Cannibal* installation as relying on aporias of meaning (public lecture, Princeton University, March 24, 2006).

Conclusion

1. In 2013 an adoption case before the Supreme Court rehearsed these very issues again. In the Baby Veronica case, which pitted the child's biological father, a Cherokee Nation citizen, against settler adoptive parents, indigenous media turned to the Cherokee Nation's sovereignty and its jurisdictional purview resulting from the 1978 Indian Child Welfare Act to explain why the lower courts had ruled in favor of the father. But reporters for the *New York Times* and other mainstream settler press venues, along with a chorus of informal commentators, expressed outrage at the apparent disregard for the child's best interest—which they understood as linked to having a normative settler home rather than an extended tribal family—and in the process ignored a complex web of political and legal considerations impinging on the case. Also in 2013, Iroquois Nationals continued to struggle with the consequences of the 2010 passport incident. Their decision to forfeit the World Cup in England in order to claim their political status as Haudenosaunee rather than US citizens led to their disqualification from participation in the 2014 World Cup, ironically to take place in Colorado.

Works Cited

Adams, David Wallace. *Education for Extinction: American Indians and the Boarding School Experience, 1875–1928*. Lawrence: UP of Kansas, 2007.

Aguilar, Dugan. "Tuolumne Rancheria Roundhouse." <http://theautry.org/ptp/aguilar.swf>. Accessed Nov. 6, 2014.

Alexie, Sherman. *Flight*. New York: Grove, 2007.

———. *Indian Killer*. New York: Warner, 1996.

Alfred, Taiaiake. *Peace, Power, Righteousness: An Indigenous Manifesto*. Oxford: Oxford UP, 1999.

———. *Wasáse: Indigenous Pathways of Action and Freedom*. Peterborough: Grove, 2003.

Alison, Jane, ed. *Native Nations: Journeys in American Photography*. London: Barbican Art Gallery and Booth-Clibborn Editions, 1998.

Allen, Chadwick. *Blood Narrative: Indigenous Identity in American Indian and Maori Literary and Activist Texts*. Durham: Duke UP, 2002.

———. "Indigeneity Inside and Outside the Metropolitan Conversation." *Conciliation and Reconciliation: Art and Literature in the Pacific*. Ed. Maryvonne Nedeljkovic. Vol. 2. Paris: L'Harmattan, 2008, 105–18.

Allen, Paula Gunn. *Pocahontas: Medicine Woman, Spy, Entrepreneur, Diplomat*. San Francisco: Harper, 2003.

Alvin, Joseph, and Joanne Nagel. *Red Power: American Indians Fight for Freedom*. Lincoln: U of Nebraska P, 1991.

Anderson, Benedict. *Imagined Communities: Reflections on the Origin and Spread of Nationalism*. London: Verso, 1991.

Aperture Foundation, Inc. *Strong Hearts: Native American Visions and Voices*. New York: Aperture, 1995.

Archuleta, Elizabeth. "Gym Shoes, Maps, and Passports, Oh My!: Creating Community or Creating Chaos at the NMAI?" *The American Indian Quarterly* 29.3/4 (Summer/Fall 2005): 426–39.

Atalay, Sonya. "No Sense of the Struggle: Creating a Context for Survivance at the NMAI." *The American Indian Quarterly* 30.3/4 (Summer/Fall 2006): 597–618.

Atanarjuat (The Fast Runner). Dir. Zacharias Kunuk. VTape, 2001.

Backbone of the World. Dir. George Burdeau. Berkeley Media LLC, 1997.

Batchen, Geoffrey. *Burning with Desire: The Conception of Photography*. Cambridge: MIT P, 1999.

———. *Each Wild Idea: Writing, Photography, History*. Cambridge: MIT P, 1999.

———. "Ectoplasm: Photography in the Digital Age." Squiers 9–23.

Baudrillard, Jean. "The System of Collecting." *The Cultures of Collecting*. Ed. John Elsner and Roger Cardinal. Cambridge: Harvard UP, 1994. 7–24.

Bazin, André. "The Ontology of the Photographic Image." Trachtenberg 237–44.

Before Tomorrow. Dir. Marie-Hélène Cousineau and Madeline Ivalu. VTape, 2009.

Benhabib, Seyla. *The Claims of Culture: Equality and Diversity in the Global Era*. Princeton: Princeton UP, 2002.

Benjamin, Walter. "A Short History of Photography." Trachtenberg 199–216.

Bennett, Tony. *The Birth of the Museum. History, Theory, Politics*. London: Routledge, 1995.

Bercovitch, Sacvan. *The American Jeremiad*. Madison: U of Wisconsin P, 1978.

Berger, John. "Understanding Photography." Trachtenberg 291–94.

———. *Ways of Seeing*. London: Penguin, 1972.

Bergland, Renée. *The National Uncanny: Indian Ghosts and American Subjects*. Dartmouth: Dartmouth College P, 2011.

Berman, Howard. "Perspectives in American Indian Sovereignty and International Law, 1600–1776." Lyons et al. 125–88.

Bernadin, Susan, Melody Graulich, Lisa MacFarlane, and Nicole Tonkovich. *Trading Gazes: Euro-American Women Photographers and Native North Americans, 1880–1940*. New Brunswick: Rutgers UP, 2003.

Berry, Susan. "Voices and Objects at the National Museum of the American Indian." *Public Historian* 28.2 (Spring 2006): 63–67.

Bhabha, Homi. "Double Visions." *Grasping the World: The Idea of the Museum*. Preziosi and Farago 236–41.

Bibby, Brian. *Deeper Than Gold: A Guide to Indian Life in the Sierra Foothills. Photographs by Dugan Aguilar*. Berkeley, CA: Heyday, 2004.

Black Robe. Dir. Bruce Beresford. Samual Goldwyn Company, 1991.

Blue Spruce, Duane, ed. *Spirit of a Native Place: Building the National Museum of the American Indian*. Washington, DC: National Museum of the American Indian, Smithsonian Institution in association with National Geographic, 2004.

Brody, Hugh. *The People's Land: Eskimos and Whites in the Eastern Arctic*. London: Penguin, 1977.

Browder, Laura. *Slippery Characters: Ethnic Impersonators and American Identities*. Chapel Hill: U of North Carolina P, 2000.

Buck-Morss, Susan. *Dialectics of Seeing: Walter Benjamin and the Arcades Project*. Cambridge: MIT P, 1991.

Burnham, Phillip. *Indian Country, God's Country: Native Americans and National Parks*. Washington, DC: Island, 2000.

Buscombe, Edward. *Cinema Today*. London: Phaidon, 2005.

The Business of Fancydancing. Dir. Sherman Alexie. Outrider Pictures, 2002.

Calloway, Colin G. *First Peoples: A Documentary Survey of American Indian History*. Boston: Bedford/St. Martin's, 2008.

Carbonell, Bettina Messias, ed. *Museum Studies: An Anthology of Contexts*. Chichester and Oxford, England; Malden, MA; India: Blackwell, 2004.

Cardozo, Christopher. *Native Nations: First North Americans as Seen by Edward Curtis*. Boston: Bulfinch, 1993.

Carpio, Myla Vicenti. "(Un)disturbing Exhibitions: Indigenous Historical Memory at the NMAI." *The American Indian Quarterly*. 30.3/4 (Summer/Fall 2006): 619–31.

Catlin, George. *Letters and Notes on the Manners, Customs and Conditions of the North American Indians*. 2 vols. London: G.Catlin, 1841, reprinted New York: Dover Publications, 1973.

Cheyfitz, Eric. *The Columbia Guide to American Indian Literatures of the United States Since 1945*. New York: Columbia UP, 2004.

Clifford, James. "Collecting Ourselves." Pearce 258–68.

———. "Histories of the Tribal and the Modern." Preziosi and Farago 636–52.

Coming to Light: Edward S. Curtis and the North American Indians. Dir. Anne Makepeace. Seventh Art Releasing, 2001.

Conn, Steven. "Heritage vs. History at the National Museum of the American Indian." *Public Historian* 28.2 (Spring 2006): 69–73.

Cook-Lynn, Elizabeth. *Anti-Indianism in Modern America: A Voice from Tatekeya's Earth*. Champaign: U of Illinois P, 2007.

Coombes, Ania E. "Inventing the 'Postcolonial': Hybridity and Constituency in Contemporary Curating." Preziosi 468–97.

Cooper, Karen Coody. *Spirited Encounters: American Indians Protest Museum Policies and Practices*. Lanham: Altamira, 2008.

Cronon, William. *Changes in the Land: Indians, Colonists and the Ecology of New England*. New York: Hill & Wang, 1983.

Curtis, Edward S. *The North American Indian*. Seattle: E. S. Curtis, 1907.

Dances with Wolves. Dir. Kevin Costner. Orion Pictures, 1992.

Debord, Guy. *La société du spectacle*. Paris: Buchet-hastel, 1967.

Deloria, Philip J. *Indians in Unexpected Places*. Lawrence: UP of Kansas, 2004.

———. *Playing Indian*. New Haven: Yale UP, 1998.

Deloria, Philip J., and Neil Salisbury, eds. *A Companion to American Indian History*. Malden: Blackwell, 2002.

Deloria, Vine, Jr. *Custer Died for Your Sins*. Norman: U of Oklahoma P, 1969.

———, ed. *American Indian Policy in the Twentieth Century*. Norman: U of Oklahoma P, 1985.

Deloria, Vine, Jr., and Clifford M. Lytle. *The Nations Within: The Past and Future of American Indian Sovereignty*. Austin: U of Texas P, 1984.

DeLugan, Robin Maria. "South of the Border at the NMAI." *The American Indian Quarterly* 30.3/4 (Summer/Fall 2006): 558–73.

Dixon, Joseph, K. *The Vanishing Race*. New York: Bonanza, 1913.

The Doe Boy. Dir. Randy Redroad. Curb Entertainment International Corporation, 2001.

Duffy, R. Quinn. *The Road to Nunavut*. Montreal: McGill-Queen's UP, 1989.

Duncan, Carol. "Art Museums and the Ritual of Citizenship." Pearce 279–86.

Durham, Jimmie. *A Certain Lack of Coherence: Writings on Art and Cultural Politics*. Berkeley: Kala, 1992.

———. "Geronimo!" Lippard 20–25.

The Edge of America. Dir. Chris Eyre. Showtime Networks, 2003.

Elliott, Michael. *The Culture Concept: Writing and Difference in the Age of Realism*. Minneapolis: U of Minnesota P, 2002.

Elsner, John, and Roger Cardinal, eds. *The Cultures of Collecting*. Cambridge: Harvard UP, 1994.

Evans, Brad. *Before Cultures: The Ethnographic Imagination in American Literature, 1865–1920*. Chicago: U of Chicago P, 2005.

Faris, James. *Navajo and Photography*. Salt Lake City: U of Utah P, 2003.

The 5th World. Dir. Blackhorse Lowe. [no distributor available] 2004.

Fixico, Donald L. "Change Over Time: The National Museum of the American Indian." *Public Historian* 28.2 (Spring 2006): 81–84.

Four Sheets to the Wind. Dir. Sterlin Harjo. [no distributor available] 2007.

Fraser, Nancy. "Rethinking Recognition." *NLR* 3 (May–June 2000): 107–20.

Gidley, Mick. *Edward S. Curtis and the North American Indian, Incorporated*. Cambridge: Cambridge UP, 2000.

Ginsburg, Faye. "Embedded Aesthetics: Creating Discursive Space for Indigenous Media." *Planet TV: A Global Television Reader*. Ed. Lisa Parks and Shanti Kumar. New York: NYU P, 2003, 303–19.

Gittings, Christopher E. *Canadian National Cinema*. New York: Routledge, 2002.

Glazer, Nathan. *We Are All Multiculturalists Now*. Cambridge: Harvard UP, 1998.

Goodyear, Frank, III. *Red Cloud: Photographs of a Lakota Chief*. Lincoln: U of Nebraska P, 2003.

Grand Avenue. Dir. Daniel Sakheim. Warner Home Video, 2000.

Greenhill, Hooper Eileen. *Museums and the Shaping of Knowledge*. New York: Routledge, 1992.

Griffiths, Alison. *Wondrous Difference: Cinema, Anthropology and Turn-of-the-Century Visual Culture*. New York: Columbia UP, 2002.

Gunning, Tom. "Phantom Images and Modern Manifestations." *In Fugitive Images from Photography to Video*. Ed. Patrice Petro. Bloomington: Indiana UP, 1995. 42–71.

Hall, Anthony J. *The American Empire and the Fourth World*. Montreal: McGill-Queen's UP, 2003.

Harlan, Theresa. "Adjusting the Focus for Indigenous Presence." Squiers 134–52.

———. "Creating a Visual History: A Question of Ownership." Aperture Foundation 20–32.

———. "Indigenous Photographies: A Space for Indigenous Realities." In *Native Nations*, 233–44.

Hearne, Joanna. *Native Recognition: Indigenous Cinema and the Western*. Albany, NY: SUNY P, 2012.

———. *Smoke Signals: Native Cinema Rising*. Lincoln: U of Nebraska P, 2012.

———. "Telling and Retelling in the 'Ink of Light': Documentary Cinema, Oral Narratives, and Indigenous Identities." *Screen* 47.3 (Autumn 2006): 307–26.

Hilden, Patricia Penn, and Shari M. Huhndorf. "Performing 'Indian' in the National Museum of the American Indian." *Social Identities* 5.2 (1999): 161–83.

Hill, Rick. "High-Speed Film Captures the Vanishing American, in Living Color." *American Indian Culture and Research Journal* 20.3 (1996): 111–28.

———. "In Our Image: Stereotyped Images of Indians Lead to New Native Art Form." *Exposure* 29:1 (Fall 1993), 6–11.

Holinger, David. *Postethnic America: Beyond Multiculturalism*. New York: Basic, 1995.

Hollrah, Patrice. "Decolonizing the Choctaws: Teaching LeAnne Howe's *Shell Shaker*." *American Indian Quarterly* 18 (2004): 73–85.

Honey Moccasins. Dir. Shelley Niro. Women Make Movies, 1998.

Hooks, Bell. "Eating the Other: Desire and Resistance." In Bell Hooks. *Black Looks: Race and Representation*. Boston: South End, 1992. 21–39.

Horton, Jessica L. "Alone on the Snow, Alone on the Beach: 'A Global Sense of Place' in *Atanarjuat* and *Fountain*," *The Journal of Transnational American Studies* 4.1 (2012): 1–25.

Howe, LeAnne. *Miko Kings*. San Francisco: Aunt Lute, 2007.

———. *Shell Shaker*. San Francisco: Aunt Lute, 2001.

Hoxie, Frederick. *This Indian Country: American Indian Activists and the Place They Made*. London, UK: Penguin, 2012.

Hudson, Kenneth. "The Museum Refuses to Stand Still." Carbonell 85–91.

Huhndorf, Shari. "Atanarjuat, The Fast Runner: Culture, History and Politics in Inuit Media." *American Anthropologist* 105.4: 822–26.

———. *Going Native: Indians in the American Cultural Imagination*. Ithaca: Cornell UP, 2001.

———. *Mapping the Americas: The Transnational Politics of Contemporary Native Culture*. Ithaca: Cornell UP, 2009.

Inuit Knowledge and Climate Change. Dir. Zacharias Kunuk and Ian Mauro. VTape, 2010.

Isaac, Gwyneira. "What Are Our Expectations Telling Us? Encounters with the NMAI." *The American Indian Quarterly* 30.3/4 (Summer/Fall 2006): 574–96.

Itam, Hakim Hopiit. Dir. Victor Masayesva Jr. Documentary Educational Resources, 1985.

Jacknis, Ira. "A New Thing? The NMAI in Historical and Institutional Perspective." *The American Indian Quarterly* 30.3/4 (Summer/Fall 2006): 511–42.

Jessup, Linda, and Shannon Bagg, eds. *On Aboriginal Representation in the Gallery*. Hull: Canadian Museum of Civilization, 2002.

Joseph, Miranda. *Against the Romance of Community*. Minneapolis: U of Minnesota P, 2002.

The Journals of Knud Rasmussen. Dir. Zacharias Kunuk. VTape, 2006.

Justice, Daniel Heath. *Our Fire Survives the Storm: A Cherokee Literary History*. Minneapolis: U of Minnesota P, 2006.

Kanehsatake: 270 Years of Resistance. Dir. Alanis Obomsawin. Bullfrog Films, 1993.

Kauanui, Khaulani, J. "Contradictions and Celebrations: A Hawaiian Reflection on the Opening of the NMAI." *The American Indian Quarterly* 30.3/4 (Summer/Fall 2006): 496–504.

Keller, Robert H., Jr., and Michael F. Turek, eds. *American Indians and National Parks*. Flagstaff: U of Arizona P, 1999.

Kidwell, Clara Sue, et al. "Every Last Dishcloth: The Prodigious Collecting of George Gustav Heye." Krech and Hail 232–58.

———. *Native American Theology*. New York: Orbis, 2001.

Kolodny, Annette. *The Lay of the Land: Metaphor as Experience and History in American Life and Letters*. Chapel Hill: The U of North Carolina P, 1975.

Konkle, Maureen. *Writing Indian Nations: Native Intellectuals and the Politics of Historiography 1827–1863*. Chapel Hill: The U of North Carolina P, 2004.

Krech, Shepard, III, and Barbara A. Hail. *Collecting Native America 1870–1960*. Washington, DC: Smithsonian Institution P, 1999.

Krinsky, Carole H. *Contemporary Native American Architecture*. Oxford: Oxford UP, 1996.

Kupperman, Karen Ordahl. *Indians and English Facing Off in Early America*. Ithaca: Cornell UP, 2000.

Kymlicka, Will. *Multicultural Citizenship*. Oxford: Clarendon Press, 1995.

———. *Politics in the Vernacular: Nationalism, Multiculturalism, and Citizenship*. Oxford: Oxford UP, 2001.

Lawlor, Mary. *Public Native America: Tribal Self-Representation in Museums, Powwows, and Casinos*. New Brunswick: Rutgers UP, 2006.

Lippard, Lucy, ed. *Partial Recall*. New York: New Press, 1992.

Lonetree, Amy. "Continuing Dialogues: Evolving Views of the National Museum of the American Indian." *Public Historian* 28.2 (Spring 2006): 57–61.

———. "Critical Engagements with the NMAI." *The American Indian Quarterly* 30.3/4 (Summer/Fall 2006): 507–10.

———. "Missed Opportunities: Reflections on the NMAI." *The American Indian Quarterly* 30.3/4 (Summer/Fall 2006): 632–45.

Looking Hot. Dir. Melina Matsoukas. 2011.

Louis, Adrian. *Skins*. Granite Falls, MN: Ellis Press, 1995.

Lujan, James. "A Museum of the Indian, Not for the Indian." *The American Indian Quarterly* 29.3/4 (Summer/Fall 2005): 510–15.

Lyman, Christopher. M. *The Vanishing Race and Other Illusions: Photographs of Indians by Edward S. Curtis*. Washington, DC: Smithsonian Institution P, 1982.

Lyons, Oren, et al., eds. *Exiled in the Land of the Free: Democracy, Indian Nations, and the U.S. Constitution*. Santa Fe: Clear Light, 1992.

Lyons, Scott R. "Rhetorical Sovereignty: What Do American Indians Want from Writing?" *College Composition and Communication* 51.1 (2000): 447–68.

———. *X-Marks: Native Signatures of Assent*. Minneapolis: U of Minnesota P, 2010.

Mann, Charles. *1491: New Revelations of America before Columbus*. New York: Vintage, 2006.

Markell, Patchen. *Bound by Recognition*. Princeton: Princeton UP, 2003.

Martin, Joel W. *The Land Looks After Us. A History of Native American Religions*. Oxford and New York: Oxford UP, 1999.

McCullough, Ken. "If you See Buddha at the Stomp Dance, Kill Him!: The Bicameral World of LeAnne Howe's *Shell Shaker.*" *SAIL* 15.2 (Summer 2003): 58–69.

Melville, Herman. *Moby Dick*. New York: Random House, 1950.

Menchú, Rigoberta. *I, Rigoberta Menchú*. Ed. Elisabeth Burgos-Debray. London: Verso, 2010.

Miller, J. R. *Skyscrapers Hide the Heavens: A History of White-Indian Relations in Canada*. Toronto: U of Toronto P, 2000.

Mitchell, William. *The Reconfigured Eye: Visual Truth in the Post-Photographic Era*. Boston: MIT P, 1992.

Momaday, N. Scott. *The House Made of Dawn*. New York: Harper & Row, 1968.

Mulvey, Laura, and Dick Snauwaert, eds. *Jimmie Durham*. London: Phaidon, 1995.

Nanook Revisited. Dir. Claude Massot. [no distributor available] 1988.

Native Nations: Journeys in American Photography. London: Barbican Art Gallery and Booth-Clibborn Editions, 1998.

Naturally Native. Dir. Valerie Red-Horse and Jennifer Farmer. Shenandoah Film, 1998.

The New World. Dir. Terrence Malick. New Line Cinema, 2005.

The NMAI Guide. Washington, DC: Smithsonian Institution P, 2004.

Older than America. Dir. Georgina Lightning. IFC Films, 200.

On the Ice. Dir. Andrew Okpeaha MacLean. WME Entertainment, 2011.

Ostrowitz, Judith. "'Concourse and Periphery' in Perspective: Well Past Planning." *The American Indian Quarterly* 29.3/4 (Summer/Fall 2005): 384–425.

Owens, Louis. *Mixedblood Messages*. Norman: U of Oklahoma P, 1998.

———. "Their Shadows before Them: Photographing Indians." Bernadin et al. 187–92.

Passalacqua, Veronica. "Hulleah J. Tsinhnahjinnie." <http://www.hulleah.com/essay.htm>. Accessed June 11, 2014.

Paz, Octavio. *The Labyrinth of Solitude*. New York: Grove, 1994.

Pearce, Roy Harvey. *Savagism and Civilization*. Berkeley: U of California P, 1988.

Pearce, Susan, ed. *Interpreting Objects and Collections*. London: Routledge, 1994.

Pfister, Joel. *Individuality Incorporated: Indians and the Multicultural Modern*. Durham: Duke UP, 2004.

Phillips, Ruth B. "Disrupting Past Paradigms: The National Museum of the American Indian and the First Peoples Hall at the Canadian Museum of Civilization." *Public Historian* 28.2 (Spring 2006): 75–80.

———. "A Proper Place for Art of the Proper Arts of Place? Native American Objects and the Hierarchies of Art, Craft, and Souvenir." Jessup and Bagg 45–72.

———. *Trading Identities: The Souvenir in the Native American Art from the Northwest, 1700–1900*. Montreal: McGill-Queen's UP, 1998.

Povinelli, Elizabeth. *The Cunning of Recognition: Indigenous Alterities and the Making of Australian Multiculturalism*. Durham: Duke UP, 2002.

Powell, Malea. "How American Indians Use Writing." *College Composition and Communictation* 53.3 (2000): 396–434.

Prakash, Gyan. "Museum Matters." Carbonell 208–15.

Pratt, Mary Louise. *Imperial Eyes: Travel Writing and Transculturation*. New York: Routledge, 1992.

Preziosi, Donald. "The Art of Art History." Preziosi, 507–25.

———, ed. *The Art of Art History: A Critical Anthology*. Oxford: Oxford U, 1998.

Preziosi, Donald, and Claire Farago, eds. *Grasping the World: The Idea of the Museum*. Burlington: Ashgate, 2004.

Prucha, Francis Paul. *The Great Father: The United States Government and the American Indian*. Lincoln: U of Nebraska P, 1984.

Raheja, Michelle. *Reservation Reelism: Redfacing, Visual Sovereignty and Representations of Native Americans in Film*. Lincoln: The U of Nebraska P, 2011.

Rassmussen, Brigit. *Queequeg's Coffin: Indigenous Literacies and Early American Literature*. Durham: Duke UP, 2011.

Reel Injun. Dir. Neil Diamond. Kino International, 2009.

Reinhardt, Akim D. *Defining the Native: Local Print Media Coverage of the NMAI. The American Indian Quarterly* 29.3/4 (Summer/Fall 2005): 450–65.

Renan, Ernest. "What Is a Nation?" in Homi Bhabha, ed. *Nation and Narration*. New York: Routledge, 1990, 8–22.

Rickard, Jolene. "Exposures: Photographs of Native Americans." In *Native Nations*.

———. "Indigenous Is the Local." Jessup and Bagg 115–23.

———. "The Occupation of Indigenous Space as 'Photograph.'" In *Native Nations* 57–71.

———. "Sovereignty: A Line in the Sand." Aperture Foundation 51–54.

Ritchin, Fred. *After Photography*. New York: Norton, 2009.

Rony, Fatima Tobing. *The Third Eye: Race, Cinema and Ethnographic Spectacle*. Durham: Duke UP, 1996.

Rosaldo, Renato. "Citizenship and Educational Democracy." *Cultural Anthropology* 9.3 (August 1994): 402–11.

Samson, Colin. *A Way of Life That Does Not Exist: Canada and the Extinguishment of the Innu*. London: Verso, 2003.

Samuels, Shirley. *Romances of the Republic*. Oxford: Oxford UP, 1996.

Sandler, Irving. *Art of the Postmodern Era*. Boulder: Westview, 1997.

Sandweiss, Martha A. *Print the Legend: Photography and the American West*. New Haven: Yale UP, 2002.

San Juan, E., Jr. *Racism and Cultural Studies: Critiques of Multiculturalism Ideology and the Politics of Difference*. Durham: Duke UP, 2002.

Sekula, Allan. "The Body and the Archive." *October* 39 (Winter 1986): 3–64.

———. "The Traffic in Photographs." *Art Journal* 41.1 (Spring 1981): 15–25.

Shoemaker, Nancy. *Clearing a Path: Theorizing the Past in Native American Studies*. New York: Routledge, 2002.

Silent Enemy. Dir. H. P. Carver. 1930.

Silko, Leslie Marmon. *Almanac of the Dead*. New York: Penguin, 1992.

———. *Ceremony*. New York: Penguin, 2006.

———. *Yellow Woman and a Beauty of the Spirit: Essays on Native American Life Today*. New York: Simon & Shuster, 1996.

Singer, Beverly R. *Wiping the War Paint Off the Lens: Native American Film and Video*. Minneapolis: U of Minnesota P, 2001.

Skins. Dir. Chris Eyre. First Look Pictures, 2002.

Smith, Linda Tuhiwai. *Decolonizing Methodologies: Research and Indigenous People.* London: Zed, 1999.

Smith, Paul Chaat. "Ghost in the Machine." Aperture Foundation 6–9.

Smoke Signals. Dir. Chris Eyre. Miramax Films, 1998.

Solnit, Rebecca. *Savage Dreams: A Journey into the Landscape Wars of the American West.* Berkeley: The U of California P, 2000.

Sommer, Doris. *Proceed with Caution, When Engaged by Minority Writing in the Americas.* Cambridge: Harvard UP, 1999.

Sontag, Susan. *On Photography.* 6th ed. New York: Farrar, 1978.

Spence, Mark David. *Dispossessing the Wilderness: Indian Removal and the Making of National Parks.* Oxford: Oxford UP, 2000.

Squiers, Carol, ed. *Overexposed: Essays on Contemporary Photography.* New York: New Press, 1999.

Starting Fire with Gunpowder. Dir. David Posey and William Hansen. Icarus Films, 1991.

Tagg, John. *Burden of Representation.* Minneapolis: U of Minnesota P, 1988.

Taylor, Charles. *Multiculturalism.* Ed. Amy Gutmann. Princeton: Princeton UP, 1992.

Teuton, Christopher B. *Deep Waters: The Textual Continuum in American Indian Literature.* Lincoln: The U of Nebraska P, 2010.

Thornton, Russell, ed. *Studying Native America: Problems and Prospects.* Madison: U of Wisconsin P, 1998.

Trachtenberg, Alan, ed. *Classic Essays on Photography.* New Haven: Leete's Island, 1980.

———. *Shades of Hiawatha: Staging Indians, Making Americans, 1880–1930.* New York: Hill and Wang, 2004.

Treuer, David. *Rez Life: An Indian's Journey through Reservation Life.* Boston: Atlantic Monthly Press, 2012.

Tully, James. *Strange Multiplicity: Constitutionalism in an Age of Diversity.* Cambridge: Cambridge UP, 1995.

Waters, Anne, ed. *American Indian Thought: Philosophical Essays.* Malden: Blackwell, 2004.

Weaver, Jace, Craig S. Womack, and Robert Warrior. *American Indian Literary Nationalism.* Albuquerque: U of New Mexico P, 2005.

———. *That the People Might Live.* New York: Oxford UP, 1997.

White, Jerry. "Frozen But Always in Motion: Arctic Film, Video and Broadcast." *The Velvet Light Trap* 55 (2005): 52–64.

Wilkins, David E., and K. Tsianina Lomawaima. *Uneven Ground: American Indian Sovereignty and Federal Law.* Norman: U of Oklahoma P, 2001.

Williams, Carol. *Framing the West: Race, Gender and the Photographic Frontier in the Pacific Northwest.* Oxford: Oxford UP, 2003.

Williams, Robert A. *Like a Loaded Weapon: The Renquist Court, Indian Rights, and the Legal History of Racism in America.* Minneapolis: U of Minnesota P, 2005.

Wilson, James. *The Earth Shall Weep: A History of Native America.* New York: Grove, 1998.

Womack, Craig S. *Red on Red: Native American Literary Separatism*. Minneapolis: U of Minnesota P, 1999.

Young, Robert J. C. *Colonial Desire: Hybridity in Theory, Culture and Race*. London: Routledge, 1995.

Yúdice, George. *The Expediency of Culture: Uses of Culture in the Global Era*. Durham: Duke UP, 2003.

Žižek, Slavoj. "Multiculturalism, Or, the Cultural Logic of Multinational Capitalism." *NLR* I/225 (1997): 28–51.

Index